AA004422

# SECURWARE 2023

The Seventeenth International Conference on Emerging Security Information, Systems and Technologies

September 25 - 29, 2023

Porto, Portugal

**SECURWARE 2023 Editors**

Erik Buchmann, ScaDS.AI, Leipzig University, Germany
Eric Veith, Carl von Ossietzky University Oldenburg, Germany
Dirceu Cavendish, Kyushu Institute of Technology/UCLA, Japan/USA

**Printed from e-media with permission by:**

Curran Associates, Inc.
57 Morehouse Lane
Red Hook, NY 12571

**Some format issues inherent in the e-media version may also appear in this print version.**

Copyright© (2023) by International Academy, Research, and Industry Association (IARIA)
Please refer to the Copyright Information page.

Printed with permission by Curran Associates, Inc. (2024)

International Academy, Research, and Industry Association (IARIA)
412 Derby Way
Wilmington, DE 19810

Phone: (408) 893-6407
Fax: (408) 527-6351

petre@iaria.org

**Additional copies of this publication are available from:**

Curran Associates, Inc.
57 Morehouse Lane
Red Hook, NY 12571 USA
Phone: 845-758-0400
Fax: 845-758-2633
Email: curran@proceedings.com
Web: www.proceedings.com

## Table of Contents

# SECURWARE 2023

# Forward

The Seventeenth International Conference on Emerging Security Information, Systems and Technologies (SECURWARE 2023), held on September 25-29, 2023, continued a series of events covering related topics on theory and practice on security, cryptography, secure protocols, trust, privacy, confidentiality, vulnerability, intrusion detection and other areas related to low enforcement, security data mining, malware models, etc.

Security, defined for ensuring protected communication among terminals and user applications across public and private networks, is the core for guaranteeing confidentiality, privacy, and data protection. Security affects business and individuals, raises the business risk, and requires a corporate and individual culture. In the open business space offered by Internet, it is a need to improve defenses against hackers, disgruntled employees, and commercial rivals. There is a required balance between the effort and resources spent on security versus security achievements. Some vulnerability can be addressed using the rule of 80:20, meaning 80% of the vulnerabilities can be addressed for 20% of the costs. Other technical aspects are related to the communication speed versus complex and time consuming cryptography/security mechanisms and protocols.

Digital Ecosystem is defined as an open decentralized information infrastructure where different networked agents, such as enterprises (especially SMEs), intermediate actors, public bodies and end users, cooperate and compete enabling the creation of new complex structures. In digital ecosystems, the actors, their products and services can be seen as different organisms and species that are able to evolve and adapt dynamically to changing market conditions.

Digital Ecosystems lie at the intersection between different disciplines and fields: industry, business, social sciences, biology, and cutting edge ICT and its application driven research. They are supported by several underlying technologies such as semantic web and ontology-based knowledge sharing, self-organizing intelligent agents, peer-to-peer overlay networks, web services-based information platforms, and recommender systems.

To enable safe digital ecosystem functioning, security and trust mechanisms become essential components across all the technological layers. The aim is to bring together multidisciplinary research that ranges from technical aspects to socio-economic models.

We take here the opportunity to warmly thank all the members of the SECURWARE 2023 technical program committee, as well as all the reviewers. The creation of such a high quality conference program would not have been possible without their involvement. We also kindly thank all the authors who dedicated much of their time and effort to contribute to SECURWARE 2023. We truly believe that, thanks to all these efforts, the final conference program consisted of top quality contributions.

We also thank the members of the SECURWARE 2023 organizing committee for their help in handling the logistics and for their work that made this professional meeting a success.

We hope that SECURWARE 2023 was a successful international forum for the exchange of ideas and results between academia and industry and to promote further progress in the area of security information, systems and technologies. We also hope that Porto provided a pleasant environment during the conference and everyone saved some time to enjoy the historic charm of the city.

**SECURWARE 2023 Chairs**

**SECURWARE 2023 Steering Committee**
Steffen Fries, Siemens, Germany
George O. M. Yee, Aptusinnova Inc. / Carleton University, Ottawa, Canada
Ki-Woong Park, Sejong University, South Korea
Rainer Falk, Siemens AG, Corporate Technology, Germany
Hans-Joachim Hof, INSicherheit - Ingolstadt Research Group Applied IT Security, CARISSMA – Center of Automotive Research on Integrated Safety Syst, Germany

**SECURWARE 2023 Publicity Chair**
Lorena Parra Boronat, Universitat Politecnica de Valencia, Spain
Laura Garcia, Universitat Politecnica de Valencia, Spain

# SECURWARE 2023

## Committee

**SECURWARE 2023 Steering Committee**

Steffen Fries, Siemens, Germany
George O. M. Yee, Aptusinnova Inc. / Carleton University, Ottawa, Canada
Ki-Woong Park, Sejong University, South Korea
Rainer Falk, Siemens AG, Corporate Technology, Germany
Hans-Joachim Hof, INSicherheit - Ingolstadt Research Group Applied IT Security, CARISSMA – Center of Automotive Research on Integrated Safety Syst, Germany

**SECURWARE 2023 Publicity Chair**

Lorena Parra Boronat, Universitat Politecnica de Valencia, Spain
Laura Garcia, Universitat Politecnica de Valencia, Spain

**SECURWARE 2023 Technical Program Committee**

Aysajan Abidin, imec-COSIC KU Leuven, Belgium
Abbas Acar, Florida International University, Miami, USA
Rabin Acharya, University of Florida, USA
Afrand Agah, West Chester University of Pennsylvania, USA
Chuadhry Mujeeb Ahmed, University of Strathclyde, UK
Sedat Akleylek, Ondokuz Mayis University, Samsun, Turkey
Oum-El-Kheir Aktouf, Greboble INP | LCIS Lab, France
Mamoun Alazab, Charles Darwin University, Australia
Ashwag Albakri, University of Missouri-Kansas City, USA / Jazan University, Saudi Arabia
Asif Ali laghari, SMIU, Karachi, Pakistan
Luca Allodi, Eindhoven University of Technology, Netherlands
Mohammed Alshehri, University of Arkansas, USA
Eric Amankwa, Presbyterian University College, Ghana
Prashant Anantharaman, Dartmouth College, USA
Mohammadreza Ashouri, Virginia Tech, USA
Alexandre Augusto Giron, Federal University of Santa Catarina (UFSC) / Federal University of Technology (UTFPR), Brazil
Antonio Barili, Università degli Studi di Pavia, Italy
Ilija Basicevic, University of Novi Sad, Serbia
Luke A. Bauer, University of Florida, USA
Malek Ben Salem, Accenture, USA
Smriti Bhatt, Purdue University, USA
Catalin Bîrjoveanu, "Al. I. Cuza" University of Iasi, Romania
Robert Brotzman, Pennsylvania State University, USA
Francesco Buccafurri, University Mediterranea of Reggio Calabria, Italy
Arun Balaji Buduru, IIIT-Delhi, India
Enrico Cambiaso, Consiglio Nazionale delle Ricerche (CNR) - IEIIT Institute, Italy
Paolo Campegiani, Bit4id, Italy

Juan-Vicente Capella-Hernández, Universitat Politècnica de València, Spain
Roberto Carbone, Fondazione Bruno Kessler, Trento, Italy
Juan Carlos Ruiz, Universidad Politécnica de Valencia, Spain
Christophe Charrier, Nomandie Univ. | UNICAEN | ENSICAEN | CNRS GREYC UMR 6072, France
Bo Chen, Michigan Technological University, Houghton, USA
Liquan Chen, Southeast University, China
Zelei Cheng, Purdue University, USA
Tan Saw Chin, Multimedia University, Malaysia
Jin-Hee Cho, Virginia Tech, USA
Stelvio Cimato, University of Milan, Italy
Jun Dai, California State University at Sacramento, USA
Dipanjan Das, University of California, Santa Barbara, USA
Avani Dave, Intel Corp., USA
Alexandre Debant , Université de Lorraine | CNRS | Inria | LORIA, Nancy, France
Raffaele Della Corte, "Federico II" University of Naples, Italy
Jean-Christophe Deneuville, ENAC | University of Toulouse, France
Jintai Ding, Tsinghua University, Beijing
George Drosatos, Athena Research Center, Greece
Navid Emamdoost, University of Minnesota, USA
Alessandro Erba, CISPA Helmholtz Center for Information Security, Germany
Rainer Falk, Siemens AG, Corporate Technology, Germany
Yebo Feng, University of Oregon, USA
Eduardo B. Fernandez, Florida Atlantic University, USA
Anders Fongen, Norwegian Defence University College, Norway
Steffen Fries, Siemens Corporate Technologies, Germany
Chrystel Gaber, Orange, France
Olga Gadyatskaya, LIACS - Leiden University, The Netherlands
Clemente Galdi, University of Salerno, Italy
Kevin Gomez Buquerin, Technical University Ingolstadt, Germany
Nils Gruschka, University of Oslo, Norway
Bidyut Gupta, Southern Illinois University, Carbondale, USA
Saurabh Gupta, IIIT-Delhi, India
Emre Gursoy, Koc University, Istanbul, Turkey
Muhammad Shadi Hajar, Robert Gordon University, UK
Amir Mohammad Hajisadeghi, Amirkabir University of Technology (Tehran Polytechnic), Iran
Mohammad Hamad, Technical University of Munich, Germany
Jinguang Han, Southeast University, China
Petr Hanáček, Brno University of Technology, Czech Republic
Dan Harkins, Hewlett-Packard Enterprise, USA
Mohamed Hawedi, École de Technologie Supérieure Montreal, Canada
Zecheng He, Princeton University, USA
Hans-Joachim Hof, INSicherheit - Ingolstadt Research Group Applied IT Security, CARISSMA – Center of Automotive Research on Integrated Safety Syst, Germany
Gahangir Hossain, West Texas A&M University, Canyon, USA
Fu-Hau Hsu, National Central University, Taiwan
Yuncong Hu, Shanghai Jiao Tong University, China
Fatima Hussain, Royal Bank of Canada, Toronto, Canada
Mauro Iacono, Università degli Studi della Campania "L. Vanvitelli", Italy

Ibifubara Iganibo, George Mason University, USA
Sergio Ilarri, University of Zaragoza, Spain
Nikolay Ivanov, Michigan State University, USA
Mariusz Jakubowski, Microsoft Research, USA
Prasad M. Jayaweera, University of Sri Jayewardenepura, Sri Lanka
Kun Jin, Ohio State University, USA
Hugo Jonker, Open Universiteit, Netherlands
Taeho Jung, University of Notre Dame, USA
Kaushal Kafle, William & Mary, USA
Sarang Kahvazadeh, Centre Tecnològic de Telecomunicacions de Catalunya (CTTC), Spain
Harsha K. Kalutarage, Robert Gordon University, UK
Georgios Kambourakis, University of the Aegean, Greece
Mehdi Karimi, The University of British Columbia, Vancouver, Canada
Georgios Karopoulos, European Commission JRC, Italy
Sokratis K. Katsikas, Norwegian University of Science and Technology, Norway
Basel Katt, Norwegian University of Science and Technology, Norway
Joakim Kävrestad, University of Skövde, Sweden
Ferdous Wahid Khan, Airbus Digital Trust Solutions, Munich, Germany
Hyunsung Kim, Kyungil University, Korea
Paris Kitsos, University of the Peloponnese, Greece
Andreas Kogler, Graz University of Technology (TU-Graz) | Institute of Applied Information Processing and Communications (IAIK), Austria
Harsha Kumara, Robert Gordon University, UK
Hiroki Kuzuno, SECOM Co. Ltd., Japan
Hyun Kwon, Korea Military Academy, Korea
Romain Laborde, University Paul Sabatier Toulouse III, France
Cecilia Labrini, University of Reggio Calabria, Italy
Yosra Lakhdhar, SUP'COM / Digital Research Centre of Sfax, Tunisia
Vianney Lapôtre, Université Bretagne Sud, France
Martin Latzenhofer, AIT Austrian Institute of Technology | Center for Digital Safety and Security, Vienna, Austria
Wen-Chuan Lee, Apple Inc., USA
Ferenc Leitold, University of Dunaújváros, Hungary
Albert Levi, Sabanci University, Istanbul, Turkey
Shimin Li, Winona State University, USA
Wenjuan Li, The Hong Kong Polytechnic University, China
Zhihao Li, Meta Platform Inc., USA
Stefan Lindskog, SINTEF Digital, Norway / Karlstad University, Sweden
Guojun Liu, University of South Florida, Tampa, USA
Shaohui Liu, School of Computer Science and Technology | Harbin Institute of Technology, China
Shen Liu, NVIDIA, USA
Yi Liu, University of Massachusetts Dartmouth, USA
Giovanni Livraga, Universita' degli Studi di Milano, Italy
George Lord, University of Chicago, USA
Jakob Löw, Technische Hochschule Ingolstadt, Germany
Giuseppe Loseto, LUM "Giuseppe Degennaro" University, Italy
Flaminia Luccio, University Ca' Foscari of Venice, Italy
Duohe Ma, Institute of Information Engineering | Chinese Academy of Sciences, China

Rabi N. Mahapatra, Texas A&M University, USA
Mahdi Manavi, Mirdamad Institute of Higher Education, Iran
Anuradha Mandal, University of Arizona, USA
Soundes Marzougui, Technical University of Berlin, Germany
Michele Mastroianni, University of Salerno, Italy
Antonio Matencio Escolar, University of the West of Scotland, UK
Wojciech Mazurczyk, Warsaw University of Technology, Poland
Weizhi Meng, Technical University of Denmark, Denmark
Aleksandra Mileva, University "Goce Delcev" in Stip, Republic of N. Macedonia
Paolo Modesti, Teesside University, UK
Adwait Nadkarni, William & Mary, USA
Vasudevan Nagendra, Plume Design Inc., USA
Priyadarsi Nanda, University of Technology Sydney, Australia
Duc Cuong Nguyen, HCL Technologies, Vietnam
Liang Niu, New York University (NYU) Abu Dhabi, UAE
Nicola Nostro, Resiltech, Italy
Jason R. C. Nurse, University of Kent, UK
Rajvardhan Oak, Microsoft, India
Bogdan Oancea, University of Bucharest, Romania
Livinus Obiora Nweke, Norwegian University of Science and Technology, Norway
Catuscia Palamidessi, INRIA, France
Carlos Enrique Palau Salvador, Universitat Politècnica de València, Spain
Lanlan Pan, Guangdong OPPO Mobile Telecommunications Corp. Ltd., China
Brajendra Panda, University of Arkansas, USA
Ki-Woong Park, Sejong University, Republic of Korea
Balázs Pejó, CrySyS Lab - BME, Budapest, Hungary
Wei Peng, University of Oulu, Finland
Travis Peters, Montana State University, USA
Josef Pieprzyk, Data61 | CSIRO, Sydney, Australia / Institute of Computer Science | Polish Academy of Sciences, Warsaw, Poland
Nikolaos Pitropakis, Edinburgh Napier University, UK
Tassilo Pellegrini, St. Pölten University of Applied Sciences, Austria
Bernardo Portela, University of Porto, Portugal
Mila Dalla Preda, University of Verona, Italy
Maxime Puys, Univ. Grenoble Alpes | CEA | LETI | DSYS, Grenoble, France
Yiyue Qian, University of Notre Dame, USA
Alvise Rabitti, Università Ca'Foscari - Venezia, Italy
Khandaker "Abir" Rahman, Saginaw Valley State University, USA
Mohammad Saidur Rahman, Rochester Institute of Technology, USA
Keyvan Ramezanpour, ANDRO Computational Solutions LLC, USA
Mohammad A. Rashid, Massey University, New Zealand
Alexander Rasin, DePaul University, USA
Danda B. Rawat, Howard University, USA
Leon Reznik, Rochester Institute of Technology, USA
Martin Ring, Bosch Engineering GmbH, Germany
Vera Rimmer, KU Leuven, Belgium
Heiko Roßnagel, Fraunhofer IAO, Germany
Salah Sadou, IRISA - Universite de Bretagne Sud, France

Nick Scope, DePaul University, USA
Rodrigo Sanches Miani, Universidade Federal de Uberlândia, Brazil
Stefan Schauer, AIT Austrian Institute of Technology | Center for Digital Safety and Security, Vienna, Austria
Stefan Schiffner, University of Münster, Germany
Savio Sciancalepore, Hamad Bin Khalifa University (HBKU), Doha, Qatar
Giada Sciarretta, Fondazione Bruno Kessler (FBK), Trento, Italy
Tanmoy Sen, University of Virginia, USA
Avi Shaked, University of Oxford, UK
Jain Shalabh, Robert Bosch LLC, USA
Haoqi Shan, University of Florida, USA
Amit Kumar Sikder, Georgia Institute of Technology, USA
Christian Skalka, University of Vermont, USA
Rocky Slavin, University of Texas at San Antonio, USA
Liwei Song, Princeton University, USA
Christoph Stach, University of Stuttgart, Germany
Dean Sullivan, University of New Hampshire, USA
Zhibo Sun, Drexel University, USA
Sheng Tan, Trinity University, USA
Michael Tempelmeier, Giesecke+Devrient, Germany
Nils Ole Tippenhauer, CISPA Helmholtz Center for Cybersecurity, Germany
Scott Trent, IBM Research - Tokyo, Japan
Yazhou Tu, University of Louisiana at Lafayette, USA
Vincent Urias, Sandia National Labs, USA
Andrea Visconti, Università degli Studi di Milano, Italy
Qi Wang, University of Illinois Urbana-Champaign / Stellar Cyber Inc., USA
Shu Wang, George Mason University, USA
Wenhao Wang, Institute of Information Engineering | Chinese Academy of Sciences, China
Wenqi Wei, Georgia Institute of Technology, USA
Ian Welch, Victoria University of Wellington, New Zealand
Zhonghao Wu, Shanghai Jiao Tong University, China
Nian Xue, New York University (NYU), USA
Ehsan Yaghoubi, University of Beira Interior, Portugal
Limin Yang, University of Illinois at Urbana-Champaign, USA
Ping Yang, Binghamton University, USA
Wun-She Yap, Universiti Tunku Abdul Rahman, Malaysia
Qussai M. Yaseen, Jordan University of Science and Technology, Irbid, Jordan
George O. M. Yee, Aptusinnova Inc. / Carleton University, Ottawa, Canada
Kailiang Ying, Google, USA
Amr Youssef, Concordia University, Montreal, Canada
Chia-Mu Yu, National Yang Ming Chiao Tung University, Taiwan
Wei Yu, Institute of Information Engineering | Chinese Academy of Sciences, China
Thomas Zefferer, Secure Information Technology Center Austria (A-SIT), Austria
Dongrui Zeng, Palo Alto Networks, Santa Clara, USA
Linghan Zhang, Florida State University, USA
Penghui Zhang, Meta Platforms Inc., USA
Tianwei Zhang, Nanyang Technological University, Singapore
Yubao Zhang, Palo Alto Networks, USA

Yue Zheng, Nanyang Technological University, Singapore
Tommaso Zoppi, University of Florence, Italy

**Copyright Information**

For your reference, this is the text governing the copyright release for material published by IARIA.

The copyright release is a transfer of publication rights, which allows IARIA and its partners to drive the dissemination of the published material. This allows IARIA to give articles increased visibility via distribution, inclusion in libraries, and arrangements for submission to indexes.

I, the undersigned, declare that the article is original, and that I represent the authors of this article in the copyright release matters. If this work has been done as work-for-hire, I have obtained all necessary clearances to execute a copyright release. I hereby irrevocably transfer exclusive copyright for this material to IARIA. I give IARIA permission or reproduce the work in any media format such as, but not limited to, print, digital, or electronic. I give IARIA permission to distribute the materials without restriction to any institutions or individuals. I give IARIA permission to submit the work for inclusion in article repositories as IARIA sees fit.

I, the undersigned, declare that to the best of my knowledge, the article is does not contain libelous or otherwise unlawful contents or invading the right of privacy or infringing on a proprietary right.

Following the copyright release, any circulated version of the article must bear the copyright notice and any header and footer information that IARIA applies to the published article.

IARIA grants royalty-free permission to the authors to disseminate the work, under the above provisions, for any academic, commercial, or industrial use. IARIA grants royalty-free permission to any individuals or institutions to make the article available electronically, online, or in print.

IARIA acknowledges that rights to any algorithm, process, procedure, apparatus, or articles of manufacture remain with the authors and their employers.

I, the undersigned, understand that IARIA will not be liable, in contract, tort (including, without limitation, negligence), pre-contract or other representations (other than fraudulent misrepresentations) or otherwise in connection with the publication of my work.

Exception to the above is made for work-for-hire performed while employed by the government. In that case, copyright to the material remains with the said government. The rightful owners (authors and government entity) grant unlimited and unrestricted permission to IARIA, IARIA's contractors, and IARIA's partners to further distribute the work.

# Lightweight Fine-Grained Access Control Mechanism Based on Zero Trust in CPS

Nakul D. Ghate
NEC Corporation, Japan
Tokyo, Japan
email: te.nak14@nec.com

Shohei Mitani
NEC Corporation, Japan
Tokyo, Japan
email: s.mitani@nec.com

Hirofumi Ueda
NEC Corporation, Japan
Tokyo, Japan
email: h-ueda_cb@nec.com

*Abstract*— **The paper explores the trade-off between security and workload when enforcing fine-grained access control in Cyber Physical Systems network. The paper describes a novel approach to select the access control granularity based on dynamic environment conditions by distributing a part of fine-grained application-level policy on a network-level access controller to reduce the workload while ensuring security. Under the desk evaluation, we achieved a workload reduction of over 90% compared to the input policy, with a granularity degrade of just 15%. Although, some mis-control due to denying essential requests can be observed in the distribution-based approach, the presented algorithms are conceptualized to minimize it. The preliminary experimental results show promising improvement in the access control system performance when employing this approach.**

***Keywords- Cyber physical systems; zero trust; fine-grained; workload; distributed access control.***

## I. Introduction

Beyond 5G / 6G network has highly enabled the integration of physical systems with the cyber world in the form of Cyber Physical Systems (CPS) [1], whose applications range from smart manufacturing, healthcare, power grids, Internet of vehicles, smart homes and so on [2]. Because they are deployed in critical infrastructures, the security of such systems has become ever important. The heterogeneity of the devices utilized in the CPS is one of the fundamental issues in CPS security. Many sensors, and actuators used are constrained IOT devices, on which deploying security functions is a challenge [3]. As CPS integrates many such hardware, along with software used for monitoring and control, etc., every site in CPS network functions as an entry point for malware to intrude into organization's network [2].

Traditional network-perimeter based defense model has become obsolete in the dynamic CPS network due to (1) failure to prevent lateral movement inside the network perimeter as everything inside the perimeter is trusted [4], (2) emergence of cloud services which blur the perimeter boundary by extending the enterprise resource access through third party servers [5]. With cloud services ever evolving, achieving practical security is impossible using perimeter-based defense techniques. Zero Trust (ZT) is the term for an evolving set of cybersecurity paradigms that move defenses from static, network-based perimeters to focus on users, assets, and resources [6]. Access control mechanisms utilizing the ZT principles assume that threats exist everywhere, and no user or device is trusted solely based on its physical or network location. The ZT-based access control continuously performs authentication and authorization to ensure only the authorized entity is permitted to access protected resource(s), adapting to the principle of least privilege to prevent lateral movement. However, to achieve this effectively, it requires fine-grained access control for authorization, where access rules are defined for individual users, devices, resources, applications, and so on. An example is Attribute Based Access Control (ABAC) [7], enforced with mechanisms such as Attribute-Based Encryption (ABE) [8] and with Application-level access policy designed for secure access to resources, when the access risk is associated with attributes such as "device ID", "resource ID", "resource confidentiality", "device behavior", "user-behavior", and so on. The application-level access policy utilizes the influence of these attributes to decide access decision, and such decisions are performed at application-level access controllers which define the fine-grained authorization rules from the application-level policy. The fine-granularity contributes to the large workload of access control mechanism in terms of increased storage of enforceable rules, large computation cost of ABE, higher processing load on the access controller, etc. [9][10][11]. These drawbacks may result in latency in enforcing access decisions and can be a possible target for Distributed Denial of Service attacks (DDOS), hindering enterprise operations [12].

Implementing coarse-grained access control such as network-level access control that defines authorization rules using the network attributes such as "source IP", "destination IP", etc. reduces the access control workload by defining a single access rule for many devices and resources contained within the same IP address. But due to its coarseness, it fails in achieving least privilege security, thereby implying that a trade-off exists between the security and workload when subjected to the granularity of access control policies. Our approach implements a distributed access control mechanism which distributes the access control decisions on sequentially implemented access controllers: network-level access controllers that utilize coarse-grained access policies and application-level access controllers that deal with fine-grained application-level policies. With this, we aim to achieve both high security and low workload to overcome the existing issue. The rest of the paper is organized as follows: Section II presents the related study, Section III presents the approach to solve the problem, Section IV describes the methodology for the approach. The experimentation and results are described in Section V, while Section VI presents the discussion of our work. Finally, we conclude our work in Section VII.

## II. Related Study

The security and workload trade-off exists because the implementation of traditional ZT-based access control in the existing literature is static in terms of access granularity, i.e., it either implements coarse-grained network-level access control [13] or fine-grained application-level access control [14]. For instance, [13] embeds authentication tokens inside TCP packets and first-packet authentication, therefore, enforcing ZT principles with static rules and coarse-grained network-level access control, while [14] only considers Attribute Based Access Control (ABAC) rules to be enforced at the Policy Enforcement Point (PEP) resulting in high workload. Such static approaches to implement ZT-based access control do not result in optimal performance with respect to the workload-security trade-off.

To reduce the workload of application-level policies, existing methods [15][16] focused on controlling the access at network devices such as firewall, based on application-awareness. In [15], the access granularity of the firewall is changed from coarse-grained *packet filtering* to a finer-grained *stateful* TCP or application-level *deep packet inspection*, depending on the application security requirements and static access control policies. In [16], an application-aware network access control for IOT services is proposed based on SDN using mandatory access control (MAC). While they simplify access management of fine-grained access control, they fail to recognize the access risks from the heterogenous devices as well the dynamically changing environment conditions. This may lead to malware infection caused by wrong choice of access granularity by only considering application awareness. [17] proposed a policy-based dynamic network access control by utilizing the real-time feedback from network devices and application servers. However, it is proposed as a conceptual framework only. Several multi-layer access control methods are also provided to enhance security. In [12], the authors proposed cooperation of PEP among network-level and application-level services in the same or remote domains to facilitate defense in depth. However, the solution relies heavily on static application-level policies. In [18], a dual layer ZT architecture is proposed where the policy evaluates user's 5G network layer behavior and industry application layer behavior. In [19] a multi-layer authorization framework of Apache Hadoop is discussed which covers a range of services. Both of them do not consider the workload and scalability aspect.

In a dynamic environment such as CPS, the deployed access control method should be aware of the changing attributes of both the access subject as well as resources, and adaptively respond by enforcing access control rules with choosing appropriate granularity. For instance, enforcing network-level access control when the risk is related to the changing network attributes, such as suspicious activities from a source IP address, and on the other hand, enforcing application-layer access control when the risk is related to the changing attributes of user or device behavior, etc. We propose a novel approach of access granularity selection based on analyzing the dynamic environment.

## III. Approach

We argue that the optimal performance is achieved when the security and workloads are balanced by the access control system towards overall business growth by facilitating access continuity. We propose that dynamic selection of access control granularity promises to achieve this balance. A schematic comparison of the existing work [15] and our approach is shown in Figure 1. Due to the fact that the existing work does not take into account for dynamically changing behaviors of access subjects, such as users and (IOT) devices, it would always choose coarse-grained packet filtering for non-confidential resource as shown in Figure 1, which may result in malicious device taking control over the resource. On the other hand, it would always choose fine-grained deep inspection to protect sensitive resources, even for trusted devices, which requires large workload and induce latency in the access.

Our approach lies in dynamically distributing the (fine-grained) application-level access control towards (coarse-grained) network-level access control. Our algorithm dynamically decides which policies are safe to be distributed towards network-level access control for the intention of reducing the workload while not compromising the security. On a high level, we utilize an application-level access policy which intends to be enforced at the application-level access controller in the traditional methods, and distribute it into two sets of policies, the coarse-grained policy enforced at the network-level access controller and the remaining subset of the application-level policies enforced at the application-level access controller as shown in Figure 1.

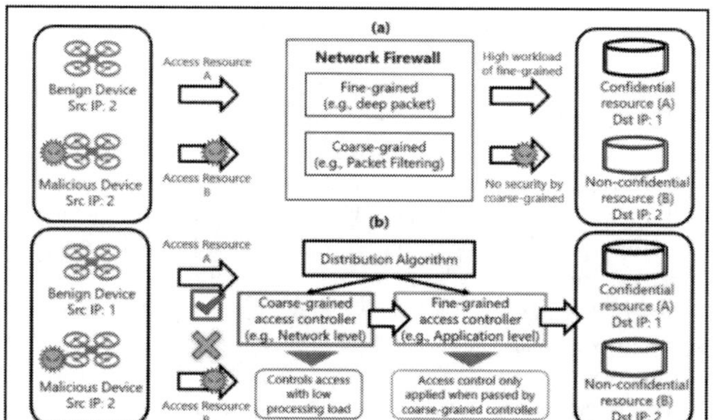


Figure 1. Comparison between (a) existing method and (b) our approach.

We take advantages of the following three properties as long as it doesn't compromise security; 1) Network-level access control requires lower processing load compared to application-level, 2) A network-level access controller deployed in front of an application-level access controller cuts off access requests, 3) The size of network-level access policy is smaller than that of application-level policy if they represent same access decision rules. In this way, the network-level access control reduces both the workload (as the application-level access controller only controls access to the requests which are passed on by the network-level access controller), as well as cuts of malicious access and attacks such as DDOS early on, securing the network against unnecessary bandwidth consumption.

## IV. METHODOLOGY

We describe the methodology to our approach in this section. Assuming an existing application-level policy, the objective of our distributed access control is to reduce the workload and operation cost of directly enforcing the application-level access control policy. Instead, we distribute and enforce it on both network-level and application-level access controller. A trivial solution is to enforce the whole policy as a network-level policy to achieve least workload. However, it has a problem. In a CPS network, many devices may share a common IP address. Assume that for accessing certain resource, one device belonging to a certain IP have "allow" decision in the application-level policy, meanwhile another device have "deny" decision. If the devices share same IP address (and same destination port number), those two devices will be assigned the same decision under the network-level access control. Hence, one of them would be mis-controlled by the decision due to policy differences. Our algorithm evaluates the mis-control rate and decides if some parts of the application-level policy can be distributed and enforced at the network-level access control. Because network-level access controller can deal with (coarse-grained) network-level policy only, we use the aggregation approach where the decisions controlling access of all *devices* from a *source IP* address to all the *resources* in the *destination IP* address can be aggregated into a single coarse-grained network-level policy enforceable at the network access controller as shown in Figure 2.

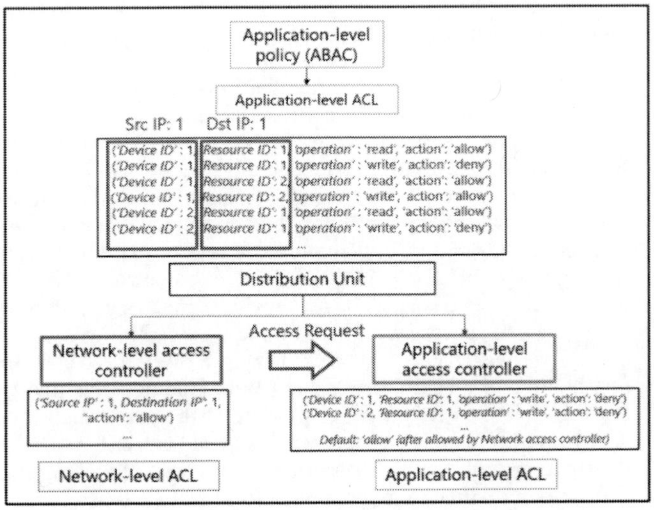


Figure 2. Distribution of application-level access control policies.

**Algorithm.** In this study, we utilized a manually defined application-level policy (such as ABAC) as the input. We assume that the application-level access policy accurately determines the authorization decisions based on the dynamic environment. For distribution algorithm to work, the policy must be defined in an enforceable form. We picked the Access Control List (ACL) [20] format for the enforceable policies. The application-level policy (ABAC) is first converted to Application-level ACL before distribution as shown in Figure 2. The distribution algorithm is described in Algorithm 1.

```
Pseudo-code of distribution of access control policies
Input: Application-level policy F = list (Device ID, Resource ID, Operation,
Decision)
1. DO
2.  Create all pairs: p = (source IP, destination IP) ∈ P
3.  Create dictionaries: nw_acl (Network-level ACL), app_acl (Application-
level ACL), D (decision), SubP (sub-Policy) with keys p for each p∈ P
4.  Initialize 'allow count' D[p][ac] = 0 and 'deny count' D[p][dc] = 0 for
      each p∈ P
5.  FOR each e = (Device ID, Resource ID, Decision) in F
6.   Find p for (Device ID, Resource ID) ∈ e
7.   If Decision == 'allow'
8.    D[p][ac] <- D[p][ac] + 1
9.   If Decision == 'deny'
10.   D[p][dc] <- D[p][dc] + 1
11.   SubP[p] <- append (e)
12. END FOR
13. FOR each p∈ P
14.  Apply policy aggregation
15. END FOR
16. RETURN (nw_acl, app_acl)

Policy aggregation
1.  Calculate allow rate AR = (ac) / (ac + dc)
2.  IF AR > threshold
3.   nw_acl[p] <- {action} = 'allow'
4.   app_acl[p] <- SubP[p]
5.  ELSE
6.   nw_acl[p] <- {action} = 'deny'
7.  END FOR
```

Algorithm 1. Distribution of application-level policy.

The input application-level policy $F$ is defined in an ACL format with attributes '*Device ID*', '*Resource ID*', '*Operation*' (such as 'read', 'write' operations, etc.) and the action decision (such as 'allow' or 'deny'). The algorithm defines the output network-level ACL '*nw_acl*' with attributes 'source IP', 'destination IP', and action decision ('allow' or 'deny') and the output application-level ACL '*app_acl*' defined with same attributes as $F$. The aggregation approach uses the attributes of the network-level ACL, i.e., *source IP, destination IP* (if the IP-level access control is enforced). The algorithm proceeds as follows: for each access pattern in $F$, it finds the pair $p$ = (*source IP, destination IP*) associated with the pair (*device ID, resource ID*) using the associated binding between device ID, resource ID and their attributes. Then, for each pair $p$ controlled by the network-level access controller, the aggregation algorithm evaluates the 'allow count' $ac$ and the 'deny count' $dc$ by calculating the total number of 'allowed' and 'denied' access patterns respectively. The decision dictionary $D$ stores this value for each $p \in P$, where P is the set of all pairs (*source IP, destination IP*). All the access patterns for each (*device ID, resource ID*) associated with the pair $p$ are stored as sub-policies of $p$ in the dictionary *SubP*. The policy aggregation algorithm calculates the 'allow rate' *AR* of access decisions for all the pairs (*device ID*, *resource ID*) belonging to $p$. The allow rate is compared against a set *threshold*. If the 'allow rate' is greater or less than the set *threshold*, the network-level acl *nw_acl* for each $p$ is set to "allow" or "deny" respectively. The policy aggregation operation is shown in algorithm 1. For each "allow" decision in the network-level ACL, an application-level ACL *app_acl* is distributed towards the application-level access controller (by appending sub-Policy *SubP* to *app_acl*). This ensures only legitimate access is permitted to access the resources (at the application-level) while the rest is denied. The value of set *threshold* depends on how strict one wants to set the access control for network access control. Higher the threshold, stricter becomes the network access control. However, denying access at network-level access control may cause limitations, which along with a conceptual solution is discussed in Section VI.

## V. EXPERIMENT AND EVALUATION

We performed a desk evaluation in Python to show the effectiveness of our approach. We assume that many devices are assigned a common IP address, e.g., through Network Address Translation (NAT). Likewise, many resources are contained in a single server that has a certain IP address. Our experiment considers two source IP addresses. The number of devices is increased from 10 to 100 in a succession of 10 devices. Similarly, at destination, two resource servers, each assigned with a unique destination IP address and contain 5 resources each. Any device can request any resource and the access is controlled in a similar fashion as Figure 1(b) with two controllers: Network-level access controller and Application-level access controller. In our first evaluation, we considered the effect of applying policy distribution on the size of the ACL (number of entries in ACL). We created the input application-level ACL with *'allow'* probability of approx. 40% (from the ABAC policy). The distribution algorithm distributes this ACL into network-level and remaining set of application-level ACL enforced at network-level access controller and application-level access controller respectively. Figure 3 shows the ACL size comparison before and after applying policy distribution.

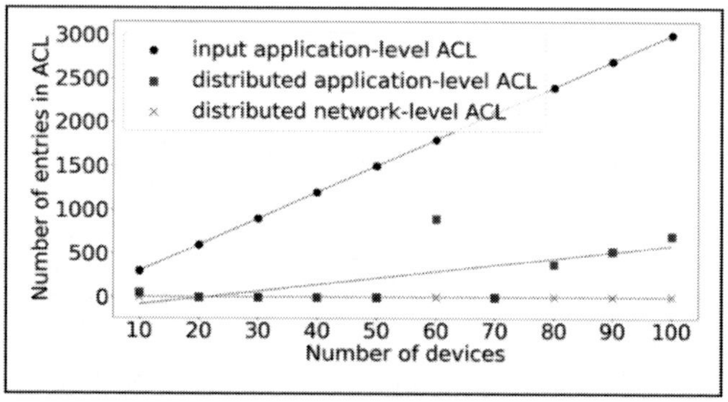


Figure 3. Comparison of the size of the policy before and after distribution.

It can be observed that with the increase in the number of devices, the difference between the size of the input and distributed application-level ACL is increased. This is due to the presence of network-level access controller which cuts the access before reaching application-level access controller. As the ACL is a list of sequentially arranged filters or commands, the throughput is inversely proportional to the size of the ACL [21]. The increase in the difference between the application-level ACL size suggests that the throughput for the distributed application-level ACL will be higher compared to the original application-level ACL, indicating latency reduction.

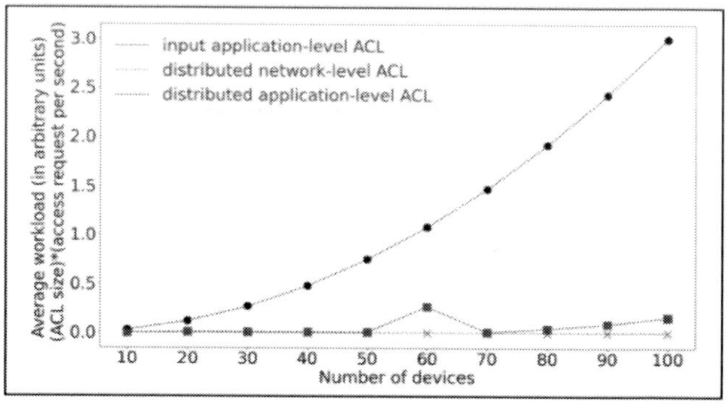


Figure 4. Comparison of the average workload on each controller before and after distribution algorithm.

TABLE I. PERFORMANCE COMPARISION BETWEEN ORIGINAL AND DISTRIBUTED ACL.

| Metric | Original Application-level ACL | Network-level ACL | **Proposed method** |
|---|---|---|---|
| **Access workload** | (100%) | 1% | **7%** |
| **Access granularity** | (100%) | 38% | **85%** |

We compare the security and workload trade-off of our proposed method through two metrics: **average access workload** and **access granularity**. The average access workload is described here, as the average time to process all the access requests on the given access controller at an instance, and it is approximated as the product of the size of the ACL used by the controller and the number of access requests falling on it [22]. For this, we artificially created 100 access requests patterns in the format ('device ID, 'resource ID', 'operation') for every device and resource pair. Figure 4 shows the comparison of access workload (defined in arbitrary units) between input policy and distributed policies. Without the distribution algorithm in place, all the access requests will be managed by the application-level access controller. As the number of access requests increase with the increase in number of devices, the access workload on the application-level access controller will keep on increasing. However, when the distribution is applied, the access workload will be divided among both the network-level as well as the application-level access controllers. This, together with smaller ACL size after distribution will result in significant workload reduction after distribution relative to input application-level ACL as shown in Figure 4. For the case of 100 devices, relative to the access workload at original application-level ACL (taken as 100%), the total access workload (network-level ACL + application-level ACL) after distribution is only around **7%**, which is comparable to simply implementing only network-level ACL as shown in Table I.

To evaluate the impact on security after distribution, we utilized access granularity metric. We measure the access granularity of a given ACL as the fraction of all access decisions enforced by the ACL which match the input application-level ACL, given the same access patterns. We assume that the input application-level ACL is carefully constructed to provide accurate access decisions with fine granularity. Therefore, any access deviations from the input application-level ACL will result in degrade of access granularity, and thus a degrade in security, as the new access decisions enforced by the access controllers after the policy distribution would not be correct. If we only use network-level ACL for access control, then in case of 100 devices, as expected, the access granularity of a network-level ACL is only 38% relative to the input application-level ACL. However, our proposed method achieves access granularity of **85%**, significantly greater than the network-level ACL. Our method thus, suggests **greater reduction in access control workload** of application-level ACL by distributing the workload among the network-level and application-level access controllers **without degrading the satisfaction of security requirements**.

## VI. DISCUSSION

In our method, the ACLs are dynamically distributed. Meaning, once the environmental conditions are changed, i.e., the attribute values belonging to the subject, resource or context change, or when new device join, etc., new ACL rules are distributed, and the previous ones are revoked (by any internal mechanism inside the controllers). The ACL enforced by our distributed mechanism sharply reduce the access control workload of application-level access controller by transferring many of the application-level policies from application-level access controller to the network-level access controller, which controls the access with low processing load. The access requests which are decided to be *"denied"* on the network-level access controller are dropped, and thus cannot reach the application-level access controller. Therefore, those requests results in no workload at the application-level access controller. Such distribution also reduces the size of the application-level ACL which now contains access rules corresponding to only those patterns which are decided to be *'allowed'* by the network-level access controller. As we increase the number of devices, more and more access requests are controlled on the network-level access controller, resulting in significant reduction of workload relative to the input application-level ACL. This is particularly useful in CPS, which contain large number of connected devices accessing data for real-time applications. A large access workload on the application-level access controller may induce latency in the access decisions, thus degrading the application's performance. By employing the distributed control approach, therefore enables to realize the real-time access. Our approach also enhances security, in terms of early rejection of malicious activities. With only using application-level ACL, every request reaches the application-level access controller, usually located close to a resource (such as implemented inside the resource server). This may allow an attacker to compromise availability by launching DDOS. Meanwhile, with our approach, such access requests can be rejected early-on by the network-level access controller, thus minimizing the risk of DDOS and congestion of enterprise bandwidth. This may also improve the CPS performance by allocating the saved bandwidth to mission-critical and other necessary services. Hence, the approach balances the security and workloads towards overall business growth.

In our evaluation, the access granularity after policy distribution was around 15% less relative to the input ACL. Investigating further, we observed that our approach correctly mimicked the input application-level ACL in case of "DENY" decisions, but in some cases failed to mimic the "ALLOW" cases. It means that some access patterns got rejected on the network-level ACL but were originally allowed in the application-level ACL, resulting in additional mis-control and thus causing granularity degradation. The reason of this additional mis-control being that these access patterns belong to a (Source IP, Destination IP) pair which mainly contains access from devices which are intended to be rejected. As our aggregation approach uses a general network allow-rate based mechanism, in such cases, "DENY" decision would be enforced on the network-level access controller when the allow-rate is small. However, it is possible that in some cases, those access patterns which were mis-controlled on the network-access controller may represent critical workflow, such as emergency situations, or mission critical services, which should not be disrupted for maintaining business continuity. Stopping them may result in a loss of availability to those services and may degrade the reliability of the access control system. To overcome this, we conceptualize an algorithm which would intend to balance the workload, security along with the business requirements. Simplistically, to decide the access granularity, the algorithm would evaluate the negative business impacts caused by the general policy aggregation approach, and then utilize several algorithms or techniques to reduce this impact. It may select any one or more techniques depending on the use-case and dynamic environmental conditions.

One example of such an algorithm is the use of attributes of application-level policy defined with attributes such as 'location', 'resource-confidentiality', 'access needs", etc., as an additional method for policy aggregation. It utilizes the impact of these attributes on the access decision for a given access pattern. For instance, consider **confidential** resources such as *employee personal details*. If the access to such resources is mistakenly permitted (mis-controlled), then it causes a large impact of information leakage. On the other hand, resources such as *server monitoring API-calls*, *diagnostics*, *updates*, etc. are essential-workflow resources that have high **access-needs** for business continuity, and it would cause large impact on customer services and revenue, if the access to them is mistakenly denied (mis-controlled). Likewise, the mis-control impact (termed attribute impact) is estimated using access attributes, such as "resource-confidentiality" and "access-needs' respectively. The attribute-impact may dynamically decide access granularity between network-level and application-level access control. For instance, in case of large attribute impact, application-level access control can be chosen for fine-granularity. In the foresight, it is necessary to consider which attributes lead to optimization between access granularity and workload. The implementation of such concept is left for future work. The evaluation performed in the current study assumes the input application-level ACL to be 100% accurate and the performance objective of the distributed policies is to mimic the original policy as close as possible with low access control workload. Thus, the current results are limited by the accuracy of the application-level ACL itself. As we obtained the accurate (input) ACL through a manually defined application-level ABAC policy, the evaluation of accuracy of the application-level ACL was out of the scope of this study. The current research fulfils the objective to show case a lightweight mechanism to achieve efficient fine-grained access control. The construction and evaluation of the improved method as well as the performance evaluation of the distributed ACLs in a real network scenario is a task for the future work.

## VII. Conclusion

For optimal performance of any access control mechanism, balancing the security and access control workload is a key challenge which is explored in this research. We proposed a novel approach of achieving a lightweight fine-grained access control mechanism by distributing the application-level access control policy towards coarse-grained access controller to reduce the workload while not compromising the security. Our results show a significant reduction in the access workload compared to the input application-level ACL without degrading the security when evaluated on an artificially created desk evaluation. The study observed the occurrence of mis-control for the cases of essential access requests in the presented algorithm. The second improved method is conceptualized which intends to lower such mis-control occurred in the first method while balancing the workload. The results of our work show a promising direction towards innovative solutions for optimal performance in the field of efficient access control.

## Acknowledgment

These research results were (partially) obtained from the commissioned research of National Institute of Information and Communications Technology (NICT) [0120101], JAPAN.

## References


[1] Z. Wang, W. Xie, B. Wang, J. Tao, and E. Wang, "Survey on recent advanced research of CPS security", Applied Sciences, vol. 11, no. 9, pp. 3751, 2021.

[2] A. Humayed, J. Lin, F. Li, and B. Luo, "Cyber-physical systems security—A survey", IEEE Internet of Things Journal, vol 4, no. 6, pp. 1802-1831, 2017.

[3] S.V. Sudarsan, O. Schelén, and U. Bodin, "Survey on delegated and self-contained authorization techniques in CPS and IoT", IEEE Access, vol. 9, pp. 98169-98184, 2021.

[4] J. Kindervag, and S. Balaouras, "No more chewy centers: Introducing the zero trust model of information security" Forrester Research 3, 2010.

[5] Amoroso, and G. Edward, "From the enterprise perimeter to a mobility-enabled secure cloud", IEEE Security and Privacy, vol. 11, no. 1, pp. 23-31, 2013.

[6] S. Rose, O. Borchert, S. Mitchell, and S. Connelly, "Zero trust architecture", National Institute of Standards and Technology, 2020.

[7] V. C. Hu, D. R. Kuhn, D. F. Ferraiolo and J. Voas, "Attribute-based access control", Computer, vol. 48, no. 2, pp. 85-88, 2015.

[8] J. Bethencourt, A. Sahai, and B. Waters, "Ciphertext-policy attribute-based encryption", IEEE symposium on security and privacy (SP'07), pp. 321-334, May, 2007

[9] S. Patil, M. Polte, K. Ren, W. tantisiriroj, L. Xiao, J. Lopez, G. Gibson, A. Fuchs, and B. Rinaldi, "Ycsb++ benchmarking and performance debugging advanced features in scalable table stores", ACM Symposium on Cloud Computing, vol. 2, pp. 1-14, Oct. 2011.

[10] L. Touati, Y. Challal, and A. Bouabdallah, "C-cp-abe: Cooperative ciphertext policy attribute-based encryption for the internet of things", International Conference on Advanced Networking Distributed Systems and Applications, IEEE, pp. 64-69, June, 2014.

[11] N. Oualha, and K. T. Nguyen, "Lightweight attribute-based encryption for the internet of things", International Conference on Computer Communication and Networks (ICCCN), vol. 25, pp. 1-6, Aug. 2016.

[12] A. Shaghaghi, M.A. Kaafar, S. Scott-Hayward, S. S. Kanhere, and S. Jha, "Towards policy enforcement point as a service (peps)", IEEE Conference on Network Function Virtualization and Software Defined Networks (NFV-SDN), pp. 50-55, Nov. 2016.

[13] C. DeCusatis, P. Liengtiraphan, A. Sager, and M. Pinelli, "Implementing zero trust cloud networks with transport access control and first packet authentication", IEEE International Conference on Smart Cloud (SmartCloud), pp. 5-10, Nov. 2016.

[14] T. Ahmad, U. Morelli, and S. Ranise, "Distributed Enforcement of Access Control policies in Intelligent Transportation System (ITS) for Situation Awareness", In Proceedings of the International Conference on Availability, Reliability and Security, vol. 17, pp. 1-10, August, 2022.

[15] E. Liu, Huawei Technologies Co Ltd, "Firewall control system based on a next generation network service and method thereof", U.S. Patent No. 7,987,503, Jul. 2011.

[16] B. Alzahrani, , and N. Fotiou, "Enhancing internet of things security using software-defined networking". Journal of Systems Architecture, 110, 101779, Nov, 2020.

[17] C. Tang, X. Fu, and P. Tamg, "Policy-Based Network Access and Behavior Control Management", IEEE 20th International Conference on Communication Technology (ICCT), vol. 20, pp. 1102-1106, Oct, 2020.

[18] Z. Feng, P. Zhou, Q. Wang, and W. Qi, "A Dual-layer Zero Trust Architecture for 5G Industry MEC Applications Access Control", IEEE International Conference on Electronic Information and Communication Technology (ICEICT), vol. 5, pp. 100-105, Aug, 2022.

[19] M. Gupta, F. Patwa, J. Benson, and R. Sandhu, "Multi-layer authorization framework for a representative Hadoop ecosystem deployment", ACM on Symposium on Access Control Models and Technologies, vol. 22, pp. 183-190, June, 2017.

[20] M. M. Kocatürk, and T. İ. Gündem, "A fine-grained access control system combining MAC and RBACK models for XML", Informatica, vol. 19, no. 4, pp. 517-534, 2008.

[21] B. A. Khalaf, S. A. Mostafa, A. Mustapha, A. Ismaila, M. A. Mahmoud, M. A. Jubaira, and M. H. Hassan, "A simulation study of syn flood attack in cloud computing environment", AUS journal, vol. 26, no. 1, pp. 188-197, 2019

[22] D. Suzuki, S. Imai, and T. Katagiri, "new index of hidden workload for firewall rule processing on virtual machine", International Conference on Computing, Networking and Communications (ICNC), pp. 632-637, Jan. 2017.

# ChatIDS: Explainable Cybersecurity Using Generative AI

Victor Jüttner*, Martin Grimmer†, Erik Buchmann‡
Dept. of Computer Science, Leipzig University, Germany
Center for Scalable Data Analytics and Artificial Intelligence (ScaDS.AI) Dresden/Leipzig, Germany
Email: *juettner@informatik.uni-leipzig.de,
†grimmer@informatik.uni-leipzig.de,
‡buchmann@informatik.uni-leipzig.de

*Abstract*—**Intrusion Detection Systems (IDS) are a proven approach to secure networks. However, in a privately used network, it is difficult for users without cybersecurity expertise to understand IDS alerts, and to respond in time with adequate measures. This puts the security of home networks, smart home installations, home-office workers, etc. at risk, even if an IDS is correctly installed and configured. In this work, we propose ChatIDS, our approach to explain IDS alerts to non-experts by using large language models. We evaluate the feasibility of ChatIDS by using ChatGPT, and we identify open research issues with the help of interdisciplinary experts in artificial intelligence. Our results show that ChatIDS has the potential to increase network security by proposing meaningful security measures in an intuitive language from IDS alerts. Nevertheless, some potential issues in areas such as trust, privacy, ethics, etc. need to be resolved, before ChatIDS might be put into practice.**

*Index Terms*—**Intrusion Detection; ChatGPT; Networks**

## I. Introduction

In recent years, privately used networks have come into the focus of cyberattacks. Reasons for this include the increased use of home-office working models [1], a shift to private areas during pandemics [2] or the proliferation of smart-home devices [3]. Intrusion Detection Systems (IDS) are a well-established approach to detect and fight cyberattacks [4], [5]. IDS scan the network and/or network appliances and send alerts for suspicious network activity.

In industry, business and government, IDSs are an important line of defense in the cybersecurity infrastructure. To this end, these sectors employ well-trained cybersecurity experts to configure, manage and maintain IDS, continuously improve the IDS rule-set, distinguish false alarms from real attacks, and design, prioritize and implement appropriate countermeasures. It is feasible to pre-configure a network-based IDS for home networks [6]. However, without a solid background in cybersecurity, it is difficult for a home user to interpret IDS alerts such as "`MALWARE-CNC Harakit botnet traffic`", distinguish false alerts from real attacks, and devise appropriate and timely countermeasures. Static sets of explanations for well-known cyberattacks [7] do not solve this problem.

In this paper, we describe our work in progress on ChatIDS, our approach to let a large language model (LLM) – a generative artificial intelligence approach – explain IDS alerts and suggest countermeasures in an intuitive, non-technical way to users without cybersecurity knowledge. ChatIDS sends anonymized IDS alerts to a LLM, and allows the user to ask questions if the generated texts are not yet understandable enough. In particular, this paper makes four contributions:

- We specify the requirements for an approach that increases the network security in privately used networks by explaining the alerts of an IDS to a non-expert.
- We describe ChatIDS, our approach to let ChatGPT [8] explain alerts from Snort [9], Suricata [10] and Zeek [11]. The explanations include cybersecurity measures and hints on why/when the measures should be implemented.
- We evaluate the feasibility of this approach using a small series of experiments with typical IDS alerts.
- To explore ChatIDS' design space, we had interdisciplinary AI experts put together issues that must be researched, before ChatIDS can go into practice.

This paper is structured as follows: Section II introduces related work. In Section III, we outline ChatIDS, our approach to explain IDS messages to non-experts. Section IV describes a number of experiments to prove feasibility, and Section V contains open issues for interdisciplinary research.

## II. Related Work

In this section, we introduce related work on network security approaches and generative AI models.

### A. Network Security

**Intrusion Detection Systems** (IDS) monitor a system for unauthorized or suspicious activity. IDS can be distinguished by system type and detection type. The system type can be *host-based*, to control a single device, or *network-based* to control a network. Detection types can be *anomaly-detection*, which detect activities that significantly differ from the regular usage or *misuse-detection*, which uses signature rules to match known intrusions [12]. Popular examples for rule-based network-based IDS are Snort, Suricata and Zeek. To use these IDS it first needs a rule-set. Popular predefined rule-sets for networks are snort3-community-rules [13], suricata-rules [14], Yara [15] and Sigma [16].

### B. Generative AI

**Generative modeling** strives to create models capable of creating new data, like sound, text or images that are similar to the data the model was trained on [17]. Popular examples for generative models are WaveNet [18] that can generate speech and music, Pix2Pix that can transform images into different styles [19] or GPT-3, a large language model (LLM), that allows for the generation of human like text [20]. Another example for a LLM is ChatGPT [8]. Like a chatbot, ChatGPT engages in a conversational manner and can generate detailed responses to questions. Bard [21] follows a similar approach. There are generative models trained for cybersecurity problems like Microsoft Security Copilot [22] but these are aimed at experts and therefore not suitable for our purpose.

**ChatGPT's** reliability varies across domains, it shows high levels of accuracy in recreation and technology domains but struggles with science and law. Problems that reduce the accuracy of ChatGPT are false information, biases and hallucinations [23]. ChatGPT and LLMs in general are capable of generating text that appears natural and to be grounded in the real context, but is unfaithful and nonsensical. This is called *hallucinated text* and much like psychological hallucinations, they can be difficult to distinguish from real perception [24].

**Prompts** are the input for a generative model, they can be a text or image that give the model instructions for the requested output. Prompts provide an intuitive way to engage with generative models [25]. For image generation a prompt could be a different image or a text description. For LLMs a prompt is a text that provides context for the desired output e.g., a question or a command to summarize information.

**Prompt Engineering** deals with optimizing prompts to achieve better responses from LLMs. For recurring problems design patterns can be used to form prompts and optimize the output, analogous to software patterns [26]. For example, the *Persona Pattern* lets the LLM assume a certain role. This can help if the LLM should respond in a special way. If the output must follow a structure, a *template* can be given in the prompt. The *Context Manager* Pattern enables the user to provide or remove context from a prompt.

## III. ChatIDS: Explainable Security

We aim at integrating a network-based IDS in privately used networks, to protect the network against cyberattacks from the Internet. For this purpose, we distinguish two roles:

An ***expert*** has the cybersecurity expertise necessary to operate and maintain an IDS, to understand its alarms, and respond to alarms with appropriate and timely actions.

A ***user*** lacks this type of expertise. A user may follow manuals written without technical vocabulary. It is difficult for a user to figure out if an IDS alert is from a real attack or due to false detection of the IDS, and to act accordingly.

An IDS [6] can be preconfigured for home networks, and integrated into a security process [27]. However, without knowledge of cybersecurity the user is left with only three possible actions: (a) do nothing, (b) turn off the device, or (c) ask an expert for help. Our ChatIDS approach strives to provide intuitive and understandable explanations of IDS alerts to give users a wider range of appropriate security measures. Therefore, ChatIDS must meet three requirements:

**R1: (Errors)** The user must assess the probability that the IDS has sent a false alert. For example, the IDS might have detected by mistake an attack that is impossible on the device.

**R2: (Urgency)** The user must assess the urgency of the alert, i.e., if it calls for immediate action, or not.

**R3: (Actions)** The user must identify appropriate measures, e.g., to execute a factory reset and install a security patch.

To explore the solution space for a generative AI approach fulfils these requirements for IDS, we use a constructive research method. In particular, we (a) model ChatIDS, we use it (b) to evaluate its technical feasibility, and (c) to discuss potential issues with interdisciplinary AI experts.

### A. Our ChatIDS Approach

The information flow of ChatIDS is illustrated in Figure 1.

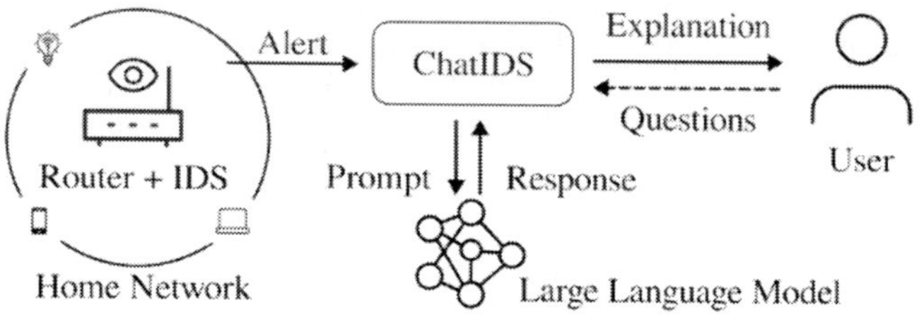


Fig. 1. Information Flow of ChatIDS

A **network-based IDS component** inspects the network packets that pass a router for suspicious traffic, and generates alerts. The IDS should be a signature-based IDS so that its alert messages are specific enough for the LLM.

The **LLM component** contains a large language model that is responsible for translating the alerts from the IDS into a language a non-expert can understand. Furthermore, this component can be used in an interactive way: If the users do not understand the explanation or the suggested measures, they can ask for details. Similarly, to the IDS the LLM is also an external component to ChatIDS.

The **ChatIDS component** is the core of our approach. ChatIDS accepts alerts from the IDS component, sends them to the LLM component for a translation into an intuitive explanation, and presents a user interface with the explanations to the user. If the user requires further support, they can use the interface to send follow up questions to the LLM. To translate alerts into intuitive explanations, the ChatIDS component contains pre-defined templates for LLM prompts.

For privacy reasons, the alerts are anonymized in three ways, before being sent to the LLM component: First, ChatIDS removes any device identifiers or network information from the alert. Second, ChatIDS sends the anonymized alert together with a set of dummy alerts to the LLM component, so that this component does not learn the real alert with certainty. The explanations from the LLM component are stored in a cache, so that the same explanation must not be requested twice.

## IV. Experimental Evaluation

Since this paper contains work in progress, we exemplarily evaluate ChatIDS with selected use cases.

TABLE I
EVALUATION OF ALERTS AND RESPONSES

| Alert | Corr. | Desc. | Cons. | Meas. | Urg. | Int. |
|---|---|---|---|---|---|---|
| MALWARE-CNC Harakit botnet traffic | ✓ | ✓ | ✓ | x | x | x |
| SERVER-WEBAPP NetGear router default password login attempt admin/password | ✓ | ✓ | ✓ | x | ✓ | x |
| SURICATA MQTT unassigned message type (0 or >15) | ✓ | ✓ | ✓ | ✓ | x | ✓ |
| SURICATA HTTP Response abnormal chunked for transfer-encoding | ✓ | x | ✓ | ✓ | ✓ | x |
| Mirai Botnet TR-069 Worm - Generic Architecture | ✓ | ✓ | ✓ | x | ✓ | x |
| Linux.IotReaper | ✓ | ✓ | ✓ | x | ✓ | ✓ |
| Identifies IPs performing DNS lookups associated with common Tor proxies. | ✓ | x | ✓ | x | ✓ | x |
| Detects remote task creation via at.exe or API interacting with ATSVC namedpipe | ✓ | ✓ | ✓ | x | ✓ | x |

### A. Experimental Setup

In line with Figure 1, we assume a home network with several smart-home devices. A router connects the network to the Internet and can observe any network packets. We assume a Philips Hue Bridge [28] is attacked. To implement the network-based IDS they are installed on the router and execute either the Snort [13], Suricata [14], Yara [15] or Sigma [16] ruleset. From each IDS implementation, we experiment with two alerts, as shown in the first column of Table I. The alerts are classified as important, and a user intervention is required.

The Intrusion Detection System in a home network has detected an intrusion and sent out the alert [ALERT MSG]. Your job is to inform [USER] about the alert in a warning message. You're in the role of a cybersecurity expert that interprets the alert and explains the alert in a warning message to [USER]. Your goal is to inform Jon about the intrusion in a way he understands and motivate the user to take steps to stop the intrusion. [USER] has no cybersecurity expertise and won't understand technical instructions, you need to provide clear, easy and non-technical instructions to follow. Don't use technical terms like "two-factor-authentication", "Intrusion Detection System", "intrusion" or "unassigned message", use simple non-technical terms instead. Don't use the term "Intrusion Detection System". Your explanation and instructions have to align with how [USER] thinks about cyberattacks. The Smart Home consists of several Smart Home Devices, the Intrusion Detection System has detected the intrusion on [DEVICE]. The warning message has to follow this order: Explain the intrusion, explain the potential consequences for the user if he won't comply with the warning message and give instructions on how to stop the intrusion in an itemized list.

Fig. 2. Template for a ChatGPT Prompt

We realized ChatIDS using ChatGPT (gpt-3.5-turbo) [8]. To generate an explanation, ChatIDS embeds each alert into a ChatGPT prompt, as shown in Figure 2. This prompt implements the patterns "Template", "Persona" and "Context Manager", as explained in Section II. Since the training data for ChatGPT comes from the Internet and much of the text on the Internet deals with security issues, we do not expect ChatGPT to produce hallucinations.

### B. Results

Figure 3 shows an example of the output produced by ChatGPT. For a better understanding, the figure shows the non-anonymized output that includes names and devices. We have tested the prompts from the first column of Table I, one by one, and we have evaluated the output of ChatGPT according to our three requirements *R1: (Errors)*, *R2: (Urgency)* and *R3: (Actions)*. To evaluate R1, we test how well the generated explanation describes the problem (Column "Desc." in Table I),

Dear Jon,

We have detected an unauthorized access attempt to your Philips Hue Bridge, which is a device in your Smart Home. This access attempt was classified as "MALWARE-CNC Harakit botnet traffic" by our system, which means that a group of computers infected with malware is trying to control your device without your permission.

If you don't take any action, your Smart Home devices, including your Philips Hue Bridge, could be used to conduct malicious actions without your knowledge. For example, attackers could use your devices to perform Distributed Denial of Service (DDoS) attacks, steal your personal data or control your devices to cause harm.

To stop the intrusion and protect your Smart Home, please follow these simple instructions:

1. Isolate the Philips Hue Bridge by disconnecting it from the internet.
2. Reset the Philips Hue Bridge to its default factory settings.
3. Configure the Philips Hue Bridge with a new username and password.
4. Check for any suspicious activity in your other Smart Home Devices.

Please don't hesitate to contact us in case you need further assistance or have any questions.

Best regards, your ChatIDS

Fig. 3. Example for an Explanation

and how intuitively understandable it is (Column "Int."). For R2, we assess the description of the consequences of ignoring the alert (Column "Cons.") and how urgent the description is (Column "Urg."). For R3 we search for a meaningful description of countermeasures (Column "Meas."). We also evaluate the correctness of the explanation (Column "Corr.").

As expected, each generated explanation was correct. Furthermore, the table shows that ChatGPT was able to explain the consequences of not taking actions in any case. In the majority of cases, ChatGPT produced a good description of the security issue that has caused the alert, and transported a sense of urgency. The description of countermeasures and the use of non-intuitive terminology leave room for improvement.

## V. OPEN RESEARCH ISSUES

As a part of our ongoing work, we have conducted a pre-study with experts from the Center for Scalable Data Analytics and Artificial Intelligence Dresden/Leipzig to compile open issues for interdisciplinary research. Our AI experts cover the topics applications, cybersecurity, ethics, jurisprudence and privacy. We presented our ChatIDS approach, asked for potential problems, and consolidated the answers:

**Security:** ChatIDS potentially increases network security, compared to a scenario where a non-expert is left alone with the alert. However, an external LLM can be a new attack surface, and incorrect or incomprehensible explanations might lead to inappropriate actions.

**Privacy:** With ChatIDS, the LLM learns that a cyberattack may have occurred on a particular network. Anonymizing device IDs and sending dummy alerts still allows the LLM to infer some information, e.g., if none of the (dummy) alerts sent to the LLM is possible for a particular type of device.

**Compliance:** ChatIDS has an impact on cybersecurity. However, it is unclear yet, how to conduct a risk analysis on LLMs and on components building upon these, how to evaluate and mitigate associated risks, and to integrate ChatIDS into security frameworks such as the Common Criteria [29].

**Jurisprudence:** If an alert is not explained well enough, the network could be successfully attacked. Conversely, ChatIDS could convince the user to take action upon false alerts. This creates legal issues. Do special liabilities exist, e.g. from user expectations into a superior AI? How to prove that a harm was caused by a misconducting or negligent AI engineer?

**Trust:** Users might have a non-rational view on AI approaches, and could fear that a persuasive, non-human intelligence plots against their interests. Conversely, if a user trusts ChatIDS too much, false alerts might result in false actions.

**Ethics:** ChatIDS could provide explanations that are not only convincing, but manipulative, even if this is in the interest of the user. This raises ethical and moral questions. How drastic can explanations be formulated to induce them to take action (which may even be harmful due to a false positive)? At what point does this limit the autonomy of the user?

## VI. Conclusion and Future Work

Comprehensibility is important for any security approach in privately used networks. This paper outlines our work in progress on ChatIDS, our approach to explain alerts from an intrusion detection system to non-experts.

ChatIDS sends anonymized alerts to ChatGPT, a large language model, to explain the alert in an intuitive way and suggest meaningful countermeasures for cyberattacks. Our experiments show that ChatIDS can be implemented easily, although more work is needed on prompt engineering to ensure intuitive explanations in the first attempt. Furthermore it needs to be analyzed if the anonymization of the data could remove relevant context or affect the report. It is difficult to measure if ChatIDS actually increases network security, because this depends on the user. Our interdisciplinary experts have provided valuable insights. In the future, we will improve ChatIDS regarding security and privacy, and consider interdisciplinary aspects such as compliance, ethics and trust.

## Acknowledgement

We would like to thank Prof. Dr. Birte Platow, Dr. Hermann Diebel-Fischer, and Prof. Dr. Johannes Eichenhofer for their valuable contributions on ethical and legal questions.

## References

[1] N. Vakakis *et al.*, "Cybersecurity in smes: The smart-home/office use case," in *2019 IEEE 24th International Workshop on Computer Aided Modeling and Design of Communication Links and Networks (CAMAD)*. IEEE, 2019, pp. 1–7.

[2] R. O. Andrade, I. Ortiz-Garcés, and M. Cazares, "Cybersecurity attacks on smart home during covid-19 pandemic," in *2020 Fourth World Conference on Smart Trends in Systems, Security and Sustainability (WorldS4)*, 2020, pp. 398–404.

[3] Y. Shah and S. Sengupta, "A survey on classification of cyber-attacks on iot and iiot devices," in *2020 11th IEEE Annual Ubiquitous Computing, Electronics & Mobile Communication Conference (UEMCON)*. IEEE, 2020, pp. 0406–0413.

[4] I. Butun, S. Morgera, and R. Sankar, "A survey of intrusion detection systems in wireless sensor networks," *IEEE Communications Surveys & Tutorials*, vol. PP, pp. 266 – 282, 05 2013.

[5] R. Mitchell and I.-R. Chen, "A survey of intrusion detection techniques for cyber-physical systems," *ACM Computing Surveys (CSUR)*, vol. 46, no. 4, pp. 1–29, 2014.

[6] C. Haar and E. Buchmann, "Securing smart homes using intrusion detection systems," in *Proceedings of the 14th International Conference on Emerging Security Information, Systems and Technologies (SECURWARE'20)*, 2020.

[7] P. Datta *et al.*, "A user-centric threat model and repository for cyber attacks," in *37th ACM/SIGAPP Symposium on Applied Computing*. Association for Computing Machinery, 2022, p. 1341–1346.

[8] Introducing ChatGPT. OpenAI. (Accessed on: 8.6.2023). [Online]. Available: https://openai.com/blog/chatgpt

[9] What is Snort? Cisco. (Accessed on: 8.6.2023). [Online]. Available: https://www.snort.org/

[10] Suricata. Open Information Security Foundation. (Accessed on: 8.6.2023). [Online]. Available: https://suricata.io/

[11] The Zeek Project. An open source network security monitoring tool. (Accessed on: 8.6.2023). [Online]. Available: https://zeek.org/

[12] T. S. Sobh, "Wired and wireless intrusion detection system: Classifications, good characteristics and state-of-the-art," *Computer Standards & Interfaces*, vol. 28, no. 6, pp. 670–694, 2006.

[13] Snort community rules. Cisco. (Accessed on: 8.6.2023). [Online]. Available: https://www.snort.org/downloads/

[14] Open Information Security Foundation. (Accessed on: 8.6.2023). [Online]. Available: https://github.com/OISF/suricata/tree/master/rules

[15] Yara-rules. YaraRules Project. (Accessed on: 8.6.2023). [Online]. Available: https://github.com/Yara-Rules/rules

[16] Sigma rules. SigmaHQ. (Accessed on: 8.6.2023). [Online]. Available: https://github.com/SigmaHQ/sigma/tree/master/rules

[17] A. Lamb, "A brief introduction to generative models," *Computing Research Repository*, vol. abs/2103.00265, 2021.

[18] Wavenet. Alphabet Inc. (Accessed on: 8.6.2023). [Online]. Available: https://www.deepmind.com/research/highlighted-research/wavenet

[19] P. Isola, J. Zhu, T. Zhou, and A. A. Efros, "Image-to-image translation with conditional adversarial networks," *Computing Research Repository*, vol. abs/1611.07004, 2016.

[20] GPT-3 powers the next generation of apps. OpenAI. (Accessed on: 8.6.2023). [Online]. Available: https://openai.com/blog/gpt-3-apps

[21] Meet Bard. Google Ireland Limited. (Accessed on: 8.6.2023). [Online]. Available: https://bard.google.com/

[22] Introducing Microsoft Security Copilot. Microsoft. (Accessed on: 9.8.2023). [Online]. Available: https://www.microsoft.com

[23] X. Shen, Z. J. Chen, M. Backes, and Y. Zhang, "In ChatGPT we trust? measuring and characterizing the reliability of ChatGPT," *Computing Research Repository*, vol. abs/2304.08979, 2023.

[24] Z. Ji, N. Lee, R. Frieske, T. Yu, D. Su, Y. Xu, E. Ishii, Y. J. Bang, A. Madotto, and P. Fung, "Survey of hallucination in natural language generation," *ACM Comput. Surv.*, vol. 55, no. 12, mar 2023.

[25] Y. Zhou *et al.*, "Large language models are human-level prompt engineers," *Computing Research Repository*, vol. abs/2211.01910, 2022.

[26] J. White *et al.*, "A prompt pattern catalog to enhance prompt engineering with ChatGPT," 2023.

[27] C. Haar and E. Buchmann, "It-security compliance for home offices," in *Proceedings of the 15th International Conference on Emerging Security Information, Systems and Technologies (SECURWARE'21)*, 2021.

[28] Philips Hue Bridge. Signify Holding. (Accessed on: 8.6.2023). [Online]. Available: https://www.philips-hue.com

[29] Management Committee of the CC Recognition Arrangement, "CC:2022 Release 1," https://www.commoncriteriaportal.org/cc/, 2022.

# Privacy-preserving Vehicle Tracking Using Homomorphic Encryption

Hoang Anh Bui
HCLTech
Hanoi, Vietnam
email: anh.bui@hcl.com

Simy Chacko
HCLTech
Chenai, India
email: simy_c@hcl.com

Duc Cuong Nguyen
HCLTech
Hanoi, Vietnam
email: cuong_nguyen@hcl.com

***Abstract*—Transportation systems use location data to track and coordinate vehicle fleets. As locations pertain to sensitive information of users, privacy has become a key concern. Users can be tracked without their consent; location data could be (unintentionally) leaked, leading to costly consequences. Existing work on solving this problem often relies on using trusted servers for computation, or on masking, anonymization, obfuscation techniques on untrusted servers. Hence, either a trusted server is needed, or one must trade data utilization for privacy, unfortunately. Homomorphic encryption could be leveraged on location-based services to eliminate the need of using user's raw location while certain computations on encrypted data are still permitted. However, homomorphic encryption (1) only allows certain arithmetic (i.e., addition, multiplication) operations on encrypted data, and (2) incurs significant performance overhead. This impedes the application of homomorphic encryption in preserving the privacy of user in location-based services. This paper presents a novel approach to track a vehicle using homomorphic encryption. To this end, we propose a communication scheme that allows a vehicle to report its encrypted location to an untrusted cloud service. We design an efficient algorithm on homomorphically encrypted data to determine if vehicles are following predefined trips using advanced transformation techniques. Our evaluation shows that we can indeed flexibly employ homomorphic encryption in privacy-preserving location tracking with acceptable performance overhead. Our work only needs ≈ *6* milliseconds to compute results on encrypted location.**

***Index Terms*—Homomorphic encryption; privacy preserving; location tracking; trajectory monitoring**

## I. Introduction

Location tracking allows companies to trace and coordinate the movements of their vehicle fleets. Further, location is heavily used for different purposes such as targeted advertising [6], recommendations [16], vehicle's trajectory monitoring [18], and many more [14]. Numerous incidents related to location tracking have been reported [17].

To tackle this issue, two main lines of work have been proposed: (1) using trusted service (with sufficient security and privacy protection) and (2) techniques to mask, obfuscate, or anonymize location data. On one hand, trusted services could become a single point of failure. Once become untrusted (e.g., for financial gains), they could potentially leverage user's locations for un-ethical usages (e.g., selling, leaking). On the other hand, data obfuscation techniques, most of the time, reduce data utilization. To potentially fill this gap, Homomorphic Encryption (HE) can be utilized to provide location-based service on encrypted data. It offers two crucial benefits: data privacy-preserving and data utilization. However, it remains challenging to employ HE in location-based services for several reasons. Homomorphic encryption only allows certain arithmetic operations on encrypted data such as multiplication and addition. This impedes the practicality of HE. Homomorphic encryption further incurs significant performance overhead, which is a constraint for many applications.

In this paper, we propose a privacy-preserving approach to track vehicles using HE. To overcome the constraints of applying HE, we design an effective algorithm to determine if a vehicle is following a pre-defined trajectory with only the allowed (on encrypted data) arithmetical operations. Accompanied with the algorithm is an efficient communication protocol that only requires few rounds of data exchanges. Our evaluation shows that it is possible to bring HE into privacy-preserving location processing with acceptable performance (and communication) overhead. Our proposed algorithm needs on average *6* milliseconds to check if an encrypted location is on a specific road-segment. We further discuss techniques to work with HE and the implication of our work.

*Outline:* This paper is organized as follows. We give an overview of related work in Section II. We describe our methodology for privacy-preserving vehicle tracking in Section III. Our approach is evaluated in Section IV. Section V discusses our findings. Section VI concludes our paper.

## II. Related Work

One of the popular approaches to (partially) preserve location's privacy is reducing location's resolution. Particularly, cloaking techniques can be used to obfuscate user's location in a specific cloaked region [3]. $K$-anonymity was also proposed to obfuscate user locations [15]. The authors combined generalization (using less specific but semantically consistent locations) and suppression (completely removing the locations) techniques to achieve anonymity for user's locations. Dummy (fake) location data can also be provided together with actual (true) locations to confuse attackers [13]. However, all these data techniques degrade the utility of location data. In certain use-cases, the data might no longer be useful. Further, attackers can try to reconstruct the obfuscated data [4]

Multiple cryptography-based approaches were proposed to protect user's positions. Users could be notified if friends were in their vicinity using symmetric key to encrypt their locations [11]. For untrusted cloud services, Maris et al. introduced an architecture to distribute the management of user's location using secret sharing [10]. Recent work of Guldner et al. proposed homomorphic encryption to examine if a location is inside/outside a fencing area [5]. This however used perpendicular projection of encrypted location to examine its position, which involves approximating functions for non-basic mathematical operations (e.g., *sine*, *cosine*).

To the best of our knowledge, none of these works use homomorphic encryption with advanced transformation techniques (on encrypted data) without linear approximation involved to provide privacy-preserving location tracking.

## III. Vehicle Tracking Using Homomorphic Encryption

In this section, we provide details on how we perform vehicle tracking without learning plaintext locations. This includes details of our settings, our novel algorithm, and a few running examples on how our algorithm works.

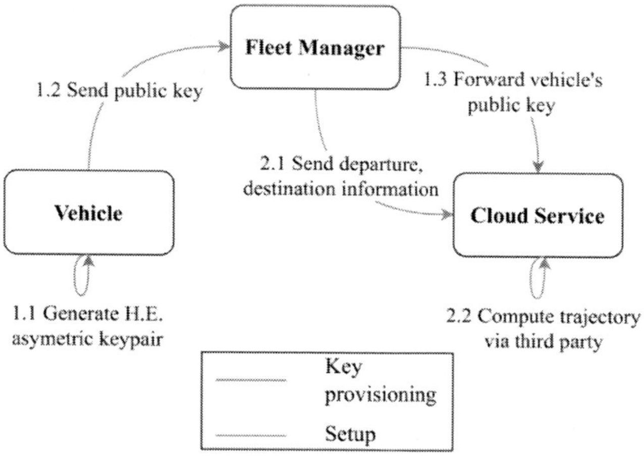


Figure 1. Setup phase.

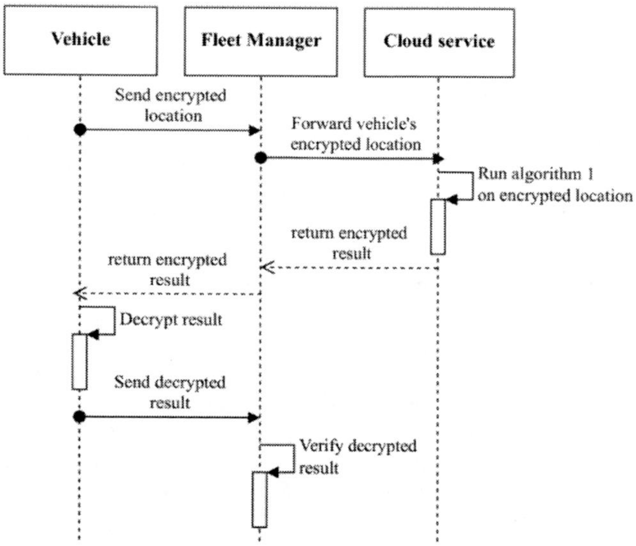


Figure 2. Communication flow.

In our settings, we assume the following parties:

- **Vehicle**: who needs to report its location periodically to a Fleet Manager. A requirement is no plaintext location can leave the vehicle.
- **Fleet Manager**: who needs to check if the aforementioned vehicle following a predefined trip. Fleet manager only needs to know whether Vehicle is following any possible route (of a predefined trip) or not. Fleet Manager is trusted, however it could be compromised.
- **Cloud Service**: who performs all computations on encrypted data to provide the answer of whether Vehicle is following any possible route (from A to B) or not. The cloud service is honest but curious, it may try to extract user's locations. In the worst scenario, cloud service could be compromised.

At the beginning of a trip, Fleet Manager provides the Vehicle a departure (A) and a destination (B) information to start the trip. Vehicle can take any route to get from A to B. Figure 1 describes the setup phase of our work. We propose this setting because it represents typical fleet management scenarios. Specifically, we want to outsource the computation to a cloud service while protecting user's privacy. In case the Cloud Service or the Fleet Manager gets compromised, it is impossible for them to learn vehicle's location as location is encrypted and only information of A and B is available in plaintext.

As we are dealing with homomorphic encryption, we are only allowed to use certain arithmetic operations on encrypted data (e.g., addition, multiplication, subtraction). However, prior algorithms to determine if a location is on a specific segment were all designed for plaintext locations. Besides, working with homomorphically encrypted data will incur significant performance overhead, we aim to tackle this by having minimal communication rounds among different communication parties. Hence, we cannot re-use existing algorithms.

*Threat model:* The adversary's goal here is to learn vehicle's location. It might try to collect vehicle's current and past location for different (unethical) purposes by attacking the Fleet Manager or the Cloud Service. In our setting, we assume the GPS location is always reported correctly (e.g., by using trusted hardware component in the vehicle [7]). We assume the Cloud Service and Fleet Manager in our setting is semi-honest (e.g., similar to prior works [9][12]). When Fleet Manager or Cloud Service is compromised, they are not able to extract vehicle's location as location is always encrypted and only the Vehicle holds the decryption key.

*Homomorphic encryption scheme:* As we work with location's coordinates in the form of longitude and latitude (e.g., float numbers), we use the *CKKS* scheme as this scheme can work with float data type.

*Key provisioning:* Our work uses the public-key scheme with four operations: (1) *KeyGen* produces a public key (*pk*) and a secrete key (*sk*); (2) *Encrypt* uses *pk* to encrypt a plaintext $m$ and produces a cipher-text $c$; (3) *Decrypt* uses *sk* to decrypt the above cipher-text $c$; (4) *Evaluate* uses *pk* to perform computation (e.g., addition and multiplication) on a set of cipher-text $C = c_1, c_2, ..., c_n$

Vehicle is responsible for setting up the encryption text with encryption (private) key and computation (public) key. The encryption key never leaves the Vehicle while the computation key is shared with the Cloud Service for running computation on encrypted data.

**Algorithm 1:** Algorithm to determine if an encrypted location is on a predefined trip

```
1  Function shift_coordinate():
       Input : coordinate, base
       Output: shifted_coordinate
2      return [coordinate.x - base.x, coordinate.y -
         base.y]
3  Function change_basis():
       Input : coordinate, vector
       Output: changed_coordinate
       /* Perform coordinates
          transformation (e.g.,
          cooridnates rotation with an
          angle called α formed by x-axis
          and the segment P). See Figure 4
          for examples.                      */
4  Function generate_noise() ():
       Input :
       Output: random_list
       /* Generate a list of random
          length. Each element is a pair
          of 2 random numbers.               */
5  Function main():
       Input : routes, loc, security_number
       Output: ret
6      ret = []
7      for segment in routes do
8          segment.start = call: shift_coordinate
            (segment.start, segment.start)
9          segment.end = call: shift_coordinate
            (segment.end, segment.start)
10         loc = call: shift_coordinate (loc,
            segment.start)
11         vector = (segment.end.x - segment.start.x,
            segment.end.y - segment.start.y)
12         segment.end = call: change_basis
            (segment.end, vector)
13         loc = call: change_basis (loc, vector)
14         lat_del = (loc.x - segment.start.x)*(loc.x -
            segment.end.x)
15         ret.append([lat_del, loc.y])
16     ret.append(call: generate_noise())
17     ret = call: shuffle(ret)
18     return ret
```

### A. Trip Tracking

The workflow of our approach is described in Figure 2. In the setup phase, the Fleet Manager shares a predefined trip — that the vehicle needs to follow — to the Cloud Service for later computation. In the running phase, the Vehicle first encrypts its current location using its encryption key and shares the encrypted location with the Fleet Manager. Upon receiving the encrypted location, Fleet Manager forwards it to the Cloud Service. Cloud Service runs algorithm 1 on the encrypted location to produce encrypted results that indicate whether a given location is on any road segment (of the predefined trip). Cloud Service further adds noise and shuffles the results of algorithm 1 before sending them back to the Fleet Manager. This makes it harder for a compromised Fleet Manager to learn about the current route segment and route that the Vehicle is following. Fleet Manager now receives the encrypted results, it will forward to the Vehicle to ask for decryption. Vehicle, upon receiving the encrypted results, decrypts them and gets the results in plain text. Vehicle then forwards the plaintext results back to the Fleet Manager. Fleet Manager first checks in the results if any number is negative. If there is a negative number, Vehicle is on a segment of a possible route. Subsequently, if a tolerance distance is defined, Fleet Manager then checks the value of the second parameters (associated with the negative number) to see if it is less than the predefined tolerance. If that is the case, the Vehicle is following the predefined trip.

### B. Algorithm 1

Pseudo code in Algorithm 1 illustrates how we perform computation on encrypted data to provide results that indicate whether a location is on a possible route of a predefined trip. In Algorithm 1, only multiplication, addition, and subtraction are used on vehicle's location as only these arithmetic operations are allowed on homomorphically encrypted data. We take as inputs (1) a set of possible routes (representing the predefined trip) that the vehicle can follow. This set of routes is represented by an array of route segments.; and (2) vehicle's current location that has been homomorphically encrypted. For each *segment* in all possible routes, Algorithm 1 first performs coordinates shifting (line 8, 9, 10) and basis change (line 12, 13) to avoid complex operations on encrypted location. The returned results (variable *ret*) are an array consisting of encrypted obfuscated distances. Once, decrypted (by the Vehicle) the Fleet Manager checks if (1) the Vehicle is on any segment of any possible route (i.e., if any number in the array is negative); and (2) the corresponding distance of the Vehicle to the segment is within the predefined tolerance.

*Running example:* Figure 3 shows the original coordinates in gray of the vehicle and the current *segment* in Algorithm 1 that we are examining. If we want to calculate the distance of the vehicle's location to *segment*, we must use some forms of advanced mathematical operations (e.g., *sine*, *cosine*). This is however not possible on homomorphically encrypted data. We therefore need to transform the current coordinates so that we can calculate the distance using only subtraction, multiplication, and addition. We shift all coordinates such that start location of the segment ($segment_{start}$)

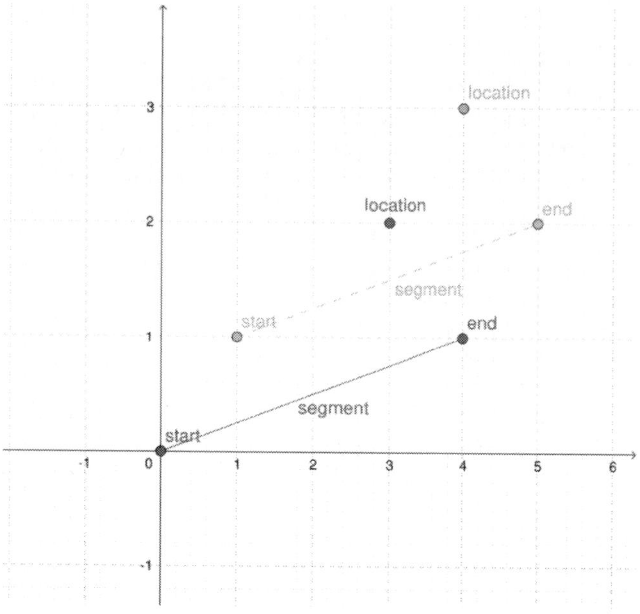


Figure 3. Coordinates shifting. New coordinates are marked blue.

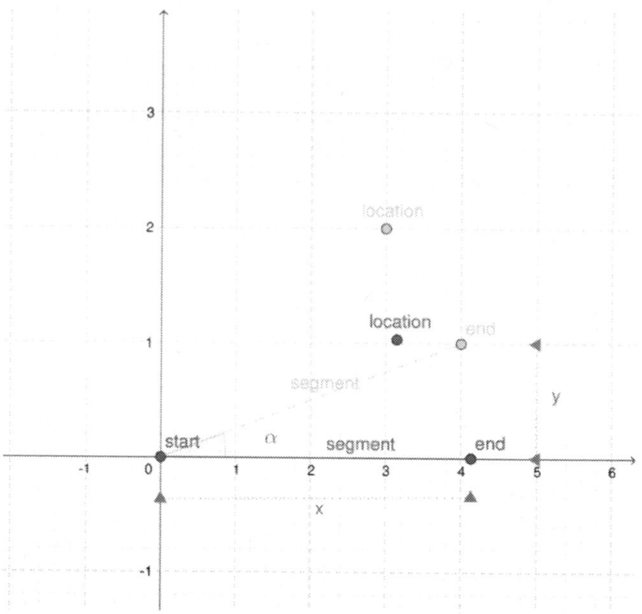


Figure 4. Coordinates with basis changed with $\alpha$ angle . New coordinates are marked blue.

becomes the origin (0, 0). Shifted coordinates are marked blue. At this point, the distance calculation related to vehicle's $\text{location}_{x,y}$ still involves complex mathematical operations (that are not allowed on homomorphically encrypted data). We then aim to rotate all coordinates such that the distance can be calculated only using allowed operations on encrypted locations. We set to rotate all coordinates so that the current segment lies on the x-axis. This gives us the distance of the current location to the segment, which is exactly the value of $\text{location}_y$ without further complex distance calculation. To this end, we apply the following equation to transform/rotate the all coordinates (i.e., change of basis [2])

$$\begin{bmatrix} x_{new} \\ y_{new} \end{bmatrix} = \begin{bmatrix} cos(\alpha) & -sin(\alpha) \\ sin(\alpha) & cos(\alpha) \end{bmatrix}^{-1} \times \begin{bmatrix} x_{old} \\ y_{old} \end{bmatrix}$$

The coordinates of vehicle's $\text{location}_{x,y}$ and segment *S* after coordinates' basis have been changed is shown in Figure 4. The functions *sin*($\alpha$) and *cos*($\alpha$) operated on plaintext data only (e.g., x and y are derived from segment *S* and the x-axis). Finally, we can see that, the closest distance between vehicle's $\text{location}_{x,y}$ and *S* is exactly the value of $\text{location}_y$.

Line 14 in Algorithm 1 performs calculation to determine if $\text{location}_{x,y}$ is with-in the segment *S*. The variable `lat_del` now indicates (after being decrypted) if a location is with-in the segment *S* (i.e., having a negative value) or not (i.e., having a positive value). The value of $\text{location}_y$ indicates the distance of the vehicle to the segment *S*. If the distance is less than (or equal to) a predefined tolerance, the Fleet Manager can consider that the Vehicle is still following the predefined trip. Otherwise, the Vehicle is not following. Line 15 adds to the results the distance from $\text{location}_{x,y}$ to segment *S*. Having the distance from an (encrypted) location to a *segment* allows us to later check if the distance is smaller than a predefined threshold (e.g., distance tolerance). If it is, the location is considered on the segment. This means, the vehicle is still following a predefined trip.

Finally, line 16 creates a random set of pairs to the returned results. This is to resemble (fake) variables loc.$y$ and `lat_del`, which represent *dummy* route segments. Hence, given a fake pair (loc.$y$ and `lat_del`), both elements must be greater than 0 (i.e., location is not on the current dummy route segment and its distance is a positive number). Subsequently, line 17 shuffles the results. This makes it harder for Fleet Manager (e.g., in case it is compromised) to associate the returned distance (of a location to a segment) with, which segments. Particularly, Fleet Manager knows the distance of vehicle's location to a segment but not the exact segment. For plaintext values (e.g., *segment.start*, *segment.end*), certain *sine*, *cosine* functions are used (*sine/cosine* of the angle of segment *S* and the x-axis), yet only on the coordinates of *segment.start* and *segment.end*. This is possible as predefined trip (and its possible routes) is not encrypted.

## IV. Evaluation

To determine the effectiveness of our solution, we measure its computation and communication overhead.

### A. Setup

Our setting environment is based on a Virtual Machine with 1 CPU 2.10 GHz and 4GB RAM, running Ubuntu 18. For our evaluation, `TenSeal` [1] is picked, as it enables quick implementation. We only care about *CKKS* scheme, since our data (location's coordinates) is represented by float numbers. Fleet Manager defines a trip that can be reached via 3 possible routes. Each possible route contains 10 segments. We choose number 10 to represent a typical (inner-city) route. This means Algorithm 1 must iterate over 30 route segments to track if the Vehicle is following the predefined route.

*B. Results*

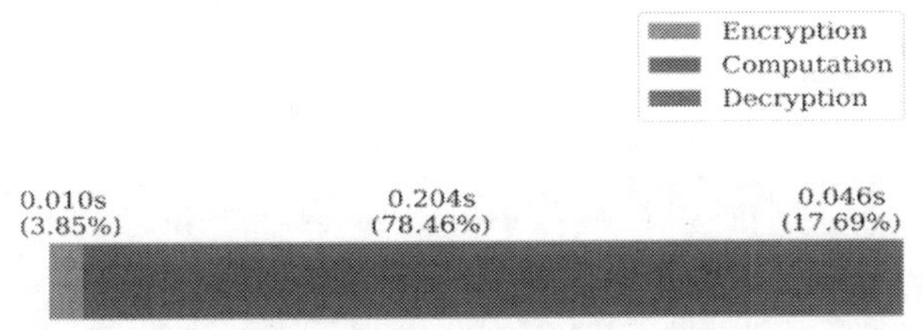


Figure 5. Execution time attribution.

We consider three phases for evaluation: encryption, computation, and decryption. In this phase, we do not consider the time spent on exchanging data among parties. Computation here refers to the execution of Algorithm 1 on the encrypted location leaves the Vehicle. We perform this evaluation 30 times on different locations to measure the execution time.

As illustrated in Figure 5, encrypting vehicle's location takes 3.85% (0.01 seconds) of the execution time. Besides, computation (running Algorithm 1 on encrypted location to return the encrypted result) takes the majority (78.46%) of the computation time with $\approx$ 0.204 seconds. Decryption on the other hand takes 17.69% the execution time with 0.046s.

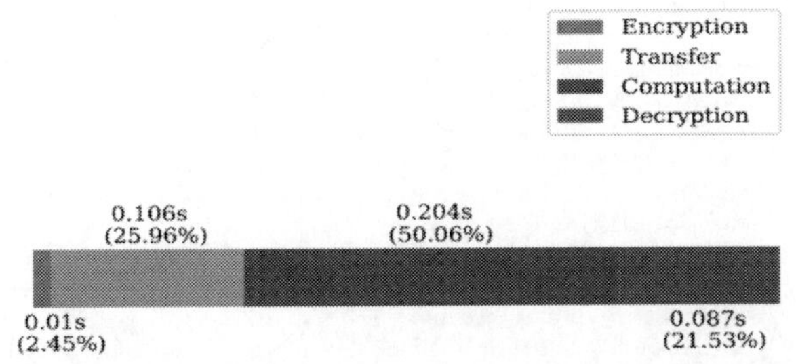


Figure 6. Total execution time attribution.

In the second evaluation, we further consider the communication time among three parties (Fleet Manager, Vehicle, and Cloud Service). As Figure 6 shows, average transfer time (among all parties) — from when encrypted location is shared by Vehicle until the decrypted results arrive at Fleet Manager — is 0.106 seconds. This means around one-forth of the total execution time is spent on exchanging data. setting. We conducted this experiment in a local network. This means the latency is negligible. Overall, the time taken for Fleet Manager to determine if a Vehicle is following a predefined trajectory is 0.407 seconds.

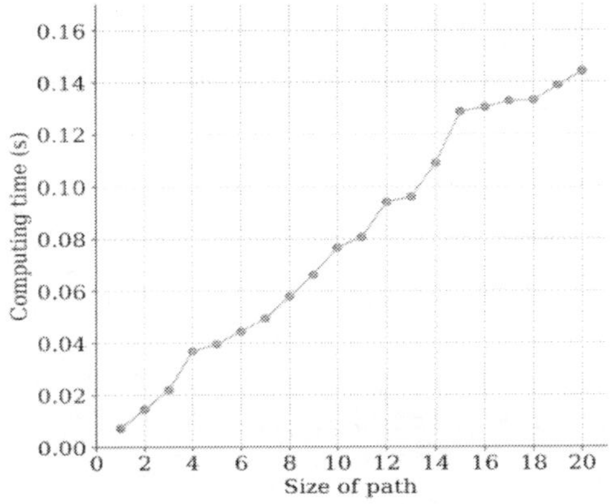


Figure 7. Correlation between execution time and N.O segments in a trajectory.

Figure 7 shows the correlation between the number of segments (segments' size) and the execution time (e.g., running Algorithm 1). We can see that the time needed to run Algorithm 1 increases linearly as the size of segments (of a predefined trajectory) increases. On average, Algorithm 1 takes $\approx 6$ milliseconds to compute results on a single segment.

*Comparison to plaintext execution:* To examine the computation overhead of our approach, we compare the execution on encrypted data against plaintext data. We run our comparison 50 times on different locations to examine the difference. On plaintext location, running Algorithm 1 takes 0.79 milliseconds while on homomorphically encrypted location it takes 60.9 milliseconds. This means, computation on encrypted location, as anticipated, takes significantly more time (77x execution time).

*Accuracy:* The accuracy of our approach depends on two factors: The approximation of the CKKS scheme and the distance tolerance set by Fleet Manager. As we use the *CKKS* implementation of `TenSeal`, we directly benefit from its precision. In our evaluation, the calculated distance has a deviation of around $\approx$ 1e-8 depending on the unit of the provided coordinates (e.g., meters, kilometers).

## V. Discussion

In this paper, we propose novel techniques to work with homomorphically encrypted data to provide vehicle monitoring service that preserve location's privacy, especially when the data processing entities (i.e., Fleet Manager or Cloud Service) are compromised. By proposing novel coordinate's transformation techniques, our work only uses arithmetic operations that are allowed on encrypted data — hence, not requiring any approximation functions, or multiple intermediates collaboration steps from the encryption key holders. Our approach prevents a compromised Fleet Manager or an untrusted Cloud Service from learning vehicle's location while still provides accurate and necessary tracking information.

### A. Limitation and Future Work

With Algorithm 1, Cloud Service needs to return a list of (encrypted) numbers. This is not optimal as future work could study a more efficient algorithm that allows checking just one number to learn vehicle's compliance.

*Performance overhead:* In our evaluation, we see a computation overhead of 77x when running Algorithm 1 on encrypted locations vs. on plaintext locations. However, we are aware that for encrypted locations, there exist other overhead such as encryption, decryption, transfer too. This will result in higher overhead overall. Hence, such a comparison only gives a rough overview of the minimal overhead of running Algorithm 1 on encrypted locations. Further, we did not consider the data sizes (to be transferred) in our experiments to judge the size overhead when applying HE. Future work could consider this aspect to provide a more comprehensive look into applying HE in location tracking.

Finally, our work relies on the security of HE schemes in-use. If adversaries can break such schemes, location data could be revealed. Specifically, CKKS scheme was shown to be vulnerable to secret key recovery under the assumption that attackers can (1) access to encryption oracle; (2) choose the function to be evaluated homomorphically; and (3) access to decryption oracle [8]. This attack exploits the linearity of the decryption function in CKKS and the hints that approximated decrypted results provide.

### B. The use of nonlinear functions

One potential direction to use nonlinear functions is to identify their corresponding approximated (linear) alternatives so that they could be applied on HE data. There are several disadvantages to this approach. Approximated functions are usually complex and could result in extreme performance overhead. With HE data, the more operations are done on it, the more noise will be accumulated. Accumulated noise could lead to the case that encrypted data cannot be decrypted any more. While bootstrapping techniques generally could remove the noise, yet it again adds more performance overhead.

### C. Application Analysis

While this work focuses on vehicle tracking, the applications of HE in location-based service is enormous. We can use HE to monitor if a person is inside a fencing area without having to collect their exact (raw) location. This protects user's privacy even in the event of data leakage (both on purpose and unintentionally). Points of interests can also be recommended to users using HE Specifically, so users can search for nearby coffee shops, restaurants, hospitals, etc. without having to provide raw location. Further, the Cloud Service, could store HE locations for future analysis. Analysis results is only be revealed with the consent of the vehicle (i.e., its owner) as the results can only be decrypted by the Vehicle.

## VI. Conclusion

This paper presents a novel privacy-preserving approach to track real-time vehicle's compliance to predefined trips. Our work leverages state of the art homomorphic encryption to protect location's privacy while still allowing computations on encrypted data to determine if a vehicle is following predefined trips. We evaluated the effectiveness of our approach and showed that homomorphic encryption can be efficiently used to protect location privacy.

## References


[1] A. Benaissa, B. Retiat, B. Cebere, and A. E. Belfedhal, "Tenseal: A library for encrypted tensor operations using homomorphic encryption," unpublished, 2021.

[2] J. G. Broida and S. G. Williamson, *A comprehensive introduction to linear algebra*. Addison-Wesley Boston, MA, USA:, 1989, vol. 4.

[3] B. Gedik and L. Liu, "Location privacy in mobile systems: A personalized anonymization model," in *25th IEEE International Conference on Distributed Computing Systems (ICDCS'05)*. IEEE, 2005, pp. 620–629.

[4] M. Gruteser and D. Grunwald, "Anonymous usage of location-based services through spatial and temporal cloaking," in *Proceedings of the 1st International Conference on Mobile Systems, Applications and Services*, ser. MobiSys '03. New York, NY, USA: Association for Computing Machinery, 2003, p. 31–42. [Online]. Available: https://doi.org/10.1145/1066116.1189037

[5] M. Guldner, T. Spieldenner, and R. Schubotz, "Nexus: Using geo-fencing services without revealing your location," in *2018 Global Internet of Things Summit (GIoTS)*. IEEE, 2018, pp. 1–6.

[6] H. Haddadi, P. Hui, T. Henderson, and I. Brown, *Targeted Advertising on the Handset: Privacy and Security Challenges*. London: Springer London, 2011, pp. 119–137. [Online]. Available: https://doi.org/10.1007/978-0-85729-352-7_6

[7] S. Hu, Q. A. Chen, J. Joung, C. Carlak, Y. Feng, Z. M. Mao, and H. X. Liu, "Cvshield: Guarding sensor data in connected vehicle with trusted execution environment," in *Proceedings of the Second ACM Workshop on Automotive and Aerial Vehicle Security*, ser. AutoSec '20. New York, NY, USA: Association for Computing Machinery, 2020, p. 1–4. [Online]. Available: https://doi.org/10.1145/3375706.3380552

[8] B. Li and D. Micciancio, "On the security of homomorphic encryption on approximate numbers," in *Advances in Cryptology – EUROCRYPT 2021: 40th Annual Internation al Conference on the Theory and Applications of Cryptographic Techniques, Zagreb, Croatia, October 17–21, 2021, Proceedings, Part I*. Berlin, Heidelberg: Springer-Verlag, 2021, p. 648–677. [Online]. Available: https://doi.org/10.1007/978-3-030-77870-5_23

[9] Y. Li and W. Xu, "Privpy: General and scalable privacy-preserving data mining," ser. KDD '19. New York, NY, USA: Association for Computing Machinery, 2019, p. 1299–1307. [Online]. Available: https://doi.org/10.1145/3292500.3330920

[10] G. Marias, C. Delakouridis, L. Kazatzopoulos, and P. Georgiadis, "Location privacy through secret sharing techniques," in *Sixth IEEE International Symposium on a World of Wireless Mobile and Multimedia Networks*. IEEE, 2005, pp. 614–620.

[11] S. Mascetti, D. Freni, C. Bettini, X. S. Wang, and S. Jajodia, "Privacy in geo-social networks: Proximity notification with untrusted service providers and curious buddies," *The VLDB Journal*, vol. 20, no. 4, p. 541–566, aug 2011. [Online]. Available: https://doi.org/10.1007/s00778-010-0213-7

[12] P. Mohassel and Y. Zhang, "Secureml: A system for scalable privacy-preserving machine learning," in *2017 IEEE Symposium on Security and Privacy (SP)*. IEEE, 2017, pp. 19–38.

[13] T. Peng, Q. Liu, D. Meng, and G. Wang, "Collaborative trajectory privacy preserving scheme in location-based services," *Inf. Sci.*, vol. 387, no. C, p. 165–179, may 2017. [Online]. Available: https://doi.org/10.1016/j.ins.2016.08.010

[14] B. Rao and L. Minakakis, "Evolution of mobile location-based services," *Commun. ACM*, vol. 46, no. 12, p. 61–65, dec 2003. [Online]. Available: https://doi.org/10.1145/953460.953490

[15] L. Sweeney, "Achieving k-anonymity privacy protection using generalization and suppression," *Int. J. Uncertain. Fuzziness Knowl.-Based Syst.*, vol. 10, no. 5, p. 571–588, oct 2002. [Online]. Available: https://doi.org/10.1142/S021848850200165X

[16] M. Xie, H. Yin, H. Wang, F. Xu, W. Chen, and S. Wang, "Learning graph-based poi embedding for location-based recommendation," in *Proceedings of the 25th ACM International on Conference on Information and Knowledge Management*, ser. CIKM '16. New York, NY, USA: Association for Computing Machinery, 2016, p. 15–24. [Online]. Available: https://doi.org/10.1145/2983323.2983711

[17] H. Yun, D. Han, and C. C. Lee, "Understanding the use of location-based service applications: do privacy concerns matter?" *Journal of Electronic Commerce Research*, vol. 14, no. 3, pp. 220–230, 01 2013.

[18] Z. Zhou, W. Dou, G. Jia, C. Hu, X. Xu, X. Wu, and J. Pan, "A method for real-time trajectory monitoring to improve taxi service using gps big data," *Inf. Manage.*, vol. 53, no. 8, p. 964–977, dec 2016. [Online]. Available: https://doi.org/10.1016/j.im.2016.04.004

# Virtual Sessions for Forensic Analysis of Video Conferencing Systems: A Novel Methodology

Jaykumar Soni, Tom Neubert, Benjamin Dietrich, Claus Vielhauer
*Department of Informatics & Media*
*Brandenburg University of Applied Sciences*
Brandenburg, Germany
{jaykumar.soni, tom.neubert, benjamin.dietrich, claus.vielhauer}@th-brandenburg.de

*Abstract*—**During the last years online meetings and consequently Video Conferencing Systems (VCS) have become more and more popular to reduce travel time and costs. Because of the dramatically increased usage of VCS, it has become more important to analyze and evaluate their security and privacy due to the huge amount of privacy related multimedia data processed by VCS. Thus, in this paper, we present a novel privacy preserving methodology to generate virtual video conferencing sessions with reproducible data to enable a comparable and reliable analysis of these systems in future work.**

*Index Terms*—**Privacy, Video Conferencing Systems, Media Security, Forensic Analysis**

## I. Introduction

In the modern world, Video Conferencing Systems (VCS) have become an essential tool for remote communication. These systems enable individuals and teams to collaborate and hold meetings from a distance, reducing travel costs and energy consumption. However, as the use of VCS continues to grow, there is an increasing need to evaluate their security, privacy, data economy and sustainability aspects. In particular, there have been reported several security and privacy issues with regard to the use of VCS (e.g. [1] and [2]) which raises concerns in the field of multimedia security. Inherently, there are privacy issues with all VCS, as facial videos and speech audios are involved, which are considered as biometric data requiring special protection. Furthermore, by analysis of the activity timelines of participants, behavioral patterns such as absence from the conference, movements, chatting behavior can be derived. These facts suggest that security analysis, especially with regard to privacy, is an important requirement within the field of multimedia security.

Due to the closed-source nature of most commercial VCS, security and privacy analysis approaches are somewhat limited to binary code analysis or behavioral analysis. e.g. by analyzing network traffic during live VC-sessions. Although VCS communication nowadays is almost 100% endpoint encrypted, but network traffic analysis can still reveal meta information about information flows, including their volumes, temporary behavior, server endpoints, streams, locations and more. In addition to deriving privacy related findings such as server operators and locations, there is also the potential to infer aspects of data economy, sustainability and reliability by these multimedia data. The network traffic analysis approach of VCS also brings along privacy issues in itself, as it requires real persons to actually use the VCS under investigation, exposing their aforementioned sensitive traits to potentially untrusted VCS service providers.

### A. Research Gap

These previously mentioned aspects leads to the need of a new approach to conceptually generate virtual video conferencing (VC-) sessions by injecting media data into VC clients to create reproducible virtual sessions for a comparable analysis of different VCS under the same data. Current concepts for the analysis of VCS (for example [1]) did not provide an environment with automated, simulated and virtual network traffic (video, audio, and text) to evaluate the systems. We assume that for a systematically forensic analysis and comparison of multiple VCS a novel concept is needed which provides simulated, stable and scripted network traffic data based on virtual VC-sessions without privacy concerns.

### B. Contribution

In this paper, we introduce a novel approach for the analysis of VCS using publicly available videos and pre-programmed scripts to simulate other VCS related activities like chatting, screen sharing and so on to generate network traffic. This approach allows the forensic analysis of encrypted data without the need for decryption and enables the evaluation of VCS without compromising user privacy. The use of virtual data instead of real biometric data protects the privacy of individuals and allows researchers to test and improve their algorithms and systems in a controlled and ethical manner and with the possibility of reproduction. The approach can provide a large and diverse dataset for studying the behavior of Video Conferencing Systems, enabling a more comprehensive understanding of these systems in real-world scenarios. Furthermore, the use of virtual data can lead to more accurate and reliable results compared to using noisy and unpredictable biometric data. Our methodology for generation of virtual VC-sessions to analyze VCS involves five steps:

1) Definition of user activities,
2) Data requirements and collection of data,
3) Automation of virtual VC-session,
4) Capture network data from virtual VC-session and
5) Forensic Analysis.

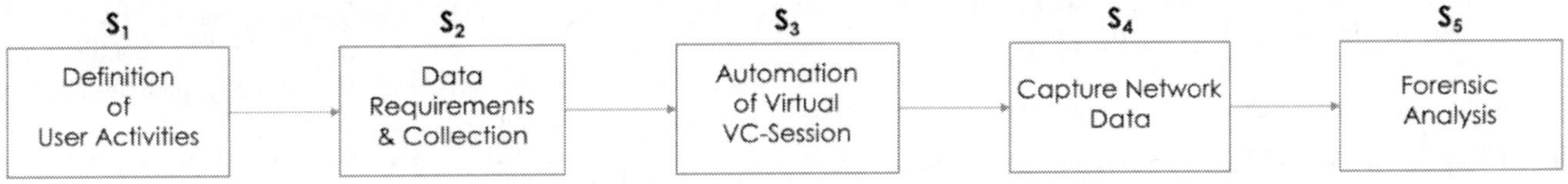


Fig. 1. Pipeline of our novel methodology

While our approach is still in its initial stages, we believe that it has the potential to offer a novel framework for the forensic analysis of VCS in future work.

### C. Structure

The work is structured as follows: In Section II, a selected State-of-the-Art of VCS analysis is presented without the claim to completeness. In Section III the novel methodology is introduced. Section IV concludes the paper with a summary, early results and future work.

## II. Selected State-of-the-Art

Forensic analysis of Video Conferencing Systems (VCS) has gained attention due to the increased use of these systems during the last years to save health, energy, costs and time. With the widespread relocation of the workplace to a private environment, security- and privacy-related aspects of Video Conferencing Systems have become more important.
Early works primarily addressed *Microsoft's Skype*™ software as widely used VCS during the last decade. Relevant papers address the following topics:

- Physical memory analysis to reconstruct user activities [3],
- Identification of *Skype*™ packets in network traffic [4],
- NAND and RAM analysis of *Skype*™ using an emulator [5] and
- Forensic analysis of *Skype*™ behavior on hard drive image on *Windows 10*™ [6].

The authors of [7] have investigated the *Cisco WebEx VCS*™ application in 2021. A forensic analysis of memory, hard disk, and a recording of network traffic was performed. In [1] Altschaffel et al. presented an approach of a forensic examination process based on heuristics and meta data analysis of VCS-related multimedia network streams. Based on the general definition of seven multimedia data streams (audio, video, screen-sharing, sharing of video, text, file-transfer and other spatial streams) 20 events could be identified that revealed sensitive user or activity related information.

## III. Methodology to Generate Virtual Sessions for Analysis of VCS

Our methodology for generating virtual video conferencing (VC-) sessions to analyze different Video Conference Systems (VCS) consists of five basic steps ($S_1$ - $S_5$, see Fig. 1). In the initial step $S_1$ the user activities for the virtual VC-sessions are defined (see Section III-A). In the second step $S_2$ the video and audio data without privacy concerns is gathered. The requirements for this data are described detailed in Section III-B. During the third step $S_3$ the automation of a virtual VC-session based on a screenplay (from $S_1$) is implemented (see Section III-C). In $S_4$ the network traffic produced by the virtual VC-session is recorded and post-processed (Section III-D). The last step $S_5$ features the potential analysis of the VCS with the recorded virtual VC-session (Section III-E).

### A. Definition of User Activities ($S_1$)

In the first step of the methodology for analyzing VCS, we define user activities $A_n$ (in this work, $n$ denotes an index number for each individual activity $A_n$, event $E_n$ or user $U_n$) to trigger VCS relevant events $E_n$ (based on [1]) in order to ensure a consistent and reproducible evaluation process. This includes creating a screenplay, which specifies different activities $A_n$ that users would carry out during the VC-session. $A_n$ are based on the functionalities present in the particular VCS that shall be analyzed in $S_5$ with the intention of identifying specific events $E_n$ of VCS. The screenplay includes details such as the number of users $U_n$ who will participate in the session and what activities $A_n$ they will perform, for example: join and leave the session, start sharing their virtual camera and audio and so on. By defining activities $A_n$ in advance, we can control user behavior and ensure consistency across different simulations, allowing for more accurate comparison of different VCS. This step is critical for eliminating variations that could potentially influence an evaluation or a comparison of different VCS and enables a more reliable analysis (in $S_5$). The output result of this step is a screenplay that details the activities $A_n$ for users $U_n$ in the virtual VC-session.

### B. Data Requirements and Collection of Data ($S_2$)

After defining the activities $A_n$ for users $U_n$ in $S_1$, the next step $S_2$ is to collect the media data required for the analysis of various VCS. Our primary goal in this step is to collect video and audio data without privacy concerns. To ensure this, we collect our data from publicly available sources such as news video platforms, which typically obtain consent from the individuals being recorded before making the footage available for public viewing. The collected data reflects the types of content and communication styles commonly encountered in real-world video conferencing scenarios. This helps us to create more accurate and relevant virtual VC-sessions. Before the collected data is used for analysis, it should be preprocessed to comply with defined requirements and standards. This may involve tasks such as formatting the data in a specific way (e.g. converting video to a particular file format or resizing of video media to a defined resolution to simulate a web cam), removing any irrelevant or extraneous information such as in-image text, or applying various filters or transformations to the data. The output result of this step is the collection of publicly available video and audio data for use in the subsequent steps.

### C. Automation of Virtual VC-Session ($S_3$)

Step $S_3$ of our methodology is the automation of the VC-session. Therefore a simulation script is implemented that takes different media like audio, video and text data as input and carries out activities $A_n$ for users $U_n$ as defined in $S_1$ in a chronological order without the need for manual intervention. As a result this step reduces the workload of manually carrying out activities $A_n$ on different clients and allows a reproducible data recording. What programming language is used for scripting the activities $A_n$ of users $U_n$ from $S_1$ with the collected data from $S_2$ should be decided by individual preferences (we used *Python 3.10*).

### D. Capture Network Data from Virtual Session ($S_4$)

In Step $S_4$, network traffic data is captured from VCS of defined user activities $A_n$ from $S_1$ with collected multimedia data from $S_2$, automated with the simulation script from $S_3$. For capturing network traffic data, we utilize a Switch $SW$ that mirrors the traffic of all *Ethernet* connected systems (from users $U_n$) to a Data Collector $DC$ (see Fig. 2). Thus, $DC$ captures the network data. It is noteworthy that in our work we can only gather network traffic data for the client-side, since we usually do not have access to the server-side (*VCS-SV*) for most commercial VCS. This approach guarantees that the data we collect accurately reflects real-world VCS scenarios. When the data is captured, it has to be post-processed to ensure that it contains only relevant data for the subsequent and use case specific forensic analysis in $S_5$ (e.g. filtering out network traffic communication based on the IP addresses of client and server along with filtering only a single protocol for analysis like *TCP* (Transmission Control Protocol) or *UDP* (User Data Protocol). Thus, $S_4$ provides a post-processed dataset of selected network traffic of a virtual session for a specific VCS scenario, with controlled and consistent user behavior.

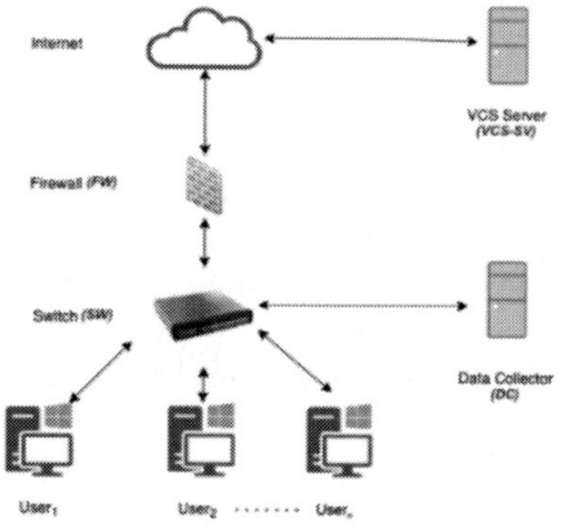


Fig. 2. Setup to capture network data of virtual VC-session $S_4$

### E. Forensic Analysis ($S_5$)

The final step $S_5$ of the methodology involves the forensic analysis of the data provided from $S_4$. The analysis can focus on various use case specific aspects, such as privacy, reliability, user activity tracking, sustainability and more. The specific aspects chosen for analysis will depend on the goals and objectives of a potential study. To perform the forensic analysis, various statistical computational techniques such as machine or deep learning based approaches can be taken into consideration. For an initial validation of the concept, we have carried out an exemplary user activity tracking for $S_5$ (see Section IV-B).

## IV. Conclusion

### A. Summary

In this paper we introduce a novel methodology for the generation of virtual session for VCS to provide a forensic analysis of VC-sessions with reliable, comparable and reproducible data. The methodology involves four steps to create data for virtual session. In the fifth step of the methodology a forensic analysis is performed which can focus on various aspects such as privacy, reliability, sustainability, user activity tracking and so on.

### B. Early Results and Future Work

For the initial proof-of-concept validation of the new methodology presented in this paper, we perform a first user activity analysis based on visualization of multimedia streams. During this initial exemplary analysis (step $S_5$), we identified user activities based on events from [1] like webcam on/off, muted/unmuted and screen sharing on an exemplary VCS. Thus, we can expect that our concept can provide reliable and reproducible virtual VC-session, which can be used for the analysis of VCS.

We will use the methodology to provide further virtual VC-session for a machine learning based analysis of multiple VC-Systems with the intention of user activity tracking.

## References

[1] R. Altschaffel, J. Hielscher, S. Kiltz, and J. Dittmann, "Meta and media data stream forensics in the encrypted domain of video conferences," in *Proceedings of the 2021 ACM Workshop on Information Hiding and Multimedia Security*, 2021, pp. 23–33.

[2] MITRE-CVE-Program, "CVE-2022-36927," Available from MITRE, CVE-ID CVE-CVE-2022-36927, 2022. [Online]. Available: https://cve.mitre.org/cgi-bin/cvename.cgi?name=CVE-2022-36927

[3] M. Simon and J. Slay, "Recovery of skype application activity data from physical memory," in *2010 International Conference on Availability, Reliability and Security*. IEEE, 2010, pp. 283–288.

[4] A. Azab, P. Watters, and R. Layton, "Characterising network traffic for skype forensics," in *2012 Third cybercrime and trustworthy computing workshop*. IEEE, 2012, pp. 19–27.

[5] M. I. Al-Saleh and Y. A. Forihat, "Skype forensics in android devices," *International Journal of Computer Applications*, vol. 78, no. 7, 2013.

[6] A. Majeed and S. Saleem, "Forensic analysis of social media apps in windows 10," *NUST Journal of Engineering Sciences*, vol. 10, no. 1, pp. 37–45, 2017.

[7] Z. Khalid, F. Iqbal, F. Kamoun, M. Hussain, and L. A. Khan, "Forensic analysis of the cisco webex application," in *2021 5th Cyber Security in Networking Conference (CSNet)*. IEEE, 2021, pp. 90–97.

# Electric Vehicle Authentication and Secure Metering in Smart Grids

Yutaka Yamaguchi
Faculty of Engineering,
Kyushu University
Fukuoka, Japan
1TE20110W@s.kyushu-u.ac.jp

Dirceu Cavendish
Department of Computer Science and Elect.,
Kyushu Institute of Technology
Fukuoka, Japan
cavendish@net.ecs.kyutech.ac.jp

Hiroshi Koide
Research Institute of Info. Tech.,
Kyushu University
Fukuoka, Japan
koide@cc.kyushu-u.ac.jp

***Abstract*—Electric vehicles have been recently produced at a very aggressive pace as a way to curb carbon emissions in the 21st century. Public utility companies are rushing to provide electric vehicle charging station infrastructure needed to serve a rapidly growing fleet of EV users in various countries around the world. Equipped with smart meters, charging stations must check vehicle's characteristics prior to charging, as well as securely report charging data back to public utility companies. In this paper, we propose to leverage an Authentication and Key Agreement protocol used in cellular networks into an electric vehicle authentication and secure metering framework. Starting with a vehicle Subscriber Identification Module, we show how generic vehicle services can be securely provided, including mutual authentication, key agreement, and key management issues.**

***Index Terms*—*Smart Grids; Electric Vehicle Charging; Authentication and Key Agreement.***

## I. Introduction

Electric Vehicles have become very popular in recent years, with hybrid and all electric models being sold in large numbers in developed countries. In addition, residential solar panels have also become popular in new house developments across the world. As a result, power utility companies in the United States and other developed countries are installing Smart Meters at residential and business buildings, in order to manage renewable energy generation and consumption to efficiently manage the electric grid [2]. These efforts are seen as evolutionary steps towards Smart Grids, which consists of intelligent power generation and transmission utilities, equipped with meters, sensing devices, and information gateways that controls energy distribution and consumption in near real time. Aggressive Smart Grid projects are currently being pursuit in US, EU, and Asia [3]. As Power Utility Companies rely on accurate metering information from smart meters, secure metering is key to a reliable electric grid management system. From a consumer's perspective, accurate billing is important. For instance, some charging stations may charge extra for vehicles staying in the stations longer than needed. Authentication and encryption mechanisms for reliably transmitting and recording data consumption of users between power companies and users via smart meters are needed.

Symetric key based authentication and encryption requires a Public Key Infrastructure (PKI) that is complex to manage, in addition to requiring more computational power than symmetric key based counterparts. About complexity, maintaining a mobile device uptodate about certificates that have been revoked is not a trivial matter. As far as processing power, although smart meters are not typically limited in power consumption, they do not necessarily come equipped with state of the art processing chipsets. Finally, symmetric key encryption is more suitable to cellular wireless interface, usually the interface of choice of Smart Meters. In this work, we propose a vehicle to Power Utility Company (PUC) authentication and secure metering scheme based on symmetric keys and cryptographic one way functions widely used in the cellular industry. We first advocate for an extension of Subscriber Identity Module (SIM) card industry to vehicles. Then, we show how to realize authentication and key agreement protocols between Power Utility Companies and EV vehicles, in order to support secure charging via smart meters. Provided that smart meters are physically protected within charging stations, the framework proposed obviates the need to manage meter credentials while still supporting secure metering.

There has been a number of research work on Security of Smart Grids in the last several years. A comprehensive survey on security issues in Smart Grids can be found at [5]. Similar to our work, [10] have proposed authentication mechanisms using credentials stored in the Electric Vehicle, using a Hardware Security Module. Due to economy of scale, a vehicle SIM is likely to be as secure and a cheaper solution than an onboard EV HSM. A Trusted Platform Module (TPM) has been proposed to safely store credentials within EVs [11]. We see such proposal to be complementary, rather than competing with our framework, as we can use TPM to store and process master keys generated by the AKA algorithm safely.

The paper material is organized as follows. Section II describes EV charging Ecosystem, its functionalities, security requirements and credential management. Section III shows how to leverage cellular authentication and key agreement protocols to provide EV/PUC mutual authentication and secure metering of charging services. Section IV discusses smart grid standards and their relation to or aka authentication protocol proposal. Section VI provides a security threat analysis of our protocol proposal. Section VII summarizes our contributions and discusses future work.

## II. Smart Grid EV System and Security

Figure 1 defines the scope of the system our work is focused on. A Public Utility Company (PUC) retails energy from distribution grid via sub-stations (not shown). For that purpose,

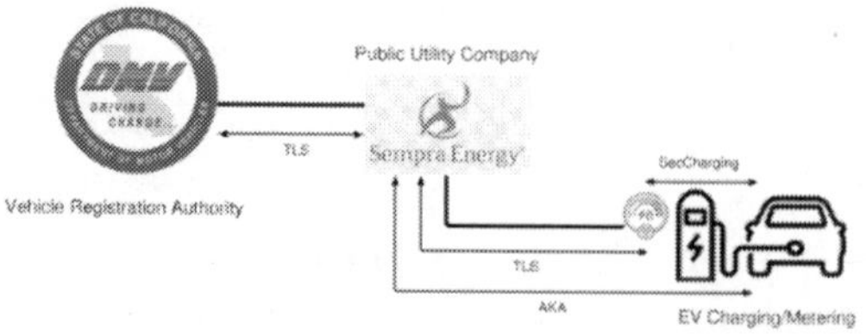


Figure 1: EV Registration and Public Utility Company Ecosystem

PUCs own and control smart meters (SM), which provides energy metering of users at energy consumption end-points, such as residential homes and commercial buildings. SMs are connected to EV charging stations, which provide both home and on the road EV charging services. Consumers EV ownership is controlled by a Vehicle Registration Authority, which manages vehicle ownership during the lifetime of the vehicle, issuing registration and license plates.

### A. Secure EV charging

Secure EV charging consists of the following components:

- **Mutual authentication of service provider (PUC) and consumer/vehicle:** PUC needs to recognize a licensed vehicle and associate it with a legitimate owner upon which charging fees are assessed. Consumers, on the other hand, need to have trust that the charging station and its SM belongs to a trustworthy PUC.
- **Secure charging metering:** Energy consumption metering needs to be reliable and confidential between PUC service provider and user/vehicle. In this paper, we assume a separate mechanism to ensure Smart Meters/EV chargers can be trusted by the PUC. Several mechanisms are possible to authenticate a SM, from a X.509 certificate to Physically Unclonable Functions [6].

For authentication between PUCs and user/vehicle, we propose a symmetric cryptographic based Authentication and Key Agreement mechanism, similar to the one widely used in cellular networks [1]. We advocate that an alternative asymmetric key scheme, based on Public Key Infrastructure (PKI), is not appropriate for mobile devices, due to complexities in managing certificate revocations and other key management issues.

### B. Vehicle SIM Credential

A Subscriber Identity Module is an integrated circuit that securely stores an International mobile subscriber number (IMSI) and a unique cryptographic symmetric key. Authentication of the mobile device is predicated on the verification of the device possession of the key, and hence the key must be kept hidden into the Universal Integrated Circuit Card (SIM card/UICC) at all costs. The authentication of the device is based on the sharing of this key only between the user and the service provider, in this case the mobile network operator. The sharing of the device key with operators is executed between UICC manufacturer and network operators via secure ceremonies, which are secure protocols to ensure that no other entity has knowledge of a valid mobile cryptographic key and its IMSI association.

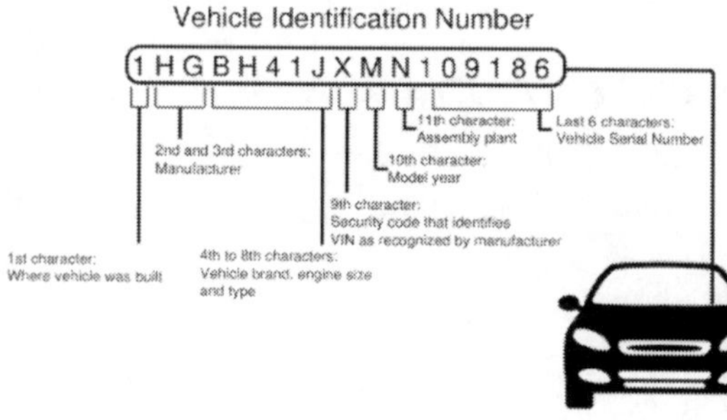


Figure 2: Vehicle Identification Number

TABLE I: LIST OF VARIABLES

| | |
|---|---|
| K | EV Vehicle key: shared secret between user and provider |
| RAND | Random challenge: challenges user identity |
| SQN | Sequence number: prevents replay attacks |
| AMF | Authentication Management Field: manages multiple AKA protocols |
| CK | Confidentiality key: encrypts data between user and provider |
| IK | Integrity key: provides data integrity between user and provider |
| AK | Anonymity key: obfuscates SQN |
| MAC | Message authentication code: verifies integrity of authentication msgs. |
| XMAC | Expected message authentication code: verifies provider |
| RES | Challenge response: produced by user for authentication |
| XRES | Expected challenge response: verifies user response |
| PUC-MSK | Master session key between a PUC and vehicle |
| SN id | Serving Network: In EV charging context, unique id of a PUC |

As SIM card industry has proven to be reliable and scaleable, we propose the extension of it to vehicles. That is, a cryptographic key is associated with the Vehicle Identification Number (VIN), which is a unique but readily available vehicle number etched into every car chassis. As shown in Figure 2, a VIN encodes vehicle manufacturer, model, engine size, among other characteristics. For our purposes, manufacturer and model information may be used to verify the type of charger required, useful if charging stations are not standardized. In addition, charging parameters specific to a vehicle model can be supported.

## III. Vehicle and Utility Company Authentication and Key Agreement

Figure 1 depicts mutually authenticated and encrypted communication protocols for secure communication between entities. PUC communicates securely with vehicle registration authority via mutually authenticated TLS session. Secure communication between PUC and EV is supported via an Authentication and Key Agreement protocol, as per Figure 3.

Upon reading of the vehicle license plate, PUC requests authentication vectors to the vehicle registration authority for the vehicle to be charged via a secure TLS connection. A stolen/fake license plate will result in vehicle authentication failure, and hence denial of EV charging service.

Authentication vectors are generated as per Figure 4 (see Table I for a glossary), as follows. A sequence number SQN is maintained between the registration authority and the vehicle, to prevent replay attacks. A fresh random number RAND is generated for each set of authentication vectors. RAND

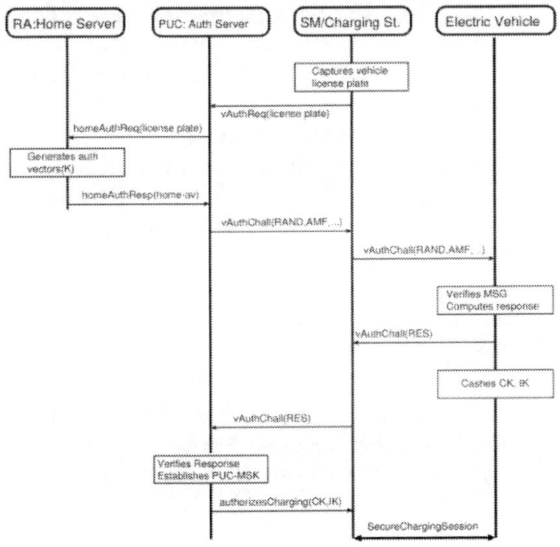


Figure 3: Home Authentication and Key Agreement

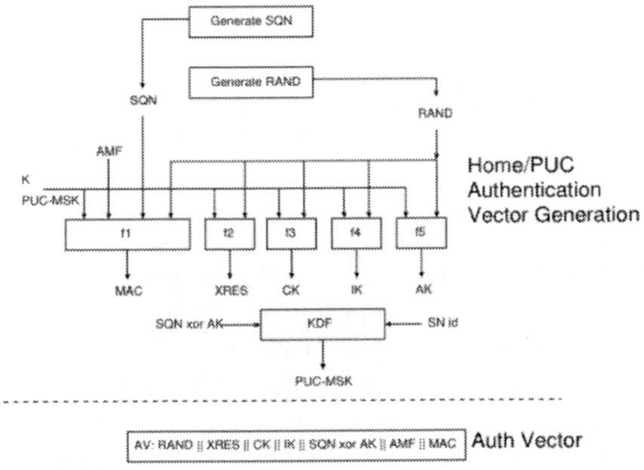


Figure 4: Authentication Vector Generation

and SQN, together with the vehicle cryptographic key K and authentication management field AMF (to be described later) are fed into five one way functions, as per [1]. A Message Authentication Code MAC is generated to verify the authenticity of the vector. An expected response XRES to challenge RAND is also produced. In addition, a confidentiality key CK (encryption), identity key IK (authentication), and anonymity key AK are produced. The authentication vector results from the concatenation of RAND, XRES, CK, IK, IK, SQN xor AK, AMF, and MAC. Upon reception of the authentication vector, PUC challenges the identity of the EV by passing the random challenge RAND, SQN xor AK, and AMF to the vehicle, for challenge response computation. It also sends MAC for message verification.

Vehicle computes challenge response as per Figure 5. Vehicle first uses RAND and its key K to retrieve AK using one way function f5. AK then is used to retrieve SQN, which, together with vehicle key K and challenge RAND, are used

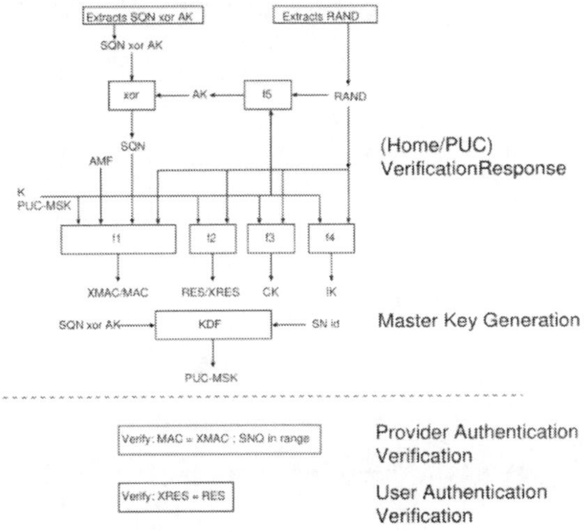


Figure 5: Provider/User Verification

to compute an expected message authentication code XMAC, a challenge response RES, and confidentiality and identity keys CK and IK, respectively. The vehicle then validates the message by comparing XMAC with MAC received from the PUC, and then sends the challenge response RES computed back to PUC, which authenticates the vehicle if XRES=RES. Finally, both PUC and vehicle use a key derivation function KDF (e.g., SHA-256) to generate a master session key PUC-MSK, which becomes a shared key between PUC and the vehicle. A serving network id is used to constraint the scope of the PUC-MSK to a specific PUC provider. We hence suggest the use of the AMF as SN id in the generation of PUC-MSK.

Once vehicle is authenticated, PUC authorizes the smart meter to initiate a charging secure session with PUC, using CK and IK keys. We assume the smart meter software has not been compromised. Mechanism to verify smart meter software vulnerabilities and secure updates is beyond the scope of this paper. Notice that during the authentication process no credential is exchanged between the parties involved. If the vehicle key K is safely stored at registration authority and the electric vehicle, authentication and key agreement process can not be compromised. In addition, user confidentiality is protected by requiring only the vehicle license plate to jump start the authentication process, and not even its VIN number. This help mitigate VIN number based cyber attacks. For additional protection, encryption of license plate information by a PUC managed symmetric key residing in the Smart Meter/charging station can mitigate even the harvesting of license plate information during authentication. This key can be securely distributed from PUC to its smart meters via secure TLS connection.

Once a master session key PUC-MSK is established between PUC and the vehicle, a variant version of the authentication protocol can be run, by replacing vehicle cryptographic key K with PUC-MSK in the figures above. This way, after first authentication of a vehicle, PUC no longer requires

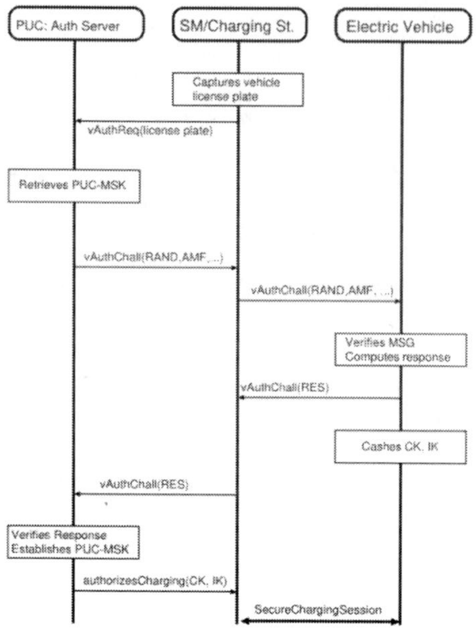


PUC Independent Authentication and Key Agreement

Figure 6: PUC Authentication and Key Agreement

contacting the registration authority to authenticate the vehicle. We call the first version of the protocol home-AKA, and the second version puc-AKA. As the vehicle needs to differentiate which AKA variant is engaging with, a different AMF is used for home-AKA and puc-AKA. Generalizing it, AMF becomes a pointer to the cryptographic key to be used by the vehicle to authenticate itself. Figure 6 illustrates PUC independent authentication protocol.

Mutual authentication of PUC/EV should be executed as a pre-requisite for every charging operation. In addition, authentication should be enabled only if the charging station cable is physically connected to the vehicle charging outlet. Any disconnect of the charging cable should trigger the need for a fresh authentication handshake upon re-establishing physical connectivity to resume charging.

### A. *Service key management*

Key management of a fleet of Smart Meters within Smart Grids is not a trivial matter. A recent survey on multiple approaches for Smart Grid Key management can be fond in [4], where various key generation and distribution schemes are compared. Our Vehicle-SIM based secure metering framework obviates the need to distribute keys across the Smart Grid, as shared master keys between PUCs and vehicles are generated at the endpoints. Key management then reduces to two issues: i- defining when these keys are generated and under which conditions they should be renewed/rotated; ii- how to support multiple PUCs.

### B. *Power Utility Company Key Rotation*

Rotation of Public Utility Company master session key PUC-MSK is driven by the following use cases:

- **New user use case:** A Smart Meter is assigned to a home, attached to a home EV charger. SM allows the running of a home-AKA algorithm, with generation of a public utility company master session key (puc-MSK).
- **Vehicle change of ownership:** A new master session key must be generated for the same vehicle. This requires the rotation of PUC-MSK at a cadence, perhaps once a month, to ensure the vehicle is still owned by the same utility user. A side use case would be a vehicle that is reported stolen. In this case, registration authority may stop issuing authentication vectors to the vehicle, effectively preventing the vehicle from being charged.
- **House change of ownership:** A new PUC-MSK must be generated, as the Home Smart Meter changes ownership.

PUC-MSK rotation may be supported by the home smart meter only. In addition, multiple PUCs will typically need to provide charging services along multiple jurisdictions. In this case, different AMFs must be used among multiple PUCs. We propose the use of a hash function with low collision probability, with a unique PUC input, such as the private key of a PUC X.509 certificate, to generate an unique AMF.

### C. *Multiple Public Utility Company key management*

As travel typically involves charging stations from multiple PUCs, each PUC requires fetching of authentication vector from the vehicle regulatory body. As each authentication vector generated increments SEQN, and given the fact that the vehicle verification involves checking a valid range of SEQNs, it is possible that the vehicle gets out of sync about the acceptable range of SEQN and RA:Home Server in a multiple PUC scenario. A synchronization mechanism between the registration authority and the vehicle needs to be established. We propose to execute this synchronization at a trusted EV charging station, such as the one at home. That is, when the smart meter engages in home-aka authentication with the vehicle, the vehicle resets its SEQN valid window around the SEQN resent in the challenge received, as per Figure 5 (replacing the SEQN in range verification with expected SEQN - XSEQN - assignment to the received SEQN).

### D. *Supporting other Smart Grid services beyond EV Charging*

The secure metering framework proposed in this work can be extended in few ways.

- **Secure Vehicle Services:** Smart devices controlling parking lot gates can be used to automatically grant entrance access to vehicles equipped with SIM cards. For instance, in some countries with advanced smart grid systems, airports may grant free parking to EV vehicles which allows one cycle charging during their stay, so as to smooth airport energy peak hours. In this case, a PUC is replaced by another service provider, which interacts with the vehicle registration authority. The authority then may provide a "authentication as a service" business model to help with operational costs.
- **Non-vehicle Secure Metering Services:** Power utility companies may use user electronic credentials other than

vehicle to generate master service keys at smart meters for smart grid services other than vehicle charging. As a first step towards that scenario, PUCs may use vehicle generated master key to provide secure metering services for smart home. In this case, a PUC would simply rotate the ev charging master key for charging, but retain the previous key in the smart meter for other home services. In future, PUCs could engage with a network operator owning a cellular network SIM card to retrieve authentication vectors, and generate master keys for generic metering services. Smart meters then could engage with user cellular phone in order to enable the generation of smart grid service keys.

## IV. Leveraging Standards and Protocols

The management of charging operation within EV charging ecosystem has evolved via different protocols, some of which have been standardized. ISO 15118 [7] allows EVs and SMs to dynamically exchange information for a proper charging. In terms of security, ISO 15118 supports a Plug & Charge feature, upon which a secure EV to SM secure communication link is established. In ISO 15118, secure EV to SM link requires agreement between EV and SM on a symmetric key - our proposal fulfills this requirement, providing a different key per EV.

Another widely used protocol is Open Charge Point Protocol (OCPP) [8], which supports all communication between the SM and its "control center" (within PUC). Various versions of the protocol exist, with version 2.0 having the most advanced security features, such as secure communication channel, secure firmware update, logging of security events. OCPP allows the SM to behave as a communication gateway between the EV and PUC backend system. This architecture blends well with our security framework. In fact, the symmetric cryptographic keys generated by our AKA framework may be used to mitigate lingering protocol vulnerabilities [9].

## V. Implementation Proof of Concept

This section describes a proof of concept implementation of the security protocols introduced in this paper. Authentication and Key Agreement algorithms were simulated in Python. Using a library called Pykka, we created an actor model of the four components of secure metering ecosystem: Home Server, PUC, Smart Meter, and Electric Vehicle (Figure 7). Pykka allows messages to be sent to other actors by tell() function. Key exchanging was implemented by using tell() with a dictionary type list in tell(), such as message = ["order": "start , "key":00112233]. Since on_receive() is a message handler, it reads the "order" of the message and performs the following conditional branching according to transactions name.

As per Figure 8, the output of the program uses print() to output the name of the actor sending message data, the name of the transaction, and the generated key to visually track how communication between entities is taking place. Even though the figure shows Home AKA output, a similar output from PUC-AKA has also been verified, omitted for space's sake.

```
class HomeServer(pykka.ThreadingActor):
    def __init__(self):
        super(HomeServer, self).__init__()

    def link_class(self, instance_name):
        self.PUC_ref = instance_name

    def on_receive(self, message):
        print("")
        print("HS")
        self.message = message
        self.order = message["order"]

        if(self.order ==
        "Send_License_Plate"):
            print("(Home_AKA)Generate_Key")
            self.license_plate =
            message["license_plate"]
            self.Generate_Key()

    def Generate_Key(self):
        self.key = 0x0011223344556677
        8899aabbccddeeff
        - self.license_plate
        self.PUC_ref.tell
        ({"order":
        "Send_Registration_Complete_Message",
        "key":self.key})
```

Figure 7: Software Implementation

## VI. Authentication and Key Agreement enhanced Charging - Security Evaluation

In this section, we evaluate our AKA EV charging framework vis a vis security threats. The analysis is structured around three actors: EV, Charging station(CS)/Smart Meter(SM), PUC/Charging control center.

- **EV:** The following threats are devised:
  - Impersonation: Impersonating an arbitrary vehicle is impossible as long as the vehicle cryptographic key is safely stored in the v-sim card. As a consequence, the protocol supports non-repudiation of charging session.
  - Denial of Service: Assuming a EV to SM (WiFi/cellular) wireless link, DoS attack may be staged, for instance, via radio jamming.
  - Distributed DOS: As charging section is initiated via AKA by the reading of the vehicle license plate, staging a DDoS from the vehicle would require multiple fake license plates. To mitigate such attacks, PUC control center may keep track of license plates that have failed authentication in the past, as in a blacklist concept, and discard charging requests coming from vehicles that have failed authentication multiple times.

```
SM
home AKA communication initiation

PUC
(Home_AKA)Send_License_Plate

HS
(Home_AKA)Generate_Authentication_Vector
SQN: 4738849701895016728
(Home_AKA)Generate_XRES_MAC
XRES: 15568641829527999796
MAC: 968201358740978223

PUC
(Home_AKA)Extract_RAND_AMF_SN_SQN_XRES_MAC

SM
(Home_AKA)Send_RAND_AMF_SQN_MAC

EV
(Home_AKA)Extract_RAND_AMF_SQN_MAC
(Home_AKA)Generate_RES_AK_CK_IK_XMAC
RES: 15568641829527999796
XMAC: 968201358740978223
AK: 22205989251187
CK: 30244256743587035516588858386965182340
IK: 204382471729976753096951681390175295497
OK! MAC = XMAC

(Home_AKA)Generate_PUC_MSK
PUC_MSK = 886499507777074393188636241814219822

SM
(Home_AKA)Forward_Encrypted_RES

PUC
(Home_AKA)Compare_RES_and_XRES
OK! XRES = RES
PUC_MSK: 886499507777074393188636241814219822
```

Figure 8: Software Output

- Data tampering: To mitigate data tampering, cryptographic storage/operations should be executed within a secure hardware in the vehicle and SM.

- **SM:** The following threats are devised:
  - Privacy: License place is read by the charging station and sent to charging control/PUC via a secure TLS session. This information does not need to be retained by the charging station/SM, once transmitted to PUC, mitigating leakage. All data exchanged between vehicle and SM is protected by the crypto keys generated by AKA algorithm, within the secure session.
  - Data tampering: Any attempt to alter data exchanged between the vehicle and the SM will be detected via the integrity key IK, and should be discarded.
- **PUC/Control Center:** The following threats are devised:
  - Denial of Service: Communication between the smart meter and the PUC can be supported via cloud service infrastructure (such as Amazon Web Services), for which DoS protection techniques do exist.
  - Data tampering: Communication between Smart Meter and PUC is protected via server authenticated TLS session. This ensures not only data integrity, but also prevents man-in-the-middle attacks.

## VII. CONCLUSION AND FUTURE WORK

We have proposed a symmetric key based authentication and key agreement protocol to support Electric Vehicle Charging in Smart Grids. PUC and vehicle mutual authentication and secure metering are achieved without the need for the Smart Meter to store credentials. In addition, new cryptographic keys are used by the smart meter on every charging session, rendering key stealing via SM tampering unprofitable. The framework hence reduces Smart Meter security requirements, as well as its attack surface. We have analyzed service keys' management on multiple Power Electricity Company scenarios. In addition, we have provided a proof of concept implementation of the authentication and symmetric keys generation involved in the framework. As future work, we plan to evaluate our proposal via prototyping.

## ACKNOWLEDGMENTS

This work is supported by JSPS Kakenhi Grant Number 21K11888 and Hitachi Systems, Ltd.

## REFERENCES

[1] "Specification of the MILENAGE algorithm Set: An Example algorithm set for the 3GPP authentication and key generation functions f1; f1*, f2, f3, f4, f5, and f5*," Document 2: Algorithm specification (3GPP TS 35.206 version 14.0.0 Release 14), 2017-04.

[2] H. M. Rehmani et al., "Integrating Renewable Energy Resources into the Smart Grid: Recent developments in information and communication technologies," In IEEE Trans. Ind. Informat., Vol. 14, no. 7, pp. 2814-2825, Jul. 2018.

[3] L. Alejandro et al., "Global Market for Smart Electricity Meters: Government policies driving strong growth," US Int. Trade Commission, Washington, DC, USA, Rep. ID-037,2014.

[4] A. Ghosal and M. Conti, "Key Management Systems for Smart Grid Advanced Metering Infrastructure: A Survey," In IEEE Communications Surveys & Tutorials, Vol. 21, No. 3, pp. 2831-2847, Third Quarter 2019.

[5] P. Kumar et al., "Smart Grid Metering Networks: A Survey on Security, Privacy and Open Research Issues," In IEEE Communications Surveys & Tutorials, Vol. 21, No. 3, pp. 2886-2927, Third Quarter 2019.

[6] B. Harishma et al., "Safe is the New Smart: PUF-Based Authentication for Load Modification-Resistant Smart Meters," In IEEE Transactions on Dependable and Secure Computing, Vol. 19, No. 1, pp. 663-680, January/February 2022.

[7] "Road vehicles - Vehicle-to-grid communication interface-Part 2: Network and application protocol requirements," Int. Org. Stand., Geneva, Switzerland, Rep. ISO/CD 15118-2, 2014.

[8] F. Buve, P. Klapwijk, and R. de Leeuw, "OCPP 2.0.1, part 0-Introduction," Open Charge Alliance, Arnhem, The Netherland, Rep. 2020-03-31, 2020.

[9] Z. Garofalaki et al., "Electric Vehicle Charging: A Survey on the Security Issues and Challenges of the Open Charge Point Protocol (OCPP)," In IEEE Communications Surveys & Tutorials, Vol. 24, No. 3, pp. 1504-1532, Third Quarter 2022.

[10] A. Fuchs et al., "HIP: HSM-based identities for plug-and-charge," In ACM 14th Int. Conf. Availability Rel. Security, Dublin, Ireland, Aug. 2020, pp. 1-33.

[11] A. Fuchs et al., "TrustEV: trustworthy electric vehicle charging and billing," In ACM 35th Annual Symposium on Applied Computing, Brno, Czech Republic, Mar. 2020, pp. 1706-1715.

# Heterogeneous Network Inspection in IoT Environment with FPGA based Pre-Filter and CPU based LightGBM

Zhenguo Hu
*Graduate School of Informatics*
*Nagoya University*
Nagoya, Japan
tu36rz9u@gmail.com

Hirokazu Hasegawa
*Center for Strategic Cyber Resilience Research and Development*
*National Institute of Informatics*
Tokyo, Japan
hasegawa@nii.ac.jp

Yukiko Yamaguchi
*Information Technology Center*
*Nagoya University*
Nagoya, Japan
yamaguchi@itc.nagoya-u.ac.jp

Hajime Shimada
*Information Technology Center*
*Nagoya University*
Nagoya, Japan
shimada@itc.nagoya-u.ac.jp

***Abstract*—With the development of modern society, IoT has entered many aspects of our daily lives. At the same time, cyber attacks in IoT environments are becoming increasingly rampant. We urgently need a method to effectively inspect and detect them such as the usage of malicious traffic detection technology. Malicious traffic detection is usually divided into two aspects: signature based method and machine learning based method. The former method usually relies on pre-defined signatures or rules and cannot effectively detect unknown threats such as zero-day attacks. Although the latter method can detect unknown attacks, most of them focus on offline traffic and cannot adapt to the current realtime IoT network environment. In this paper, we propose a heterogeneous malicious traffic detection system which combines both of them to achieve the realtime detection. In this design, we utilize the bloom array to execute pre-filter in an FPGA board, and implement a CPU based LightGBM classifier to identify the filtered traffic. We also implemented an experiment to evaluate the proposed system on both training stage and inference stage, which shows the system has the ability to identify malicious traffic in the IoT network environment.**

***Keywords*—*Malicious Traffic Detection; Machine Learning; FPGA; LightGBM***

## I. Introduction

With the development of information technology, Internet of Things (IoT) has gained more and more people's attractions in recent years. It improves the convenience of our lives by enabling communication between electronic devices and sensors through the Internet [1]. IoT depicts a world where anything can be connected in an intelligent fashion [2], including smart homes, smart cities, wearable devices, industrial automation and even healthcare and telemedicine. Although the development of the IoT has brought revolutionary changes to modern society, however, it also brings some security issues such as data leakage and identity theft. One of the famous IoT security threats is Mirai Botnet, it is a worm-like family of malware which changes IoT devices to DDoS botnets [3]. It was appeared as early as August 31, 2016 [4]. By scanning IoT devices on the Internet and controlling them, Mirai has the ability to launch DDoS attacks to the target network, which causes huge losses to companies and organizations. In order to protect the digital and property security of enterprises and users, and prevent the similar attacks from happening again, we need some effective defense approaches to resist and prevent the cyber threats.

Malicious traffic detection is an efficient mechanism to identify and mitigate potential threats and attacks. It is widely used in Intrusion Detection System (IDS) which is among the existing security methods responsible for detecting malicious activities [5]. Traditional malicious traffic detection usually adapts signature or feature based rules to achieve the traffic inspection process [6][7]. These methods rely on the pre-defined signatures or rules of malicious traffic such as packet protocols or payloads, which are essentially specific patterns associated with the known network attacks. However, if we just rely on the traditional signature matching mechanism, it may miss out many potential and undiscovered threats such as zero-day attacks [8][9][10]. Compared with signature based malicious traffic detection, machine learning (ML) based malicious traffic detection is a different detection approach which leverages the advantages of machine learning to detect unknown attacks and increase the detection efficiency. Therefore, in the IoT environments [11][12][13], it is useful to use machine learning methods to detect network attacks, which will apply machine learning models to learn corresponding features on the network traffic datasets. By extracting the traffic features from packet headers or payload contents, the machine learning algorithm can identify whether the network traffic is benign or malicious. Although machine learning based malicious traffic detection methods overcome some limitations of signature based detection methods, but most of them focus on the offline detection which can not deal with the realtime incoming network traffic [14][15][16].

In order to overcome this problem, in this paper, we present a realtime heterogeneous malicious traffic detection method based on LightGBM, which has the ability to detect malicious traffic with high accuracy. An FPGA based pre-filter is used to perform IP address blacklist filtering, while a packet capturer and parser is used to capture and parse the packet, and a LightGBM classifier is implemented to achieve precise detection of malicious network packets. The performance of our proposed system is evaluated from both detection speed and detection accuracy, which shows that our system can support realtime malicious traffic detection in the IoT environment.

The rest of the paper is organized as follows. In Section II, we discuss the related work about malicious traffic detection. In Section III, we introduce the prototype design of the heterogeneous malicious traffic detection system. We also conduct an experiment and evaluate the system in Section IV. Finally, we conclude this paper in Section V.

## II. Related Work

In the past few years, in order to alleviate security and trust issues on the Internet, there are a lot of researches focusing their attentions on inspecting and detecting network malicious traffic. In this section, we mainly review signature based malicious traffic detection including software and hardware, and machine learning based malicious traffic detection.

### A. *Signature based Malicious Traffic Detection*

On the software side, Snort [17] and Suricata [18] are the famous signature based IDS projects which are widely used in many companies or organizations. They distinguish network traffic against a set of defined signatures to identify attacks and threats. These kinds of signatures are provided by cybersecurity experts or proprietary vendors [19]. Besides, in the paper [20], J. Nam et al. propose a high-performance Suricata-based NIDS on many-core processors (MCPs) which is called Haetae to achieve traffic detection. This system adapts the parallelism of NIDS engines and uses programmable network interface cards to offload packet processing, it can also dynamically offload network traffic to host-side CPU to achieve the detection. H. Li et al. [21] design the vNIDS to offer effective detection and provisioning for NIDS virtualization by using such as detection state sharing and microservices.

On the hardware side, K. Jaic et al. [22] design a hybrid-NIDS (called SFAOENIDS), which combines the FPGA with a network interface card to provide hardware pattern matching and software post processing. In the paper [23], Z. Zhao et al. propose an FPGA-first approach called Pigasus, most of the processing and controlling of the network traffic are implemented in the FPGA to ensure the speed. Except for the FPGA components, there are also some designs which are implemented on other hardware devices. N. Cascarano et al. [24] present a regular expression matching method with a parallel engine that is implemented on GPU. T. Jepsen et al. [25] propose a string searching approach of packet payloads on a programmable network ASIC.

### B. *Machine Learning based Malicious Traffic Detection*

Recently, machine learning methods (such as supervised and unsupervised learning) are widely used on malicious traffic detection. For example, in order to detect and block bot-net C&C traffic, M. Antonakakis et al. [14] propose a method called Pleiades to identify randomly generated domains without reversing. They combine clustering and classification algorithms, monitor traffic below the local recursive DNS server and analyze streams of unsuccessful DNS resolutions to achieve detection process. In the paper [26], T. Nelms et al. present the WebWitness, which is an incident investigation system to trace back events before malware downloads happening, and leverages the paths to build effective defenses. They also deploy their system on an academic network to collect malicious download paths, which shows the system can successfully decrease the infection rate. In addition, in order to resist the threat of malware, L. Invernizzi et al. [16] propose a system called Nazca which identifies infections in large scale networks by investigating how a client downloads and installs malware in the real world. Through checking the telltale signs of the malicious network infrastructures, Nazca has the ability to detect previously-unseen malware and can not be easily influenced by code obfuscation. Y. Mirsky et al. [27] also present another approach called Kitsune which uses neural networks to distinguish normal traffic and network attacks. This method adapts the ensemble of neural networks which are called autoencoders to identify the benign and abnormal network traffic. They also propose a dataset named Mirai which includes the real network information of the Mirai botnet malware.

## III. Heterogeneous Malicious Traffic Detection System Design

The heterogeneous malicious traffic detection system is designed to detect packet-level malicious traffic in IoT environment, it mainly consists of two parts: FPGA based Pre-Filter and Machine Learning based Traffic Detection. The former is used to preliminary filter the incoming traffic, while the latter is used for further traffic detection. Figure 1 shows the overview of the system architecture.

### A. *FPGA based Pre-Filter*

*1) Description of FPGA based Pre-Filter:* In a network environment, there will be some truly malicious traffic with specific characteristics such as IP address. These traffics can be blocked by setting the software firewall and corresponding rules. Compared with the traditional firewall that uses CPU to handle traffic, an FPGA based pre-filter can be programmed with specific rules to filter or discard data with low resource consumption and high performance. At the same time, it can implement underlying protocol parsing (such as Layer 2, Layer 3) to achieve more accurate detection. Currently, we execute

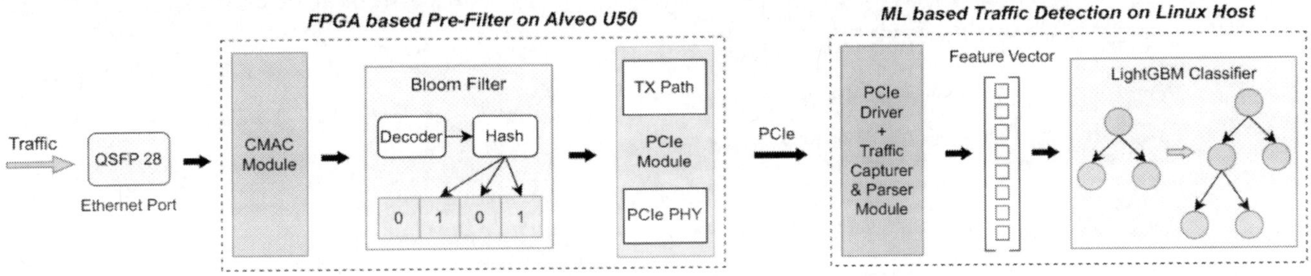


Figure 1. Overview of the system architecture.

"Source IPv4 Address" matching on the third layer of the OSI model. The main function of this pre-filter is to filter the truly malicious traffic by setting a blacklist in the FPGA board. When the irregular traffic from some IP addresses come in, it will drop these packets automatically.

In order to achieve end-to-end packet processing and detection, the FPGA based pre-filter consists of four components which are shown as follows. We implement the prototype design based on AMD OpenNIC project [28].

- Ethernet Port: Ethernet port is a physical component (such as QSFP 28 interface) which can create an ethernet connection with the network to be detected. It is used to forward the traffic to the CMAC module.
- CMAC Module: CMAC module is used to receive the traffic packet. Here we adapt the Xilinx CMAC IP core as the implementation.
- Bloom Filter: After getting the packet, the bloom filter will decode it and extract the "Source IPv4 Address" as the matching data. The result will indicate whether this packet can be reserved or blocked.
- PCIe Module: The packets that flow out through the bloom filter will be sent to the ML based traffic detection for further inspection through the PCIe interface. It relies on the PCIe driver to achieve the communication with the host machine.

*2) Bloom Filter:* Bloom filter is a space-efficient data storage mechanism to decide whether an element is located in a data set. Figure 2 shows the architecture. It utilizes a bit array and hash functions to store information of the element states. In our design, we use it as the IP blacklist implementation and the elements in bloom array map the "Source IPv4 Address". In order to add an element to the filter, it needs the hash computations. We adapt the CRC hash as the hash functions, and each hash function calculates the element location in the bloom array. When one element comes from the CMAC module, to check if it is in the bloom array, the same hash functions are applied. If any of the calculated positions are not 1, it means this element is not in the defined array.

$$\text{False Positive Probability} = \left(1 - e^{-\frac{kn}{m}}\right)^k \quad (1)$$

Another property of the bloom filter is that there is a false positive probability. Hash collision is one reason that causes

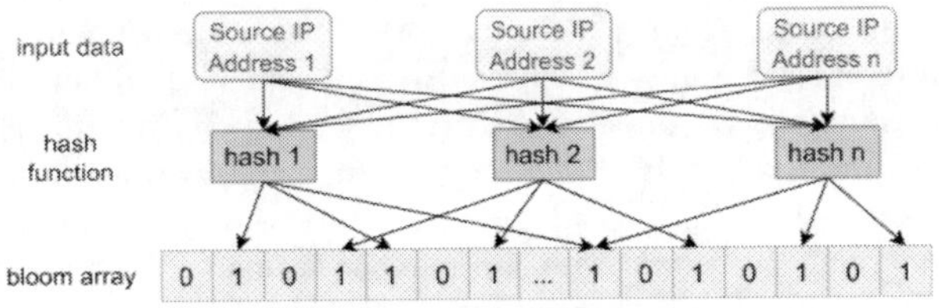


Figure 2. Architecture of the bloom filter.

the false positive probability. According to the equation (1), $k$ is the number of hash functions, $n$ is the number of elements, and $m$ is the size of the bloom array. We choose $k$=4, $m/n$=16, where the false positive probability is computed to 0.239% that meets our design goal.

## B. Machine Learning based Traffic Detection

Machine learning based traffic detection leverages the data-driven insight ability of machine learning to analyze the malicious traffic on the CPU side. Compared with the traditional signature based IDS systems, it has the adaptability and flexibility and can even detect certain undiscovered attacks. In order to ensure the realtime performance and detect the attack behaviors timely, we implement two modules including the Traffic Capturer and Parser Module, and the LightGBM Classifier that are shown in Figure 1. We focus on the implementation of the inference process.

*1) Traffic Capturer and Parser Module:* After filtering the traffic using FPGA based pre-filter, we need to capture and parse it for further detection. We adapt the *libpcap* implementation to execute the realtime capturing. It builds a connection between the FPGA board and the software stack. By capturing from the FPGA board, we can get the corresponding packet-level filtered traffic. After that, we need to analyze and preprocess each packet to get the packet features (e.g., IPv4 Length). We mainly adapt the header information instead of the content to improve the universality of our system. At the same time, considering we need to replay the traffic to achieve realtime detection, we do not use the time related features such as timestamp. We perform hierarchical splitting on each data packet and extract corresponding features according to the needs of detection. The specific features that we use and their descriptions are shown in the Table I.

TABLE I
FEATURE DESCRIPTION

| Feature | Description |
|---|---|
| IPv4 Length | The length of an IPv4 packet |
| IPv4 ID | The identification of an IPv4 packet |
| IPv4 TTL | The time to live of an IPv4 packet |
| Layer | The type of protocol |
| Source Port | The source port |
| Destination Port | The destination port |
| Source IP Address | The source IP address |
| Destination IP Address | The destination IP address |

We focus on the packet-level feature extraction. Through detecting each data packet, we can timely identify the malicious traffic. Among these features, since some of them have different categories which can not be sent into the machine learning model directly. In that case, we encode the label (such as the LabelEncoder encoding in scikit-learn) for Layer, Source IP Address and Destination IP Address to convert the category format into the number format. The processed features will be combined into a feature vector and will be transported into the LightGBM classifier for inspection.

*2) LightGBM Classifier:* LightGBM is a gradient boosting decision tree (GBDT) framework which is widely used for both classification and regression problems. It has advantages of high accuracy, speed and scalability. Compared with other traditional GBDT algorithms, it adapts some optimization technologies (e.g., Histogram Decision Tree, Gradient-based One-Side Sampling (GOSS) and Exclusive Feature Bundling (EFB)) to accelerate the training speed. The processing flow of a realtime classifier based on LightGBM is shown as follows: Firstly, import the pre-trained LightGBM model and instantiate it. The model is saved in *txt* file format in advance. Secondly, the extracted feature vectors are converted into the floating point array and fed into the instantiated LightGBM model. Next, the model conducts inference calculations to obtain the classification probability of the feature vector. Finally, we determine whether the data packet is benign or malicious based on its inference result.

## IV. EXPERIMENT AND EVALUATION

We designed an experiment to evaluate the prototype malicious traffic detection system with a specific IoT network attack dataset. We also evaluated our system from two stages: training stage and inference stage.

### A. Dataset

The experiment and evaluation dataset that we use comes from Kitsune Mirai [27]. It is presented in 2018 and it is captured from an IoT network, where the Mirai malware begins to infect other devices and scans for new victims network. Table II shows the details of the experiment dataset. It consists of 642,516 pieces of malicious data and 121,621 pieces of benign data. We selected 80% (611,309) of them as the training set and 20% (152,828) as the test set.

TABLE II
DETAILS OF THE EXPERIMENT DATASET

| Name | Year | Number | |
|---|---|---|---|
| Kitsune Mirai | 2018 | ***Num of Malicious*** | ***Num of Benign*** |
| | | 642,516 | 121,621 |
| | | ***Num of Train*** | ***Num of Test*** |
| | | 611,309 | 152,828 |

### B. Evaluation on Training Stage

The evaluation on the training stage can reflect the accuracy of our method. The specific details of the evaluation metrics are shown as follows.

*1) Evaluation Metric:* We use the following evaluation metrics to evaluate the performance of our system:

- **False Positive (FP)** represents the negative samples predicted to be positive.
- **False Negative (FN)** represents the positive samples predicted to be negative.
- **Accuracy (ACC)** is adapted to evaluate the overall performance of our system:

$$\text{ACC} = \frac{TP + TN}{TP + TN + FP + FN} \tag{2}$$

- **Precision** is used to measure the accuracy of positive predictions:

$$\text{Precision} = \frac{TP}{TP + FP} \tag{3}$$

- **Recall** evaluates the ability of the model to detect positive samples:

$$\text{Recall} = \frac{TP}{TP + FN} \tag{4}$$

- **F1-score** is a harmonic mean between the precision and the recall:

$$\text{F1-score} = 2 \times \frac{Precision \times Recall}{Precision + Recall} \tag{5}$$

*2) Evaluation Results:* Table III shows the comparison of evaluation results on different classifiers. We set four other models including Support Vector Machine (SVM), K-Nearest Neighbor (KNN), Random Forest and Decision Tree as the comparisons. From the results, we can get that using the packet-level features extracted from traffic achieves good detection performance, which proves that the features in Table I are effective. At the same time, we observe that LightGBM achieves the highest evaluation in all the classifiers on ACC, Precision, Recall and F1-score. It reaches 0.9589, 0.9774, 0.9736 and 0.9755 respectively. This is one of the reasons that we choose LightGBM as the classifier in the ML based traffic detection. We also make a comparison between Decision Tree and LightGBM models with heatmap representations in Figure 3 to indicate the metrics of FP and FN, which shows that our method has a better performance than other approaches.

### C. Evaluation on Inference Stage

The evaluation on the inference stage can reflect the realtime detection capability of our system. It is separated into two aspects: FPGA Resource Utilization and Throughput.

TABLE III
COMPARISON OF EVALUATION RESULTS

| Classifier | ACC | Precision | Recall | F1-score |
|---|---|---|---|---|
| SVM | 0.9104 | 0.9706 | 0.9214 | 0.9453 |
| KNN | 0.9494 | 0.9740 | 0.9656 | 0.9698 |
| Random Forest | 0.9525 | 0.9766 | 0.9668 | 0.9716 |
| Decision Tree | 0.9556 | 0.9773 | 0.9697 | 0.9735 |
| LightGBM | **0.9589** | **0.9774** | **0.9736** | **0.9755** |

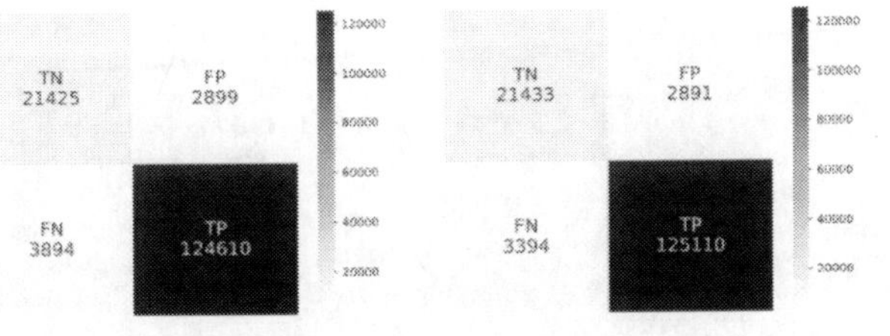


(a) Decision Tree (b) LightGBM

Figure 3. Heatmaps between different methods.

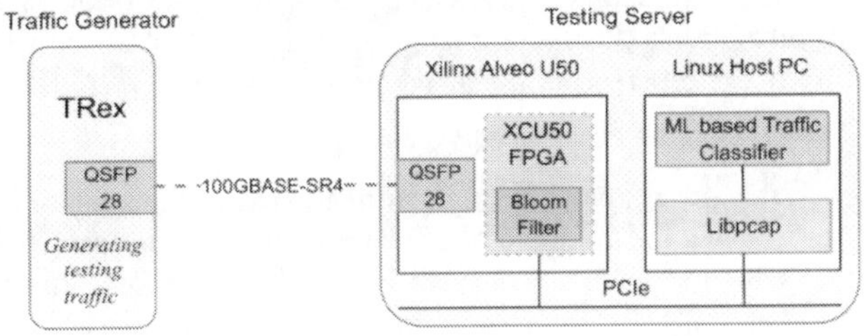


Figure 4. Overview of the experiment environment.

TABLE V
RESOURCES CONSUMPTION IN XILINX U50

| Module Name | LUT | Register | BRAM Tile |
|---|---|---|---|
| CMAC Module | 9,793 | 31,504 | 0 |
| Filter Module | 5,279 | 5,209 | 0 |
| PCIe Module | 79,576 | 84,544 | 94 |
| Proportion | 10.9% | 7.0% | 7.0% |

*1) Experiment Environment:* Table IV shows the assumed experimental IoT network according to the Kitsune Mirai dataset. The number of clients is calculated by the destination mac address. By adjusting the bloom array in the FPGA based pre-filter, we build four situations of irregular traffic which includes different types of source IPv4 addresses. The experiment environment is shown in Figure 4, we use Cisco TRex [29] as the traffic generator. On the testing server, the Xilinx Alveo U50 accelerator card [30] is our FPGA platform which has 872K LUTs, 1743K registers and 47.3 Mb BRAM. The Linux host machine is installed with an Intel i9-13900K cpu and 64GB memory. The filtered traffic will be forwarded to the ML based traffic classifier.

TABLE IV
ASSUMED EXPERIMENTAL IOT NETWORK

| Source IPv4 Address Range | Clients | Assumed Irregular Traffic filtered by FPGA based Pre-Filter | |
|---|---|---|---|
| | | ***Source IPv4 Address*** | ***Situations*** |
| 192.168.2.0/24 and 0.0.0.0 | 30 | 192.168.2.108 | Situation1 |
| | | 192.168.2.108<br>192.168.2.1 | Situation2 |
| | | 192.168.2.108<br>192.168.2.1<br>192.168.2.113 | Situation3 |
| | | 192.168.2.108<br>192.168.2.1<br>192.168.2.113<br>192.168.2.110 | Situation4 |

*2) FPGA Resource Utilization:* The resource utilization refers to the usage of hardware resources on an FPGA board. Table V indicates the consumption of LUT, Register and BRAM Tile which comes from Xilinx Vivado Design Suite 2020.2, and shows the respective proportion in Xilinx U50 accelerator card. From the result we can see, the filter module consumes 5,279 LUTs and 5,209 registers which occupies a reasonable resource consumption.

*3) Throughput:* We adjust the time interval of packets in TRex and replay the Kitsune Mirai dataset to measure the throughput. In our FPGA design, the data bus width is set to 512-bit and the clock frequency is set to 250MHz. Since we adapt the pipeline design, the throughput of the pre-filter is calculated as following:

$$\text{Throughput} = \frac{512\text{-}bit}{(1/250MHz) * 10^9} = 128Gbps \qquad (6)$$

Considering the design throughput of the Xilinx CMAC IP core is 100Gbps, the calculated throughput of the pre-filter has the ability to reach the line speed of 100Gbps.

Figure 5 shows the experiment results of the complete system. The horizontal axis represents the different situations in Table IV where truly malicious traffic will be filtered by FPGA based pre-filter, while the vertical axis represents the detection throughput. *Baseline* indicates that there are no rules being enabled in the FPGA based pre-filter. From this figure we can see, the FPGA based pre-filter can block a portion of malicious traffic by setting up an IP blacklist which reduces the burden on ML based traffic detection, and effectively improve the overall detection throughput of the system. At the same time, we also observe the current system performance

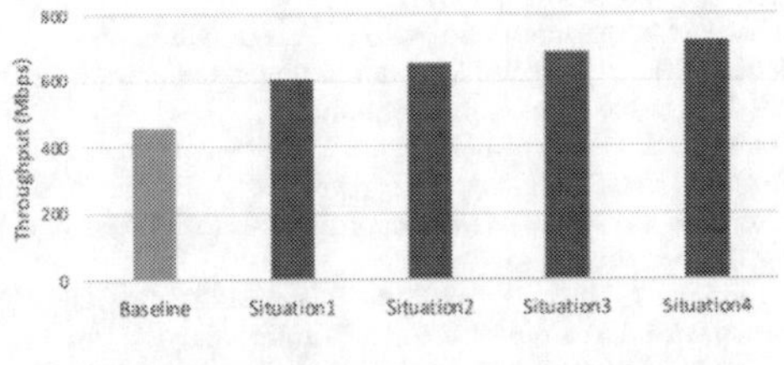


Figure 5. Throughput under different situations.

is limited with LightGBM side. If we improve LightBGM classifier part such as increasing calculation cores or changing to other packet capture methods, it still has the ability to improve the performance of the entire system.

## V. Conclusion

In this paper, we present a realtime heterogeneous malicious traffic detection method based on LightGBM classifier especially for IoT environment. We built an FPGA based pre-filter to filter the truly malicious traffic through the bloom array. A traffic capturer and parser are used to receive and extract features from the filtered traffic, while a CPU based LightGBM classifier is responsible for inspecting and detecting the traffic in realtime. In order to evaluate the prototype design, we used a malicious traffic dataset of the IoT malware to test the proposed system from both training stage and inference stage. The results on the training stage show that our method has better performance than the traditional machine learning methods. Moreover, we built an experiment environment with the traffic generator and testing server to evaluate this system on inference stage. The results indicate that our system has a low FPGA resource usage and effective throughput improvement. In future work, we will explore to add other models to our system to further improve the detection efficiency.

## Acknowledgment

This research was partially supported by "Nagoya University Interdisciplinary Frontier Fellowship" supported by Nagoya University and JST, the establishment of university fellowships towards the creation of science technology innovation, Grant Number JPMJFS2120, and the MEXT/JSPS KAKENHI, Grant Number JP23H03396.

## References

[1] S. Kumar, P. Tiwari and M. Zymbler, "Internet of Things is a revolutionary approach for future technology enhancement: a review," J. Big Data, Vol. 6, pp. 111, 2019.

[2] S. Madakam, R. Ramaswamy and S. Tripathi, "Internet of Things (IoT): A Literature Review," Journal of Computer and Communications, Vol. 03, pp. 164-173, 2015.

[3] M. Antonakakis, T. April, M. Bailey, M. Bernhard, E. Bursztein, J. Cochran, Z. Durumeric, J. A. Halderman, L. Invernizzi, M. Kallitsis, D. Kumar, C. Lever, Z. Ma, J. Mason, D. Menscher, C Seaman, N. Sullivan, K. Thomas and Yi Zhou, "Understanding the Mirai Botnet," In 26th USENIX Security Symposium (USENIX Security 2017), pp. 1093–1110, 2017.

[4] @unixfreaxjp, "Mmd-0056-2016 - Linux/Mirai, how an old ELF malcode is recycled", http://blog.malwaremustdie.org/2016/08/mmd-0056-2016-linuxmirai-just.html.

[5] F. Hussain, S. G. Abbas, G. A. Shah, I. Miguel Pires, U. U. Fayyaz, F. Shahzad, N. M. Garcia and E. Zdravevski, "A Framework for Malicious Traffic Detection in IoT Healthcare Environment," Sensors, Vol. 21, No. 9, pp. 3025, 2021.

[6] K. Borders, J. Springer and M. Burnside, "Chimera: A Declarative Language for Streaming Network Traffic Analysis," In Proceedings of the 21th USENIX Security Symposium, pp. 365-379, 2012.

[7] M. A. Jamshed, J. Lee, S. Moon, I. Yun, D. Kim, S. Lee, Y. Yi, and K. Park, "Kargus: A Highly-scalable Software-based Intrusion Detection System," In Proceedings of the ACM conference on Computer and Communications Security (CCS '12), pp. 317-328, 2012.

[8] P. García-Teodoro, J. Díaz-Verdejo, G. Maciá-Fernández and E. Vázquez, "Anomaly-Based Network Intrusion Detection: Techniques, Systems and Challenges," Comput. Secur., Vol. 28, No. 1-2, pp. 18-28, 2009.

[9] A. L. Buczak and E. Guven, "A Survey of Data Mining and Machine Learning Methods for Cyber Security Intrusion Detection," IEEE Commun. Surv. Tutorials, Vol. 18, No. 2, pp. 1153-1176, 2016.

[10] R. Tang, Z. Yang, Z. Li, W. Meng, H. Wang, Q. Li, Y. Sun, D. Pei, T. Wei, Y. Xu and Y. Liu, "ZeroWall: Detecting Zero-Day Web Attacks through Encoder-Decoder Recurrent Neural Networks," In Proceedings of the 39th IEEE Conference on Computer Communications (INFOCOM 2020), pp. 2479-2488, 2020.

[11] D. Ventura, D. C. Mansilla, J. Lopez-de-Armentia, P. Garaizar, D. López-de-Ipiña and V. Catania, "ARIIMA: A Real IoT Implementation of a Machine-Learning Architecture for Reducing Energy Consumption," In Proceedings of the 8th International Conference on Ubiquitous Computing and Ambient Intelligence, pp. 444-451, 2014.

[12] R. Xue, L. Wang and J. Chen, "Using the IoT to Construct Ubiquitous Learning Environment," In Proceedings of the Second International Conference on Mechanic Automation and Control Engineering, pp. 7878-7880, 2011.

[13] M. A. Alsheikh, S. Lin, D. Niyato and H. P. Tan, "Machine Learning in Wireless Sensor Networks: Algorithms, Strategies, and Applications," IEEE Commun. Surv. Tutorials, Vol. 16, No. 4, pp. 1996-2018, 2014.

[14] M. Antonakakis, R. Perdisci, Y. Nadji, N. Vasiloglou, S. Abu-Nimeh, W. Lee and D. Dagon, "From Throw-Away Traffic to Bots: Detecting the Rise of DGA-Based Malware," In Proceedings of the 21th USENIX Security Symposium, pp. 491-506, 2012.

[15] L. Bilge, D. Balzarotti, W. K. Robertson, E. Kirda and C. Kruegel, "Disclosure: Detecting Botnet Command and Control Servers Through Large-Scale NetFlow Analysis," In Proceedings of the 28th Annual Computer Security Applications Conference (ACSAC 2012), pp. 129-138, 2012.

[16] L. Invernizzi, S. Miskovic, R. Torres, C. Kruegel, S. Saha, G. Vigna, S. Lee and M. Mellia, "Nazca: Detecting Malware Distribution in Large-Scale Networks," In Proceedings of the 21st Annual Network and Distributed System Security Symposium (NDSS 2014), 2014.

[17] Snort, https://www.snort.org/.

[18] Suricata, https://suricata.io/.

[19] Snort Rules, https://www.snort.org/downloads#rules.

[20] J. Nam, M. Jamshed, B. Choi, D. Han and K. Park, "Haetae: Scaling the Performance of Network Intrusion Detection with Many-Core Processors," In Proceedings of the 18th International Symposium on Research in Attacks, Intrusions, and Defenses, pp. 89-110, 2015.

[21] H. Li, H. Hu, G. Gu, G. Ahn and F. Zhang, "VNIDS: Towards Elastic Security with Safe and Efficient Virtualization of Network Intrusion Detection Systems," In Proceedings of the 2018 ACM SIGSAC Conference on Computer and Communications Security (CCS '18), pp. 17-34, 2018.

[22] K. Jaic, M. C. Smith and N. Sarma, "A Practical Network Intrusion Detection System for Inline FPGAs on 10GbE Network Adapters," In Proceedings of the 25th IEEE International Conference on Application-Specific Systems, Architectures and Processors (ASAP 2014), pp. 180-181, 2014.

[23] Z. Zhao, H. Sadok, N. Atre, J. C. Hoe, V. Sekar and J. Sherry, "Achieving 100Gbps Intrusion Prevention on a Single Server," In Proceedings of the 14th USENIX Conference on Operating Systems Design and Implementation (OSDI'20), pp. 1083-1100, 2020.

[24] N. Cascarano, P. Rolando, F. Risso and R. Sisto, "INFAnt: NFA Pattern Matching on GPGPU Devices," Comput. Commun. Rev., Vol. 40, No. 5, pp. 20-26, 2010.

[25] T. Jepsen, D. Alvarez, N. Foster, C. Kim, J. Lee, M. Moshref and R. Soulé, "Fast String Searching on PISA," In Proceedings of the 2019 ACM Symposium on SDN Research (SOSR '19), pp. 21-28, 2019.

[26] T. Nelms, R. Perdisci, M. Antonakakis and M. Ahamad, "WebWitness: Investigating, Categorizing, and Mitigating Malware Download Paths," In Proceedings of the 24th USENIX Conference on Security Symposium, pp. 1025-1040, 2015.

[27] Y. Mirsky, T. Doitshman, Y. Elovici and A. Shabtai, "Kitsune: An Ensemble of Autoencoders for Online Network Intrusion Detection," In Proceedings of the 25th Annual Network and Distributed System Security Symposium (NDSS 2018), 2018.

[28] AMD OpenNIC, https://github.com/Xilinx/open-nic.

[29] Cisco TRex, https://trex-tgn.cisco.com/.

[30] Xilinx Alveo U50 Data Center Accelerator Card, https://www.xilinx.com/products/boards-and-kits/alveo/u50.html.

# Stego-Malware Attribution: Simple Signature and Content-based Features Derived and Validated from Classical Image Steganalysis on Five Exemplary Chosen Algorithms

Bernhard Birnbaum
*Dept. of Computer Science*
*Otto-von-Guericke University*
Magdeburg, Germany
email: bernhard.birnbaum@ovgu.de

Christian Krätzer
*Dept. of Computer Science*
*Otto-von-Guericke University*
Magdeburg, Germany
email: christian.kraetzer@ovgu.de

Jana Dittmann
*Dept. of Computer Science*
*Otto-von-Guericke University*
Magdeburg, Germany
email: jana.dittmann@ovgu.de

***Abstract*—Stego malware, which hides malicious functionality using steganographic communication channels, is becoming increasingly common in today's attack scenarios. Cybersecurity capabilities against such malware include prevention, detection, response and attribution tasks. In this paper, we focus on JPEG images and the attribution task by investigating a set of very simple signature-based steganalysis features for stego-malware attribution by attempting to identify the embedding algorithm used in a multi-class problem. First, the communication scenario in stego-malware is discussed by showing how the warden (observer) setting differs from the typical communication setup in steganography (known as the 'Alice and Bob (A-B) scenario') to be used for a simple (non-blind) cover-stego pair analysis besides blind steganalysis. For our considered stego-malware case, the stego communication is redefined as an attacker-to-attacker (A-A) scenario by extending the capabilities of the warden. Second, due to the very simple nature of stego approaches often used in malware, basic assumptions in steganography are not well incorporated in the malware design. This motivates us to study simple, classically known steganography approaches to simulate stego-malware attribution capabilities using five long-standing, well-known steganography tools. Four simple signature-based and two content-based features are derived for the attribution of five stego algorithms and their performance is validated in a multi-class comparison. Using a test set of 1000 randomly selected original cover images from the Alaska2 dataset, the feature set for attribution of the five algorithms used and their individualisation properties are investigated exemplarily for two different capacities (low: 26 bytes and high: 2.1 kBytes) and two different embedding keys (one long and one short), also considering a recompression case for the low capacity. A single and double recompression of the 1000 Alaska2 images used and the Flickr dataset with its 31,783 images are performed to determine the false positive detection performance within image data without steganographic embedding. The results show the differences in stego-algorithm attribution performance per feature and algorithm.***

***Keywords*—stego-malware communication scenario; multi-class steganalysis and attribution.**

## I. Introduction

According to [1], attackers started to use information hiding techniques to make malicious software (malware) stealthier and harder to detect more than a decade ago. In the last 10 years, the volume of malware using steganography and information hiding to prevent detection (bypass security mechanisms), implement evasion or anti-forensics techniques, as well as create hidden communication channels to orchestrate attacks, has been growing on a yearly basis [2]. For such malware using information hiding the term *stego-malware* was created and the following taxonomy was proposed [1]:

- Group 1) malware hiding information by modulating shared resources (e.g., a CPU register)
- Group 2) malware hiding information within network traffic
- Group 3) malware hiding information in digital media objects (covers, e.g., digital images in JPEG formats)

This taxonomy partially reflects the goal of the information hiding mechanism implemented by the attacker: Methods belonging to group 1 are primarily used to allow two processes to exchange data within the same machine or to bypass hardware isolation, methods in group 2 are primarily used to implement Internet-wide covert communication, and methods belonging to group 3 are used for data infiltration, exfiltration or storage. For instance, images modified via steganographic techniques have been used to store information on the local file system of the infected host, to conceal configuration files and malicious code when spreading the infection, or to implement simple command and control (C&C) channels by making them available in social networks or other network services.

Today's cybersecurity capabilities against malware include prevention, detection, response and attribution tasks. For stego-malware detection, for example, the authors from MalJPEG [3] provide an overview of existing work and show that JPEG images are often used. Further [4] summarises available stego-malware approaches by also concluding that JPEG is often used as cover media type. For the detection, the authors in [5] propose an approach to locate stego content in JPEG images by analysing JPEG header markers. In our paper, we also have selected to follow this idea of using JPEG header analysis (file/header integrity as well as the characteristics of specific markers). We focus on an attribution task: Finding traces indicating on the source of the malware. Such a source can be for example malware creation kits on one or more computers, malicious cyber activities of a human intruder or an ultimately responsible party, see e.g., in [6]. As summarized in [7], attribution contains the identification of such sources, the collection of artefacts, extracting relevant information from the data and answering attribution questions besides the source, such as e.g., the time of a malware infestation and activities that where performed on the target. This is similar to the attribution approach presented by Jennifer Newmans group in [8].

In this paper, we address in particular the following in attribution: The identification of the source and collection of artefacts to try to determine the used stego algorithm in stego-malware that is hiding information in digital images (media objects used as covers group 3 in the taxonomy discussed above).

Starting in 2015, the volume of attacks observed 'in the wild' using such methods increased in numbers but also reduced in terms of variety. In fact, the majority of malware exploiting steganographic techniques seems to only take advantage of images as the preferred type of cover media object. As detailed in surveys on that topic (e.g., [2] and [4]), it seems that attackers are capitalizing on the techniques offered by related literature, publicly available source code and libraries, or third-party information-hiding-capable malicious routines offered on a Crime-as-a-Service basis (usually malware creation kits which also contain steganography modules/plugins).

In contrast to the academic research on traditional (end-to-end) steganography (as discussed, e.g., in [9] or [10]), stego-malware relies on much simpler basic assumptions on the communication scenario that will be discussed in more detail in Section II. As done in recent work in [5], we also use existing simple steganography tools from [11], easily available to potential stego-malware creators: *jphide*, *jsteg*, *outguess*, *steghide* and *f5*. Amongst other tools *f5* was also used in [5].

Focusing on stego-malware that uses JPEG images as cover, the paper contributions are as follows to identify the embedding algorithm used in a multi-class problem:

- The disscussion of the warden setting in the stego-malware communication scenario, calling it attacker-to-attacker (A-A) setup by also showing differences in the corresponding basic assumptions for traditional steganographic end-to-end communication (also known as the 'Alice and Bob (A-B) scenario').
- Considerations on the attribution of steganographic methods in stego-malware, aiming at providing indicators of compromise (IoC) for malware detection by trying to identify the algorithm used in a multi-class attribution problem on the example of five algorithms.
- Introduction of a set of light-weight (i.e., easy to compute) features derived from observed artefacts during embedding: Four simple, blind signature-based features and two non-blind, content-based features. The signatures are derived by using existing forensic tools (here *foremost* and *binwalk*) as well as by header analysis on the JPEG files (considering the JFIF version from the JPEG APP0 marker segment as well as a string-search in the JPEG COM marker segments). While the first is novel to this paper, the second follows the methodology in [3] and [5] but determines novel signatures for the string-search performed. The content-based, non-blind features, which analyse in our case the (re-)compression behaviour as well as the embedding impact to the colour distribution in the image, are motivated by the typical, content-focused steganalysis methods discussed, e.g., in [10]. The feature extraction and attribution functionalities are presented in detail in Section III and in Figure 2.
- An empirical investigation on five simple, classical steganography approaches with two different capacities and key sizes based on 1000 randomly chosen images from the Alaska2 image steganalysis reference database [12] to derive a tendency for malware detection and algorithm individualisation by additionally testing for false positives (wrongful stego attribution on cover data with no embedding) with (1) single and double re-compressed Alaska2 images without embeddings and (2) the Flickr30k data set from [13] with 31,783 images in total. The results show in the multi-class decision the following: Unique attribution of *jsteg* is possible with two blind features with no errors and one blind feature with 0.18 percent errors, four stego algorithms can be attributed using file header signatures. *jphide* is difficult to attribute with our features set. Those promising results motivate further work for stego-malware detection and attribution focusing on JPEG image header analysis.

The rest of the paper is structured as follows: First, the A-A communication scenario of stego-malware and corresponding attribution challenges for the Warden are introduced in Section II. In Section III, the attribution concept with the summary of the used steganography tools, the used image sets, the embedding options and the set of attribution features are discussed. Section IV contains implementation details and Section V summarizes the results, followed by a last section with a summary and conclusion.

## II. Scenario and attribution background for Stego-Malware

Stego-malware has firmly established itself as a dangerous and still growing malware trend since 2015. A recent example for such malware relying on steganographic channels is an incident that has been reported in November 2022 by (among many other sources) [14]. In [15] this stego-malware is discussed in some detail by security specialists that where reacting to this attack early on and who were responsible for limiting its spread by providing involved actors with indicators of compromise (IoC). The details in [15] provide first insights, with more detailed information presented here:

In late October 2022 malicious source code projects from this attack started to appear on the Python code repository PyPi. They were claiming to be libraries to be useful for web development tasks and were soon added (in a kind of supply chain attack) as includes to other repositories on PyPi and GitHub. In those malicious packages, the existing steganography library 'judyb' [16] (itself a fork from the well known Python steganography module 'stegano' [17]) was used to manage the communication. On *infestation* on a target machine, the malware tried to post-fetch/infiltrate malicious routines steganographicaly hidden in PNG images from a fixed remote source (in this case a channel on imgur.com), *establish on site control* (this only worked on MS Windows machines due to the execution methods used), *execute the actual malicious function* (a fork of W4SP-Stealer [18], trying to steal saved passwords, two-factor-authentication tokens, wallet keys, etc. and uploading them to the command & control (C&C) server; here, this W4SP fork is different from other forks by the fact that it uses the steganographic channel to exfiltrate the stolen data instead of simply posting it on Discord) and *communicate it back to the C&C server*. The code of the malicious libraries also contained hookups for a spreader module to try to infest also other MS Windows machines in the same Active Directory domain, but corresponding code was defunct in the sources analyzed here. Figure 1 illustrates the activities of this stego-malware.

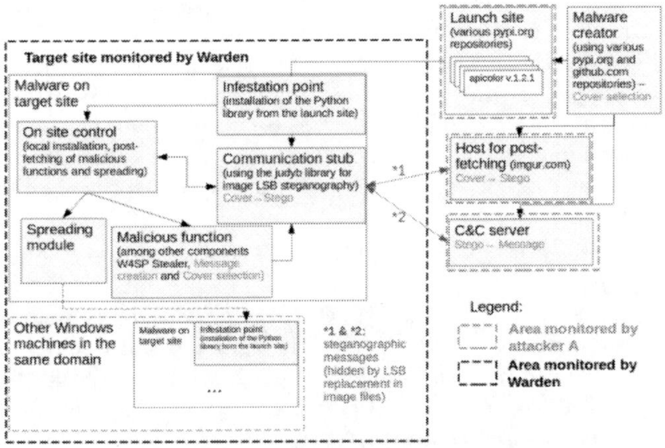


Fig. 1. Activities of the exemplary discussed stego-malware and the A-A communication scenario discussed in this paper.

In their initial report [15], the authors summarize that '*little more than 80 projects containing the malicious packages*' were detected in this supply chain attack. It can be assumed that this number is too low, since over more than two weeks many different versions of the initial libraries were created on PyPi under different names and were then be used to poison other projects (on PyPi and GitHub) by adding them as includes in user contributions. The attack wave stopped after PyPi managed to find a way to automatically derive IoCs and thereby effectually take down new versions before they could be used to poison other projects.

For this representative stego-malware scenario using image steganography, the following points shall be highlighted:

- All discussed software components (the steganography library, the W4SP-Stealer as actual payload, etc.) were and still are **publicly available on platforms like GitHub**.
- Attackers make extensive use of **third party resources** (e.g., repositories like PyPi or GitHub as well as social media sites / image hosts like imgur.com) in infiltration and exfiltration activities, making blocking by application level firewalls difficult.
- The steganographic method used in the discussed example is **trivial least significant bit (LSB) replacement for PNG images** (which is still good enough to prevent usual end-point security solutions from raising an alarm during infiltration).
- The **key** used for securing the communication is not pre-shared but is instead infiltrated together with other attack components, **violating Kerckhoffs' principle**.
- The attacker embeds steganographic messages in PNG images found in **the target system observed by the warden** with the intention to communicate these stego images back to him/herself, making the whole scenario prone to cover-stego image comparison attacks.

This stego-malware example is representative for the current state-of-the-art, where the significant deviations from the traditional 'Alice and Bob' (A-B) end-to-end communication scheme can be identified:

- As the **attacker A activities at the target system are fully observable**, all attacker actions should be as limited as possible to **raise no suspicion**.
- Therefore **Non-Kerckhoffs'** setups (key-less techniques, hard-coded keys or key infiltrated together with the payload of the hidden communication) are often used.
- **Simple embedding and retrieval techniques** are used natively in the target domain or are put in place with supply-chain-attacks like the one discussed above.
- The classical 'Alice and Bob' (A-B) end-to-end communication scenario with a 'Warden' monitoring the channel is changed to a scenario with the **attacker A controlling both ends of the communication** and the **Warden observing the target system and its incoming and outgoing communication** - the A-A scenario shown in Figure 1.
- The cover selection and/or cover embedding at the target system can be observed by the warden. Blind as well as **non-blind analysis of cover and stego objects used** become possible.

For in-depth justifications on these generalizing claims, the reader is referred to [2] and [4].

## III. Attribution Concept

In the A-A communication scenario of stego-malware, the Warden has (potentially) full access to the malware injected into the target side and to all communication channels, including the steganographic communication, due to the Non-Kerckhoffs' setups. **As a consequence**, the Warden would be capable to perform **blind** steganalysis (as in the traditional Warden in an 'Alice and Bob' (A-B) end-to-end steganography scenario) but potentially also **non-blind** (stego-cover comparison) analysis, since the media used as cover in an outgoing communication would be originating within his observed domain. In stego-malware setups, the attacker A relies primarily on two things for the security/confidentiality of his malicious communication: a) a lack of suspicion from the Warden (i.e., security by obscurity) and b) the fact that an in-depth analysis of every in- and outgoing object by dedicated steganalysis engines is far to expensive (in terms of run-time, communication delays and other QoS aspects, false positives, etc.), so such an analysis would only be used as an on demand service for the scaling of methods for evidence gathering in case of a suspicions (e.g., when an IoC was found by an endpoint security solution). As a consequence, the attacker will assumedly try to perform only **simple, innocently looking operations** (like, e.g., accessing PNG files on an image hosting service as in the example discussed in the previous section) to avoid raising suspicion.

In this paper, the research idea is to **define and use a set of light-weight attribution features** that could be checked by the Warden for each communicated media object as part of the **continuous perimeter defense of the target site** (e.g., as rules in a next-generation firewall). As starting point for our empirical work, **five existing, simple steganography tools**, easily available to potential stego-malware creators, are used here, together with **simple signature- and content based-steganalysis methods** to provide a set of light-weight (i.e., easy to compute) features (five simple structural features plus two content-based features). This set of light-weight attribution features is applied on a selected image test set, processed with a fixed embedding option using two selected payload capacities and two different keys as described in the following sub-sections.

### A. Steganography and general analysis tools

Our goal is to use very simple approaches to simulate malware steganography. Therefore the well known **Steganography Toolkit** [11] is used for the empirical evaluations in this paper. It is maintained by the GitHub user 'DominicBreuker' and is one of the most popular steganography repositories on GitHub. At the time of writing of this paper it has been forked (and extended) more than 300 times by other users. The reason why it is so popular lies in the fact that it provides a large number of popular steganography and steganalysis tools in a Docker image, making them easily deployable on many platforms without complicated installation procedures. The **steganography tools selected for this paper** from this toolkit are limited to provided image steganography tools for JPEG images. The corresponding set of steganography methods contains the following five tools: *jphide*, *jsteg*, *outguess*, *steghide* and *f5*.

The following **general analysis tools** are selected from the Steganography Toolkit to compute the features/attributes for this paper: *exiftool*, *binwalk*, *foremost*, *strings*, and the *imagemagick* modules 'identify' and 'compare'. All tools used in this paper are listed in Table I.

### B. Image sets for evaluation

For a first empirical evaluation, the quality of the test data (esp. the amount of relevant and representative data) is important to obtain generalizable results. To ensure that the data used here is representative as well as diverse, 1000 randomly chosen specimen are sampled as covers from the established image steganalysis reference dataset 'Alaska2' [12]. To provide a significant amount of wide variance image data to establish potential false positive rates for the attribution in an 'in the field' scenario, additionally the 'Fickr30k' dataset from [13] is used in our evaluations.

### C. Embedding options used

In this first evaluation, an attribution based on two different message capacities (embedding data: ASCII text of 26 Bytes ('low' capacity scenario) and 2.1 kBytes ('high' capacity scenario) length) and two keys of different length (4 Bytes (='short') and 128 Bytes (='long') are used. Only *jsteg* does not support a key as a parameter and therefore the embedding that case is key-less ('no key').

### D. Our set of light-weight attribution features

Motivated from the idea to design an easy to compute feature set, the tools selected (see Section III-A) are analysed and a set of features is identified for potential attribution. Based on in-depth tool output analysis, the following set of light-weight attribution features are implemented from Table I, using pre-existing analysis tools (see marked in cursive) and used in this paper. This table also encodes for each of the attribution features whether it is relevant (`r`), unique (`u`), motivated from (`m`) or not applicable (`n.a.`) for a specific steganographic tool.

**Our six features** are motivated from the following observations:

- $\mathtt{ba}_1$: The feature extracted by *exiftool* is considered anomalous if the value cannot be successfully retrieved. As can be seen in Figure 2, the 2 bytes reserved for the JFIF version in the APP0 marker segment are zero, which is the case for all *jsteg* embedding attempts.
- $\mathtt{ba}_2$: For correctly written JPEG images, *binwalk* can also determine the data type by extracting image data, but similar to the feature $\mathtt{ba}_1$, this does not apply to *jsteg* embeddings, as the file header is corrupted by this stego tool.
- $\mathtt{ba}_3$: The tool *foremost* can produce successful output for all manipulations by carving the input image except for *jsteg*, since the *jsteg* image headers appear to be damaged, which violates JPEG image format integrity.
- $\mathtt{ba}_4$: All tools seem to leave specific traces in the COM sections of the JPEG file header. This is a weakness that many stego tools share, because they use in many cases non-standard JPEG libraries and do not write correct or plausible JPEG/JFIF metadata. As listed in Table II, $\mathtt{ba}_4$

TABLE I

THE ATTRIBUTION FEATURES USED IN THIS PAPER WITH THE CORRESPONDING ANALYSIS TOOLS AND THE ENCODING OF THE RELEVANCE FOR THE FIVE CONSIDERED STEGANOGRAPHY TOOLS (r: RELEVANT, u: UNIQUE, m: MOTIVATED FROM, n.a.: NOT APPLICABLE)

| feature id | feature name | feature type | analysis tools | *jphide* | *jsteg* | *outguess* | *steghide* | *f5* |
|---|---|---|---|---|---|---|---|---|
| **signature-based features** | | | | | | | | |
| $ba_1$ | *JFIF version* | blind | exiftool | n.a. | r, u, m | n.a. | n.a. | n.a. |
| $ba_2$ | *binwalk extraction* | blind | binwalk | n.a. | r, u, m | n.a. | n.a. | n.a. |
| $ba_3$ | *foremost carving* | blind | foremost | n.a. | r, u, m | n.a. | n.a. | n.a. |
| $ba_4$ | *file header* | blind | strings | r | r, u | r | r | r, u, m |
| **content-based features** | | | | | | | | |
| $nba_1$ | *file size* | non-blind | exiftool | r | n.a. | n.a. | r, m | n.a. |
| $nba_2$ | *difference color mean* | non-blind | imagemagick | r | n.a. | n.a. | r, m | n.a. |

TABLE II

SIGNATURES FOR FEATURE $BA_4$ - CHECKED ON ITS PRESENCES: IF $sig_1$, $sig_3$ AND $sig_5$ ARE NOT PRESENT AND $sig_2$ AND $sig_4$ ARE PRESENT THE CORRESPONDING STEGO ALGORITHM IS DETECTED

| signature id | stego algorithm | signature content |
|---|---|---|
| $sig_1$ | *jsteg* | JFIF |
| $sig_2$ | *f5* | (((((((((((((((((((((((((((((((((((((((((((((( |
| $sig_3$ | *jphide* | 56789:CDEFGHIJSTUVWXYZcdefghijstuvwxyz |
| $sig_4$ | *outguess, steghide* | !22222222222222222222222222222222222222222222222222 |
| $sig_5$ | *outguess, steghide* | Exif |

is based on different signatures, which are also shown in Figure 2. First, the identifier field in the JFIF-APP0-marker-segment is checked for $sig_1$. If it is not present, a *jsteg* embedding is assumed. Further in the file header, the COM-marker-segment is also checked for the following signatures: the presence of $sig_2$ indicates a *f5* embedding; *jphide* embeddings usually do not contain $sig_3$; whenever $sig_4$ is found but $sig_5$ is not, an *outguess* or *steghide* embedding is expected.

- $nba_1$: The idea behind this feature is to compare original and stego-image file sizes, as the stego tools *jphide* and *steghide* do not perform an image recompression during embedding. This results in a stego file size that is much closer to the original compared to other stego algorithms. The following rule was derived by empirical analysis: $\texttt{diff. size} < \frac{\texttt{orig. size}}{2} \wedge \texttt{stego size} > \frac{\texttt{orig. size}}{2}$.
- $nba_2$: This feature is also motivated by the fact that *jphide* and *steghide* do not apply a recompression. So, when creating a differential image of the stego-manipulated image (by *jphide* or *steghide*) and the original, all visible changes are directly related to the embedded data. Usually, the amount of changes is much smaller than the changes related to a re-compression, except when embedding large amount of data. As stego manipulations are also visible in the different colour channels of the image, but changes in the RGB channels due to a re-compression are much higher than for stego embeddings, the following detection rule is derived by empirical analysis: $\texttt{diff. mean} > 127 \wedge \texttt{diff. mean} == \texttt{rgb diff. mean} \pm 1\%$.

## IV. IMPLEMENTATION OF THE ATTRIBUTION

**Analysis and attribution feature extraction**: The process of feature extraction is done by first executing all given analysis tools (as outlined in Section III-A) in a so-called '**screening phase**' in the following order: *exiftool*, *binwalk*, *strings*, *foremost* and *imagemagick*. In the '**parsing phase**', the attribution features from Table I are parsed into a CSV file, where each row contains the data of one investigated JPEG files.

**Implementation of the attribution**: The attribution was implemented in two different modes, **blind** and **non-blind.** As **blind** attribution is the most common case in reality, **non-blind** attribution – often plausible for stego-malware as discussed for the A-A scenarion and the warden monioring capabilities – allows to take advantage of more powerful features (e.g., *steghide* embeddings are not detectible with only the blind attributes presented in Table III-A). Finally, multiple queries with rules/signatures specific for each steganography tool are used to interpret the extracted feature values, which performs the actual stego-tool attribution. Figure 2 illustrates the attribution process in a flowchart.

## V. RESULTS AND EVALUATION

In Table III at the end of the document, the evaluation results are summarized. The table is divided into three main column parts:

The **first** part, containing the first and second column, the features from Table I and the test configuration are listed. In the **second** part, the attribution results in terms of correct or incorrect entries to the result list as well as (true/false) positive (=stego) hits and (true/false) negative (=unmodified cover) hits are given. In the **third** main column part, all stego tool identification results are included for the corresponding test configuration.

Starting with the results for *jphide*, Table I discusses attribution results for each of the blind or non-blind attributes deemed relevant for a stego tool, using the described stego embeddings on the Alaska2 data set. This is done for all five stego tools. Second, false positive rate tests on re-compressed genuine Alaska2 and Flickr30k images are presented.

The results presented in the table can be summarised as follows:

- **Regarding different capacities and keys** for all algorithms:

(1) The **blind** simple signatures show:
  - **no influence from different capacities and keys** in the performance for ***jphide***, ***jsteg*** and ***f5***, while *jphide* and *f5* have false classifications for the file header signatures of $\texttt{ba}_4$: *jphide* with the re-compressed Alaska2 set and Flickr30k, *f5* with Flickr30k only;
  - for ***outguess*** **and** ***steghide*** the $\texttt{ba}_4$ - file header signatures are sensitive: The high capacity with the short key influences the *outguess* file header signature (for the 2.1KB message, in 437 of the 1000 cases *outguess* could not successfully embed, which results for this tool in an empty (0 Byte) output file without a header – in the evaluations these cases are counted as false negatives since they are no genuine image files any longer but are also not flagged to be the output of this steganography tool). For *steghide*, the $\texttt{ba}_4$ file header signature is (besides embedding problems that result in only 881 stego files being successfully created for the 2.1KB message) not only resulting in large numbers of false negatives for all cases except the re-compressed Alaska2 images with short capacity with the short key but it also lacks discriminatory power in regard to *steghide* and *outguess*.

(2) The **non-blind** (content-based) features motivated from *steghide* characteristics show the following:
  - both features are relevant for ***steghide*** **and** ***jphide*** but not in a unique manner;
  - the first content-based feature ($\texttt{nba}_1$) of **file size** is **in most cases capacities and keys independent** but attributes *steghide* as well as *jphide* at the same time (in a not unique manner) with errors only in high capacity with the short key and with wrong classifications in the Alaska2 re-compression tests;
  - the second non-blind feature of different **color mean** attributes ($\texttt{nba}_2$) also *steghide* as well as *jphide* and is **error prone to high capacity with the short key too** and less sensitive for all other settings with wrong classifications in the Alaska2 re-compression tests.

- **Regarding the individual algorithm identification performances**:

(1) ***jsteg***: Features $\texttt{ba}_1$, $\texttt{ba}_2$ and $\texttt{ba}_3$ are motivated from the artefacts observed after embedding and also $\texttt{ba}_4$ file header motivated from *f5* can be used with $\texttt{sig}_1$ in the file header to identify *jsteg* in a unique manner with best results. There are only a minor error in high capacity with the short key for $\texttt{ba}_2$ and JFIF signature errors for $\texttt{ba}_1$ in the Flickr30k tests of 58 errors.

(2) ***f5***: Feature file header $\texttt{ba}_4$ with signature $\texttt{sig}_2$ allows a unique identification of *f5* with only low errors in the Flickr30k test of 624 similar cases in $\texttt{sig}_2$.
In summary of (1) of (2): $\texttt{ba}_1$ and $\texttt{ba}_4$ signatures $\texttt{sig}_2$ seem to be partially occurring also in JPEG data on the example on Flickr30k causing classification errors: for $\texttt{ba}_1$ of 0.18% (58/31783) and $\texttt{ba}_4$ of 1.96% (624/31783).

(3) ***outguess***: Feature file header $\texttt{ba}_4$ with signature $\texttt{sig}_4$ is relevant for identification of *outguess* but it is not unique with errors in the high capacity embedding; it overlaps with the signature for *steghide* in the file header. For stego malware detection without the need of algorithm identification the $\texttt{sig}_4$ usage is possible. There are no errors in the re-compression and Flickr30k tests.

(4) ***steghide***: Feature file header $\texttt{ba}_4$ with signature $\texttt{sig}_4$ is relevant for identification of *steghide* but also *outguess* is attributed and therefore no unique algorithm identification is possible, but it allows with $\texttt{sig}_4$ the general stego-malware detection. Only the re-compressed embedding has no errors. As for *outguess* there are also no errors in the re-compression and Flickr30k tests.
The two blind content-based features $\texttt{nba}_1$ and $\texttt{nba}_2$ are motivated from *steghide* artefacts in JPEG files. Both features are relevant but do not allow algorithm individualization as also *jphide* causes similar artefacts in JPEG. Further it causes false positives in the re-compression and in the Flickr30k tests.
In summary from (3) and (4): the $\texttt{ba}_4$ $\texttt{sig}_4$ allows stego-malware detection but no algorithm individualization.

(5) ***jphide***: Feature file header $\texttt{ba}_4$ with signature $\texttt{sig}_3$ is relevant and unique for identification of algorithm but the lack of signature $\texttt{sig}_3$ (and the attribution based on this fact) also appears in the Flickr30k tests.
The two non-blind content-based features $\texttt{nba}_1$ and $\texttt{nba}_2$ are motivated from *steghide* artefacts in JPEG files. Both features are also relevant but does not allow algorithm individualization as also *steghide* causes similar artefacts. Further it also causes as for *steghide* false positives in the re-compression and in the Flickr30k tests.
In summary for (5): the based on $\texttt{ba}_4$ $\texttt{sig}_3$ is unique for the algorithm *jphide*, but also occurs in non stego data in re-compression of Alaska2 and Flickr30k. Content based features are also relevant, but also occur during normal re-compression. Therefore, for these three features, it is difficult to used them for stego-malware detection.

For the tested attribution features, the following summary can be drawn:

- the signature-based features $\texttt{ba}_2$ and $\texttt{ba}_3$ are capacity and key independent and perform best for *jsteg* algorithm identification with no false positives in re-compression as well as in the Flickr30k tests;
- feature $\texttt{ba}_1$ (JFIF Version) has a similar performance for *jsteg* with few errors of 0.18% in the Flickr30k tests;
- $\texttt{ba}_4$ COM signatures allow algorithm identification with:

- $\texttt{sig}_1$: *jsteg* – unique with no errors,
- $\texttt{sig}_2$: *f5* – unique with $\texttt{sig}_2$ but 1.96% errors in Flickr30k test,
- $\texttt{sig}_3$: *jphide* – relevant but with 100% errors in Alaska2 re-compression and 98.04% errors in the Flickr30k test,
- $\texttt{sig}_4$ and $\texttt{sig}_5$: *outguess* and *steghide* - relevant with errors depending on capacity and keys.

The content-based features have high error rates when the images are re-compressed and are therefore not applicable if re-compression needs to be considered.

## VI. Summary and Conclusion

**Summarizing the results** presented in Section V, it can be said that the set of light-weight attribution features used in this paper in an initial and also very simple evaluation shows a first positive tendency to potentially identify the stego algorithm used in a stego-malware scenario with the tested set of five different existing algorithms. The promising results motivate further work on attribution approaches, especially for a generalization for stego-malware detection and prevention scenarios. One research perspective might be the combination of our approach with its multi-class attribution with the localization work for embedding artefacts as discussed in [5]. The interest in this field is caused (as pointed out in Section II) by non-Kerckhoffs' setups, which are often found in combination with simple embedding techniques (like the ones practically evaluated in this paper, or even more trivial, like LSB embedding in pixel domain image formats such as PNG). Furthermore, the Warden can usually monitor all relevant communication channels as well as the potential cover objects available in the target domain. This last characteristic of such stego-malware scenarios also enables non-blind analysis and attribution methods which significantly simplify the detection and attribution tasks.

The first aspect for potential **future work** would be the **definition of additional attribution characteristics** for individualization of the attack, respectively to characterise the attacker A more precisely. An extension should cover further aspects such as different stego key usage, different capacities, message- and stego-encoding, etc. as well as further forensic approaches. During the interpretation of the results, additional knowledge was derived, that could be used for future attribution features: With the tested steganography tools, no metadata, such as geodata, used camera, or timestamps were available in the generated stego image files. In addition, all stego objects were generated by the stego tools in baseline encoded JPEGs, even if their covers were progressive DCT-based JPEGs. For non-blind attribution, initial tests with image entropy showed for a stego object a slightly larger entropy than for a double compressed version of the same cover (using the same quality factor as in the first compression again). Also, the location of the changes in the difference image indicate for some tools whether a stego embedding or a re-compression might have created the artefacts.

Second, the **list of steganography tools and methods targeted in the attribution should be significantly extended**, e.g., by including into the evaluations also the steganographic tools represented in the StegoAppDB [19]. Analyzing **different embedding capacities** might bring more individualization, like malicious content included as hidden message could potentially be classified by message length into different classes.

An extension into **inter-media attribution** would be beneficial. In this paper only JPEG images were considered, but also image formats (esp. PNG and BMP for the still popular LSB-embedders) or other media formats like audio file formats should be addressed. The Stego-Toolkit [11] would also provide a good starting point for such developments.

**Source code analysis for stego tools** would give very valuable attribution characteristics, including the used JPEG-libraries with details on quantization tables and other header details to be expected in the output of the created stego objects as a kind of software-based fingerprinting or signature-based detection.

Since some of the stego methods are also content-sensitive in the embedding (e.g., ignoring low texture regions and embedding only into high texture regions) evaluations with a focus on **content selection** and different content classes should be performed.

**Author Contributions:** Initial idea & attribution methodology: Jana Dittmann (JD); Stego-Malware scenario modelling and domain adaptation from end-to-end steganalysis: Christian Krätzer (CK); Evaluation (setup and realisation): Bernhard Birnbaum (BB); Writing – original draft: BB; Writing – review, enhancements, finalisation & editing: CK, JD and BB.

## References

[1] W. Mazurczyk and L. Caviglione, "Information hiding as a challenge for malware detection," *IEEE Security & Privacy*, vol. 13, no. 2, pp. 89–93, 2015.

[2] L. Caviglione, M. Choraś, I. Corona, A. Janicki, W. Mazurczyk, M. Pawlicki, and K. Wasielewska, "Tight arms race: Overview of current malware threats and trends in their detection," *IEEE Access*, vol. 9, pp. 5371–5396, 2021.

[3] A. Cohen, N. Nissim, and Y. Elovici, "Maljpeg: Machine learning based solution for the detection of malicious jpeg images," *IEEE Access*, vol. 8, pp. 19997–20011, 2020.

[4] R. Chaganti, V. Ravi, M. Alazab, and T. D. Pham, "Stegomalware: A systematic survey of malwarehiding and detection in images, machine learningmodels and research challenges," *CoRR*, vol. abs/2110.02504, 2021.

[5] V. Verma, S. K. Muttoo, and V. B. Singh, "Detecting stegomalware: Malicious image steganography and its intrusion in windows," in *Security, Privacy and Data Analytics* (U. P. Rao, S. J. Patel, P. Raj, and A. Visconti, eds.), (Singapore), pp. 103–116, Springer Singapore, 2022.

[6] H. S. Lin, "Attribution of malicious cyber incidents: From soup to nuts," *Legal Perspectives in Information Systems eJournal*, 2016.

[7] F. Skopik and T. Pahi, "Under false flag: using technical artifacts for cyber attack attribution," *Cybersecurity*, vol. 3, pp. 1–20, 2020.

[8] W. Chen, Y. Wang, Y. Guan, J. Newman, L. Lin, and S. Reinders, "Forensic analysis of android steganography apps," in *Advances in Digital Forensics XIV* (G. Peterson and S. Shenoi, eds.), (Cham), pp. 293–312, Springer International Publishing, 2018.

[9] J. Fridrich, *Steganography in Digital Media: Principles, Algorithms, and Applications*. Cambridge, MA.: Cambridge University Press, 2009.

[10] R. Böhme, *Advanced Statistical Steganalysis*. Information Security and Cryptography, Springer Berlin Heidelberg, 2010.

[11] D. Breuker, "Steganography-toolkit," *https://github.com/DominicBreuker/stego-toolkit - last accessed: August 21st, 2023*, 2020.
[12] Kaggle, "Alaska2 image steganalysis set," *https://www.kaggle.com/competitions/alaska2-image-steganalysis/data - last accessed: August 21st, 2023*, July 2020.
[13] P. Young, A. Lai, M. Hodosh, and J. Hockenmaier, "From image descriptions to visual denotations: New similarity metrics for semantic inference over event descriptions," *TACL*, vol. 2, pp. 67–78, 2014.
[14] F. Y. Rashid, "Malicious python package relies on steganography to download malware," *https://www.darkreading.com/threat-intelligence/malicious-pypi-package-steganography-download-malware/ - last accessed: August 21st, 2023*, 2022.
[15] Spectralops, "Check point cloudguard spectral exposes new obfuscation techniques for malicious packages on pypi," *https://research.checkpoint.com/2022/check-point-cloudguard-spectral-exposes-new-obfuscation-techniques-for-malicious-packages-on-pypi/ - last accessed: August 21st, 2023*, 2022.
[16] JUDYB, "Judyb steganography library," *https://pypi.org/project/judyb/ - last accessed: August 21st, 2023*, 2020.
[17] Stegano, "Stegano steganography library," *https://sr.ht/ cedric/stegano/ - last accessed: August 21st, 2023*, 2020.
[18] W4SP, "W4sp-stealer," *https://github.com/Im4wasp/W4SP-Stealer-Sourcecode - last accessed: August 21st, 2023*, 2020.
[19] J. Newman, "Stegoappdb," *https://forensicstats.org/stegoappdb/ - last accessed: August 21st, 2023*, 2020.

# Appendix A

Fig. 2. Flowchart of attribution

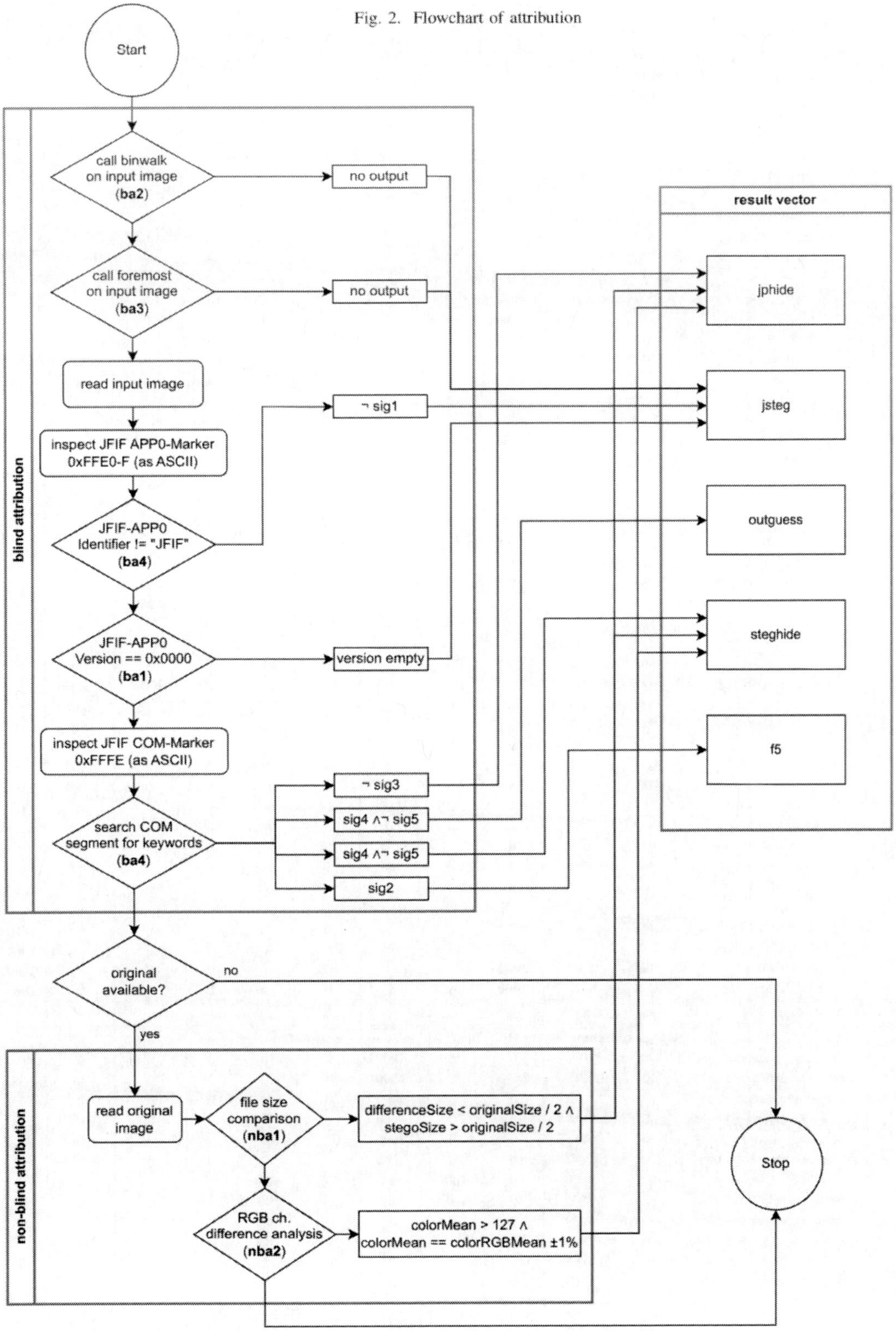

TABLE III
ATTRIBUTION RESULTS FOR THE FIVE TESTED STEGO ALGORITHMS AND THE IMPLEMENTED FEATURES

| feature | test config | in result list | | positives | | negatives | | identification results | | | | |
|---|---|---|---|---|---|---|---|---|---|---|---|---|
| | | correct | incorrect | true p. | false p. | true n. | false n. | *jphide* | *jsteg* | *outguess* | *steghide* | *f5* |
| ***jphide*** (1000 images from Alaska2) | | | | | | | | | | | | |
| $ba_4$ | 26B, long Key | 1000 | 0 | **1000** | 0 | 0 | 0 | **1000** | 0 | 0 | 0 | 0 |
| | rec; 26B, short Key | 1000 | 0 | **1000** | 0 | 0 | 0 | **1000** | 0 | 0 | 0 | 0 |
| | 26B, short Key | 1000 | 0 | **1000** | 0 | 0 | 0 | **1000** | 0 | 0 | 0 | 0 |
| | 2.1KB, short Key | 1000 | 0 | **1000** | 0 | 0 | 0 | **1000** | 0 | 0 | 0 | 0 |
| $nba_1$ | 26B, long Key | 1000 | 1000 | **0** | 0 | 0 | 0 | **1000** | 0 | 0 | 1000 | 0 |
| | rec; 26B, short Key | 1000 | 1000 | **0** | 0 | 0 | 0 | **1000** | 0 | 0 | 1000 | 0 |
| | 26B, short Key | 1000 | 1000 | **0** | 0 | 0 | 0 | **1000** | 0 | 0 | 1000 | 0 |
| | 2.1KB, short Key | 1000 | 1000 | **0** | 0 | 0 | 0 | **1000** | 0 | 0 | 1000 | 0 |
| $nba_2$ | 26B, long Key | 923 | 923 | **0** | 0 | 0 | 77 | **923** | 0 | 0 | 923 | 0 |
| | rec; 26B, short Key | 775 | 775 | **0** | 0 | 0 | 225 | **775** | 0 | 0 | 775 | 0 |
| | 26B, short Key | 921 | 921 | **0** | 0 | 0 | 79 | **921** | 0 | 0 | 921 | 0 |
| | 2.1KB, short Key | 0 | 0 | **0** | 0 | 0 | 1000 | **0** | 0 | 0 | 0 | 0 |
| ***jsteg*** (1000 images from Alaska2) | | | | | | | | | | | | |
| $ba_1$ | 26B, keyless | 1000 | 0 | **1000** | 0 | 0 | 0 | 0 | **1000** | 0 | 0 | 0 |
| | rec; 26B, keyless | 1000 | 0 | **1000** | 0 | 0 | 0 | 0 | **1000** | 0 | 0 | 0 |
| | 2.1KB, keyless | 1000 | 0 | **1000** | 0 | 0 | 0 | 0 | **1000** | 0 | 0 | 0 |
| $ba_2$ | 26B, keyless | 1000 | 0 | **1000** | 0 | 0 | 0 | 0 | **1000** | 0 | 0 | 0 |
| | rec; 26B, keyless | 1000 | 0 | **1000** | 0 | 0 | 0 | 0 | **1000** | 0 | 0 | 0 |
| | 2.1KB, keyless | 999 | 0 | **999** | 0 | 0 | 1 | 0 | **999** | 0 | 0 | 0 |
| $ba_3$ | 26B, keyless | 1000 | 0 | **1000** | 0 | 0 | 0 | 0 | **1000** | 0 | 0 | 0 |
| | rec; 26B, keyless | 1000 | 0 | **1000** | 0 | 0 | 0 | 0 | **1000** | 0 | 0 | 0 |
| | 2.1KB, keyless | 1000 | 0 | **1000** | 0 | 0 | 0 | 0 | **1000** | 0 | 0 | 0 |
| $ba_4$ | 26B, keyless | 1000 | 0 | **1000** | 0 | 0 | 0 | 0 | **1000** | 0 | 0 | 0 |
| | rec; 26B, keyless | 1000 | 0 | **1000** | 0 | 0 | 0 | 0 | **1000** | 0 | 0 | 0 |
| | 2.1KB, keyless | 1000 | 0 | **1000** | 0 | 0 | 0 | 0 | **1000** | 0 | 0 | 0 |
| ***outguess*** (1000 images from Alaska2) | | | | | | | | | | | | |
| $ba_4$ | 26B, long Key | 1000 | 1000 | **0** | 0 | 0 | 0 | 0 | 0 | **1000** | 1000 | 0 |
| | rec; 26B, short Key | 1000 | 1000 | **0** | 0 | 0 | 0 | 0 | 0 | **1000** | 1000 | 0 |
| | 26B, short Key | 1000 | 1000 | **0** | 0 | 0 | 0 | 0 | 0 | **1000** | 1000 | 0 |
| | 2.1KB, short Key | 563 | 563 | **0** | 0 | 0 | 437 | 0 | 0 | **563** | 563 | 0 |
| ***steghide*** (1000 images from Alaska2) | | | | | | | | | | | | |
| $ba_4$ | 26B, long Key | 338 | 338 | **0** | 0 | 0 | 662 | 0 | 0 | 338 | **338** | 0 |
| | rec; 26B, short Key | 1000 | 1000 | **0** | 0 | 0 | 0 | 0 | 0 | 1000 | **1000** | 0 |
| | 26B, short Key | 338 | 338 | **0** | 0 | 0 | 662 | 0 | 0 | 338 | **338** | 0 |
| | 2.1KB, short Key | 241 | 241 | **0** | 0 | 0 | 640 | 0 | 0 | 241 | **241** | 0 |
| $nba_1$ | 26B, long Key | 1000 | 1000 | **0** | 0 | 0 | 0 | 1000 | 0 | 0 | **1000** | 0 |
| | rec; 26B, short Key | 1000 | 1000 | **0** | 0 | 0 | 0 | 1000 | 0 | 0 | **1000** | 0 |
| | 26B, short Key | 1000 | 1000 | **0** | 0 | 0 | 0 | 1000 | 0 | 0 | **1000** | 0 |
| | 2.1KB, short Key | 881 | 881 | **0** | 0 | 0 | 0 | 881 | 0 | 0 | **881** | 0 |
| $nba_2$ | 26B, long Key | 992 | 992 | **0** | 0 | 0 | 8 | 992 | 0 | 0 | **992** | 0 |
| | rec; 26B, short Key | 971 | 971 | **0** | 0 | 0 | 29 | 971 | 0 | 0 | **971** | 0 |
| | 26B, short Key | 991 | 991 | **0** | 0 | 0 | 9 | 991 | 0 | 0 | **991** | 0 |
| | 2.1KB, short Key | 0 | 0 | **0** | 0 | 0 | 881 | 0 | 0 | 0 | **0** | 0 |
| ***f5*** (1000 images from Alaska2) | | | | | | | | | | | | |
| $ba_4$ | 26B, long Key | 1000 | 0 | **1000** | 0 | 0 | 0 | 0 | 0 | 0 | 0 | **1000** |
| | rec; 26B, short Key | 1000 | 0 | **1000** | 0 | 0 | 0 | 0 | 0 | 0 | 0 | **1000** |
| | 26B, short Key | 1000 | 0 | **1000** | 0 | 0 | 0 | 0 | 0 | 0 | 0 | **1000** |
| | 2.1KB, short Key | 1000 | 0 | **1000** | 0 | 0 | 0 | 0 | 0 | 0 | 0 | **1000** |
| all other | | n.a. | n.a. | n.a. | n.a. | n.a. | n.a. | n.a. | n.a. | n.a. | n.a. | n.a. |
| **imagemagick re-compression** (1000 images from Alaska2, quality factor 75%) | | | | | | | | | | | | |
| $ba_1$ | genuine recompressed | 0 | 0 | 0 | 0 | **1000** | 0 | 0 | 0 | 0 | 0 | 0 |
| | genuine recompressed twice | 0 | 0 | 0 | 0 | **1000** | 0 | 0 | 0 | 0 | 0 | 0 |
| $ba_2$ | genuine recompressed | 0 | 0 | 0 | 0 | **1000** | 0 | 0 | 0 | 0 | 0 | 0 |
| | genuine recompressed twice | 0 | 0 | 0 | 0 | **1000** | 0 | 0 | 0 | 0 | 0 | 0 |
| $ba_3$ | genuine recompressed | 0 | 0 | 0 | 0 | **1000** | 0 | 0 | 0 | 0 | 0 | 0 |
| | genuine recompressed twice | 0 | 0 | 0 | 0 | **1000** | 0 | 0 | 0 | 0 | 0 | 0 |
| $ba_4$ | genuine recompressed | 0 | 1000 | 0 | 1000 | **0** | 0 | 1000 | 0 | 0 | 0 | 0 |
| | genuine recompressed twice | 0 | 1000 | 0 | 1000 | **0** | 0 | 1000 | 0 | 0 | 0 | 0 |
| $nba_1$ | genuine recompressed | 0 | 1134 | 0 | 0 | **433** | 0 | 567 | 0 | 0 | 567 | 0 |
| | genuine recompressed twice | 0 | 2000 | 0 | 0 | **0** | 0 | 1000 | 0 | 0 | 1000 | 0 |
| $nba_2$ | genuine recompressed | 0 | 650 | 0 | 0 | **675** | 0 | 325 | 0 | 0 | 325 | 0 |
| | genuine recompressed twice | 0 | 1960 | 0 | 0 | **20** | 0 | 980 | 0 | 0 | 980 | 0 |
| **genuine Flickr30k** (31783 images from flickr) | | | | | | | | | | | | |
| $ba_1$ | original | 0 | 58 | 0 | 58 | **31725** | 0 | 0 | 58 | 0 | 0 | 0 |
| $ba_2$ | original | 0 | 0 | 0 | 0 | **31783** | 0 | 0 | 0 | 0 | 0 | 0 |
| $ba_3$ | original | 0 | 0 | 0 | 0 | **31783** | 0 | 0 | 0 | 0 | 0 | 0 |
| $ba_4$ | original | 0 | 31783 | 0 | 31783 | **0** | 0 | 31159 | 0 | 0 | 0 | 624 |

# Joining of Data-driven Forensics and Multimedia Forensics for Deepfake Detection on the Example of Image and Video Data

Dennis Siegel
*Dept. of Computer Science*
*Otto-von-Guericke-University*
Magdeburg, Germany
dennis.siegel@ovgu.de

Christian Kraetzer
*Dept. of Computer Science*
*Otto-von-Guericke-University*
Magdeburg, Germany
kraetzer@iti.cs.uni-magdeburg.de

Jana Dittmann
*Dept. of Computer Science*
*Otto-von-Guericke-University*
Magdeburg, Germany
jana.dittmann@iti.cs.uni-magdeburg.de

***Abstract*—DeepFake technology poses a new challenge to the validation of digital media integrity and authenticity. In contrast to 'traditional' forensic sub-disciplines (e.g., dactyloscopy), there are no standardized process models for DeepFake detection yet that would enable its usage in court in most countries. In this work, two existing best-practice methodologies (a data-centric model and a set of image authentication procedures) are combined and extended for the application of DeepFake detection. The extension includes aspects required to expand the focus from digital images to videos and enhancements in the quality assurance for methods (here focusing on the peer review aspect). The new methodology is applied to the example of DeepFake detection, utilizing three existing tools as methods. One for the Auxiliary data analysis and two DeepFake detectors based on hand-crafted and deep learning based feature spaces for Media content analysis are used. A total of 27 features were considered. In addition, the value types, ranges and their tendency for a DeepFake are determined for each feature. With the discussed potential extensions towards video evidence and machine learning, we identified additional requirements. These requirements are addressed in this paper as a proposal for an extended methodology to serve as starting point for future research and discussion in this domain.**

***Index Terms*—forensics, media forensics, DeepFake detection, machine learning**

## I. Introduction and Motivation

Recent advances in computer vision and deep learning enabled a new digital media manipulation technology called DeepFakes, replacing identities in digital images, videos and audio material. They pose a challenge to the integrity and authenticity of digital media and the trust placed in media objects for forensic science. With the advances in technology and also DeepFake quality, they are no longer easily recognizable as such to the bare eye. For this reason, most existing protection approaches use machine learning algorithms for DeepFake detection. The use of machine learning makes it necessary to fulfil additional requirements for artificial intelligence (AI) systems (i.e., legal regulations). In consequence, DeepFake detectors are still not suitable for court room usage. This is due to aspects such as lack of maturity, including (besides precisely validated error rates) modeling and standardization efforts so that they can be integrated into established forensic procedures.

In this paper, this gap (i.e., the lack of process modeling and investigation steps) is partially addressed by the following contributions:

- conceptional joining of IT and media forensic methodologies on the selected example of the existing *Data-Centric Examination Approach (DCEA)* [1], [2] and the *Best Practice Manual for Digital Image Authentication (BPM-DI)* from the *European Network of Forensic Science Institute (ENFSI)* [3].
- illustration of applicability and benefits of our concept on the example of three existing applications ExifTool [4], the hand-crafted DeepFake detector $DF_{mouth}$ [5] as well as the deep learning based DeepFake detector LipForensics [6].

With the focus on process modelling in the context of individual investigations, the prerequisites for the use of the individual tools are not considered in this paper. This includes essential aspects such as initial model training, appropriate benchmarking and certification of the proposed tools. For these aspects the reader is referred to [7].

The paper is structured as follows. First, a brief overview of the state of the art on digital forensics, standards and regulations as well as implications on the topic of DeepFake is presented in Section II. Following that, our concept of combining data-driven and media forensics can be found in Section III based on the DCEA [1] and BPM-DI [3]. Which is then applied to the practical example of detecting DeepFakes using three different features spaces [5] as methods in Section IV. Finally, conclusions are drawn from the evaluation results presented and future directions are outlined in Section V.

## II. Forensic Investigations in the Context of DeepFake Detection

With the potential of DeepFake manipulations in digital media it is even more important to validate integrity and authenticity of digital media especially for intended court room usage. The following sections address the current state and challenges in digital forensics, existing and upcoming regulations and the topic of DeepFake. These three aspects state fundamentals for the intended court room usage and while there are established in themselves, they are mostly considered in isolation.

### *A. Digital Forensics*

Digital forensics is a subdomain of forensics, which is defined as "*the use of scientifically derived and proven methods toward the preservation, collection, validation, identification, analysis, interpretation, documentation, and presentation of digital evidence derived from digital sources [...]*" [8]. In [9] the domain of digital forensics is further divided into computer and multimedia forensics based on their link to the outside world. Computer forensics operates exclusively in the digital domain, whereas multimedia forensics uses sensors to capture and connect with the real world.

In general, the application of media forensics is governed by national legislation. For this reason, our focus will be on European documents and views on media forensics. Here, the European Network of Forensic Science Institutes (ENFSI) provides a broad list of *Best Practice Manuals (BPM)* and guidelines in forensics. In the field of digital imaging, there are three Best Practice Manuals. The first document addresses the aspect of forensic facial image comparison [10] and formulates the respective investigation steps. This comparison is conducted by an examiner on the basis of a so-called facial feature list, including a total of 19 facial components, such as eyes, nose and mouth. The second BPM focuses on best practices of enhancement techniques for images and videos [11]. Here, approaches for enhancing image and video as well as strategies for selecting suitable frames are presented. This is also done on the basis of a human operator. The most recent document on image forensics and also the closest to the topic of DeepFake detection, is the *Best Practice Manual for Digital Image Authentication (BPM-DI)* [3]. In its own words it "*aims to provide a framework for procedures, quality principles, training processes and approaches to the forensic examination*" in the context of image authentication. For this purpose it describes a total of four aspects to categorize and structure investigation steps. These aspects consist of two different analysis methods, namely **Auxiliary data analysis** and **Image content analysis**, which are used based on different **Strategies** fulfilling different purposes. The last method class is **Peer review**, enabling the validation, interpretation and evaluation of the individual methods and their outcomes by a forensic human examiners.

At the national level, the German situation is relevant for the authors. Here, the guidelines for IT forensic by the German Federal Office for Information Security (BSI; the national cyber security authority) [38] are currently relevant. The data-centric examination approach (DCEA) is an extension of these guidelines. The DCEA has three main components: a model of the *phases* of a forensic process, a classification scheme for *forensic method classes* and *forensically relevant data types*.

The six DCEA *phases* are briefly summarized as: *Strategic preparation (SP), Operational preparation (OP), Data gathering (DG), Data investigation (DI), Data analysis (DA) and Documentation (DO)*. While the first two (*SP and OP*) contain generic (*SP*) and case-specific (*OP*) preparation steps, the three phases *DG, DI* and *DA* represent the core of any forensic investigation. At this point it is necessary to emphasize the importance of the *SP*, because it is the phase that also includes all standardization, benchmarking, certification and training activities considered. For details on the phase model the reader is referred, e.g., to [1] or [12].

In terms of data types, the DCEA proposes a total of six for digital forensics and ten for digitized forensics. In [2], the data types are specified in the context of media forensics and are referred to as *media forensic data types (MFDT)*. The resulting eight can be summarized as: digital input data *MFDT1* (the initial media data considered for the investigation), processed media data *MFDT2* (results of transformations to media data), contextual data *MFDT3* (case specific information e.g., for fairness evaluation), parameter data *MFDT4* (contain settings and other parameter used for acquisition, investigation and analysis), examination data *MFDT5* (including the traces, patterns, anomalies, etc that lead to an examination result), model data *MFDT6* (describe trained model data e.g., face detection and model classification data), log data *MFDT7* (data, which is relevant for the administration of the system e.g., system logs), and chain of custody & report data *MFDT8* (describe data used to ensure integrity and authenticity e.g., hashes and time stamps as well as the accompanying documentation for the final report).

An additional extension is made in the process modeling, in which individual processing steps are represented as atomic black box components. These components are accompanied by a description of the process performed. The individual components have four connectors input, output, parameters and log data. In addition, with the increasing use of machine learning, a fifth connection required for knowledge representation is defined. The labeled model can be found in [2].

### *B. Standards and Regulations in the Context of Media Forensics*

With the intended court room usage of forensic methods, standardization is required in investigation and analysis procedures. One of the more established standards is the United States Federal Rules of Evidence (FRE; especially FRE 702, see [13]) and the Daubert standard in the US. Although these standards only apply in the US, its usage e.g., in Europe has been discussed in [14]. In this work, the focus is on modelling media forensic methods within an investigation, whereby the following two (of five) Daubert criteria are particularly relevant [14]:

- "*whether the technique or theory has been subject to peer review and publication*";
- "*the existence and maintenance of standards and controls*".

In the context of standards and controls, the European Commission proposed the Artificial Intelligence Act (AIA), addressing the usage of Artificial Intelligence (AI) systems [15]. At the current time, the proposal has been adjusted and approved by the European Parliament [16]. This upcoming regulation places particular emphasis on the human in control aspects (Art. 14). The decisive factor is therefore not only the decision of the AI system, but the process of decision-making, which must be comprehensible for the human operator and thus enable the decision to be questioned and challenged. In addition, the International Criminal Police Organization (INTERPOL) recently published a document, addressing the usage of AI systems for law enforcement purposes [17]. Furthermore, the National Institute of Standards and Technology (NIST) currently develops a data set for DeepFake detection for validation of methods [18]. All documents have in common that a human operator should comprehend and oversee the processing and decision-making of the AI system.

### C. DeepFakes

With the advances in machine learning and computer vision DeepFake are a recent form of digital media manipulation and generation. In contrast to previous manipulation techniques, DeepFake utilizes deep learning to artificially generate or manipulate existing digital media, such as image, video and audio data. The application of DeepFakes is very versatile and can also be used for positive aspects, as described in [19]. Independently of their intended purpose, DeepFakes have to be identifiable both for integrity and authenticity of digital media and is further enforced by the recently adopted AIA [16]. DeepFake detection methods can be divided into methods utilizing spatial and temporal feature spaces [20]. This classification goes hand in hand with the diversified creation of DeepFakes, which can take place on image, video and audio files. Initially, the focus of detection was solely on the proposal of suitable deep learning based detectors without any form of explanations. More recently publications further prioritize forensic aspects in detection. In [21] DeepFake detection with the consideration of compliance with existing and upcoming regulations are shown.

## III. Conceptional Extension and Joining of data-driven and Media Forensic

For the conceptual connection of data-driven and media forensics, the BPM-DI [3] is considered as a basis and extended for the case of DeepFake detection for video. To classify this further, it should be noted that [3] proposes the application in practice on a specific investigation. According to the phase modeling, this includes the phases *OP*, *DG*, *DI* and *DA*, with *SP* being omitted. An overview of the proposed extended BPM-DI can be found in Figure 1.

The aspect of **Auxiliary data analysis** (see **Methods** in Figure 1) focuses on all traces of a media file. This includes the **Analysis of external digital context data**, which takes meta data of the file system into account. It can be used to identify potential traces of editing, for example by investigating the modify, access and change (MAC) times. The **File structure analysis** covers the examination of the file format. The format found for the examined file is compared with common formats including the specific version number. This can be a clue to the tools used to store the file. For videos, this is also useful to determine the potential origin based on the codec and its version used. **Embedded metadata analysis** takes into account all embedded metadata that can be found in the specific media. These can be used for the two main purposes of identifying the capturing device and gathering more details on the capturing process. For the identification of the capturing device the resolution and corresponding pixel format of images and videos can be used as a first indicator. For audio devices the sampling rate can be used as an equivalent. It is also possible for the device information to be specified in the metadata, but this is optional. For details on the capturing, there are optional metadata regarding the date and time of the recording and the GPS (Global Positioning System) location. In comparison to the BPM-DI [3], no extensions are required so far.

As discussed in Section II-C DeepFakes can occur in image, video as well as audio files. To address this aspect the BPM-DI [3] needs to extend the **Methods** to include spatial and temporal feature spaces in particular. This extension is suggested by a change in two steps, first the **Image content analysis** (see **Methods** Figure 1) has to become broader to also address video files by introducing **Media content analysis**. Second, a further separation of methods is presented, according to the categorization of DeepFake detection methods proposed in [20] dividing into **Spatial** and **Temporal content analysis**. **Methods** of **Spatial content analysis** correspond to BPM-DI [3] **Image content analysis**, which are **Analysis of visual content**, **Global analysis** (i.e., analysis of the entire image) and **Local analysis** (i.e., analysis of a particular image region). These Methods can be found to the left of **Spatial content analysis** in Figure 1.

In contrast, **Temporal content analysis** is another required modality of DeepFake detection. There the first **Method** utilizes the **Behavioral analysis** shown in video or audio. For example in [22] facial movement is analyzed using facial action units to detect DeepFakes of Barack Obama, which is further enforced by the availability of reference data for this person. **Physiology analysis** relies on the assumption, that DeepFake creation lack physiological signals, e.g., in heart rate [23] or eye blinking behavior [19]. **Methods** for **Synchronization analysis** utilize different types of media to validate their correlation. In most cases this is done by extracting features from both audio and video and comparing them against each other. Previous research has been done for example on emotions [24] or lip synchronization [25]. **Coherence analysis** focuses on the aspect, that DeepFakes are created on a frame by frame basis, which might result in flickers and jitters in the video.

The general purpose of the category **Strategy** (see **Methods** in Figure 1) is to categorize previously mentioned **Methods**, both **Auxiliary data analysis** and **Media content analysis**,

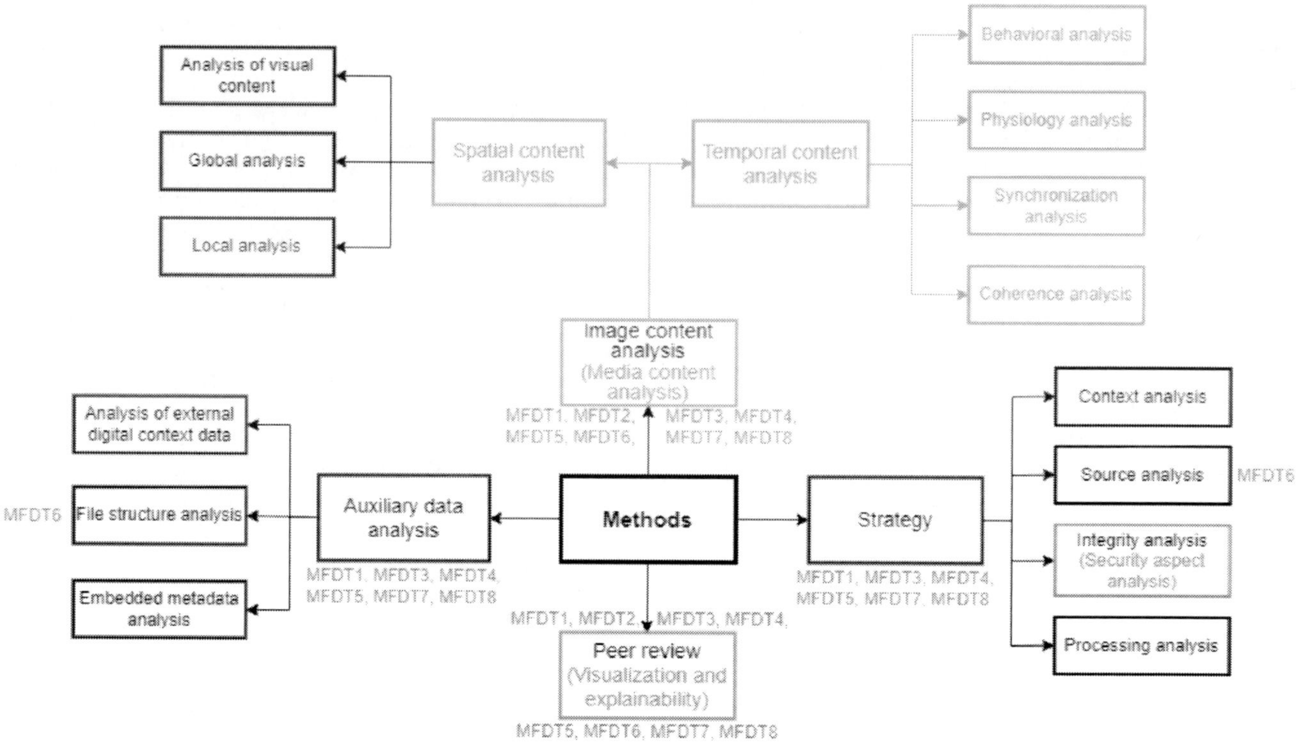


Fig. 1. Categorization of forensic methods proposed in [3], extended on the case of media forensics, especially DeepFake detection. Extensions are marked in gray. Integration of media forensic data types (MFDT) can be found in red.

based on the specific investigation goal. In this work, we consider three of the investigation goals of BPM-DI [3] as they stand and extend the other. These address the correctness of the context the media is put into (**Context analysis**), identification of the device used to capture the media (**Source analysis**) and which processing steps applied to the media (**Processing analysis**). Extensions are made to the **Integrity analysis**, which initially identifies whether the questioned media was altered after acquisition. The extension aims to take into account all security aspects and additionally leave room for future requirements (e.g., compliance with the AIA [15]). The existing method of **Integrity analysis** can be seen as method within the category of **Security aspect analysis**.

The **Peer review** (see **Methods** in Figure 1) of the BPM-DI [3] is the integration of a human examiner to analyze and interpret results during the whole process. With the introduction of machine learning techniques, especially for DeepFake detection, an extension of this aspect is proposed by introducing techniques to improve **Visualization and explainability**. Its purpose is therefore to support the human examiner in the process of investigation and decision making. With the introduction of machine learning algorithms, special attention has to be paid to the reproduceability of individual methods, their visualization and the entire examination process.

The application of data types is based on the existing 8 media forensic data types (MFDT) [2] mentioned in Section II-A and can also be seen in Figure 1 in red. Since the individual analysis **Methods** are kept generic our assignment of the data types is based on the higher level categories and is the same for the corresponding subcategories. In general, all **Methods** given require a process-accompanying documentation, which are specified to log data (*MFDT7*) and chain of custody & report data (*MFDT8*). Both **Auxilary data analysis** and **Strategy** work on the initial media representations (*MFDT1*), utilizing case specific information (*MFDT3*) and parameters (*MFDT4*) to yield examination data (*MFDT5*). In addition, model data (*MFDT6*) is required for both **File structure analysis** of and **Source analysis** to have a reference model of file structures or camera models respectively. The same can be said for **Media content analysis**, with the addition of various additional representations of the media (*MFDT2*) specific to the method of analysis and the potential usage of machine learning to introduce model data (*MFDT6*). One difference can be found in **Peer review**, in the initial proposal it suggests the analysis and interpretation of media representations (*MFDT2*) and examination data (*MFDT5*). By extending this category to **Visualization and explainability** and the identification of different human operators [7] it further introduces additional data types to be explained. These human operators include, but are not limited to, the forensic investigator, who requires *MFDT2*, *MFDT3*, and *MFDT5*, and the data scientist, who requires *MFDT3*, *MFDT4*, and *MFDT6*. Independent of the human operator, the data types *MFDT1*, *MFDT7* and *MFDT8* are required. In consequence, all MFDTs must be addressed in the method of **Visualization and explainability**.

To enable a more specific and descriptive assignment of the occurring data types, the individual processing steps have to be known, which is specific to the application used for the analysis. This is shown in more detail in the practical example given in Section IV-B.

## IV. Application of DeepFake Detection on the Extended Modelling

To validate the applicability of the proposed extended **Methods** (see Figure 1), a practical application on the example of DeepFake detection is performed. To cover a wide range of applications three existing tools of different categories are used. The first tool is ExifTool [4], which does not use any form of machine learning. ExifTool is an open source tool, which is able to read, write and edit metadata for a wide range of image and video formats. In addition, two existing machine learning based DeepFake detectors are used. To diversify the approaches, one based on hand-crafted features and one based on Deep Learning were chosen.

### A. Semantics-driven DeepFake Detection Approaches as Methods in the Context of the Best Practice Manual

One of the more promising feature spaces for DeepFake detection utilizes the mouth region, addressing two flaws in DeepFake synthesis. First, the synthesis occurs on a frame-by-frame basis, which results in inconsistencies in the temporal domain, enabling aspects of lip movement analysis. In [25] the detection is performed based on lip synchronization, by considering both audio and video and detecting inconsistencies between phonemes in audio and visemes in video. A similar approach has been taken for the LipForensics detector [6] by identifying unnatural mouth movement. The second aspect utilizes the post processing, especially blurring, performed in DeepFake synthesis. In [26] and [27] texture analysis is performed on the mouth region to identify manipulations. A combination of both approaches is given in [5], where hand-crafted features are used to detect DeepFakes based on mouth movement and teeth texture analysis described as $DF_{mouth}$.

To evaluate the suitability of the proposed Ext. BPM-DI modeling for DeepFake detection the two detectors $DF_{mouth}$ [5] and LipForensics [6] are selected, representing both a hand-crafted as well as deep learning based detector.

### B. Practical Application of the Extended Methods

In the following, the individual processing steps and groups of features (hereinafter referred to as PS) as well as individual features (hereinafter referred to as ID) will be labeled and categorized in the extended BPM-DI [3] for **Auxiliary data analysis** (shown in Figure 2), **Media content analysis** (shown in Figure 3) and **Strategies** (shown in Figure 4). The first step in verifying the authenticity of the media content under study is carried out using the methods of **Auxiliary data analysis**. For this purpose the open source tool ExifTool [4] is used. It is able to read, write and edit metadata for a wide range of image and video formats. In the context of this work, it is used for extracting the metadata (PS-exif). While a variety of entries are available in the metadata, a total of eight features (ID-exif$_n$) are selected for this exemplary approach and categorized according to the Ext. BPM-DI. These can be found in the top part of Table I. The first set of three features address **Analysis of external digital context data** with the aim of **Processing analysis**. These can give first indications of possible manipulations, for example by validating timestamps for modification, access and creation (ID-exif$_1$), file size (ID-exif$_2$) or system feature flags such as user permissions (ID-exif$_3$). Furthermore, three additional features can be used for **File structure analysis**, by extracting the file format (ID-exif$_4$), its format version (ID-exif$_5$) and in case of a video file the used codec (ID-exif$_6$). The extracted information of **File structure** can then be compared to **Standard formats**, unveiling potential traces for **Processing analysis**. In addition, file formats and codecs can give an indication of the software or device to enable **Source analysis** as well. The third set, consisting of two features, which address **Embedded metadata analysis**, with the aim of **Context analysis**, by extracting the media files width and height (ID-exif$_7$) and frame rate if it is a video (ID-exif$_8$). The features ID-exif$_4$-ID-exif$_8$ can further be used to validate the suitability of subsequent DeepFake detectors. This refers in particular to media properties such as width and height of an image or frame (ID-exif$_7$), frame rate for videos (ID-exif$_8$) and format (ID-exif$_4$) or codec specific compression (ID-exif$_6$).

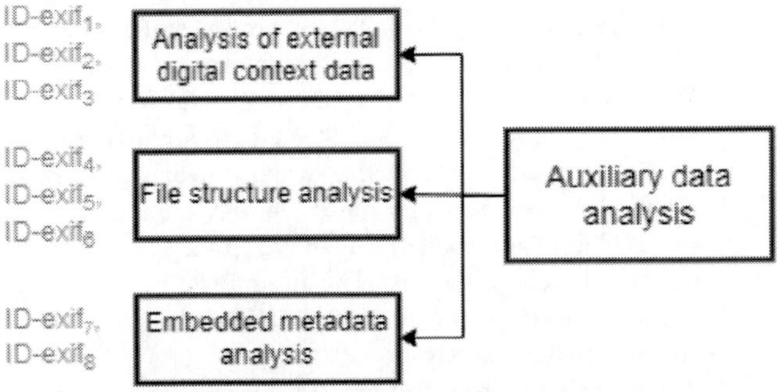


Fig. 2. Individual features extracted using ExifTool [4] (in red) categorized in the extended BPM-DI [3] for the category Auxiliary data analysis.

In terms of DeepFake detectors, both address **Media content analysis**, **Strategies** and **Peer review**. In addition, DF$_{mouth}$ utilizes the features ID-exif$_7$ and ID-exif$_8$ of **Auxiliary data analysis** for internal feature normalization. With their intention of identifying DeepFakes the general **Strategy** of application is **Integrity analysis**. Starting with DF$_{mouth}$, the detector is introduced in [5] and trained using the WEKA machine learning toolkit [28]. For the classification the decision tree classifier J48 [29] is used on the datasets Deepfake-TIMIT [30], [31], Celeb-DF [32] and DFD [33]. Detection performance peaks at 96.3% accuracy on a distinct training and test split of DFD. Considering distinct datasets for training and testing, detection performance peaks at 76.4% accuracy trained on DeepfakeTIMIT and tested on DFD. In a later benchmark approach given in [7] DF$_{mouth}$ is applied on a larger variety of DeepFake synthesis methods, including FaceForensics++ [33], DFD [33], Celeb-DF [32] and HiFiFace [34]. With an achieved detection performance of 69.9% accuracy the approaches suitability is identified only for certain DeepFake synthesis methods. With the limitations of DF$_{mouth}$ in mind, it is first split into five processing steps and categorized according the extended model. The individual features are then used for decision support by human operator, using the thresholds provided by the classifier in [5].

1) The video under investigation is first split into individual frames (PS-mouth$_1$) to first focus on **Spatial content analysis**.
2) For each frame a face detection algorithm is applied, in [5] using dlib's 68 landmark detection model [35] to extract the corresponding region for the mouth region (PS-mouth$_2$), which shows a dependency on the underlying model for face detection.
3) Then in PS-mouth$_3$, based on the keypoint geometry, it is determined whether the mouth is open (referred to as "state 1") or closed ("state 0"). Furthermore, the occurrence of teeth (referred to as "state 2") are examined based on texture analysis.
4) Based on the extracted mouth region and the information gathered, a total of 16 features are extracted. The first set of features, ID-mouth$_1$-ID-mouth$_7$ and ID-mouth$_{12}$ refer to **Physiological analysis** by describing mouth movements and the presence of teeth, by embedding individual frame features back into the temporal context of the video (PS-mouth$_4$). With the idea of DeepFakes having fewer mouth movements, values closer to 0 indicate a DeepFake for the features ID-mouth$_1$-ID-mouth$_6$. Features ID-mouth$_7$ and ID-mouth$_{12}$ aim to identify potential post-processing of the media, where lower values in ID-mouth$_{12}$ and higher values in ID-mouth$_7$ indicate a DeepFake. These are used for **Context analysis** to identify temporal inconsistencies. The normalization of features is done based on the frame rate (ID-exif$_8$) identified in **Auxiliary data analysis**.
5) The second group of features (PS-mouth$_5$), which consist of ID-mouth$_8$-ID-mouth$_{11}$ and ID-mouth$_{13}$-ID-mouth$_{16}$, refers to **Local analysis** to describe the sharpness of objects (here mouth and teeth region). In general, higher values for the features addressing state 1 (ID-mouth$_8$-ID-mouth$_{11}$) and lower values for the features addressing state 2 (ID-mouth$_{13}$-ID-mouth$_{16}$) indicate a potential DeepFake. The underlying **Strategy** is **Processing analysis**. The normalization of features is done based on the video frame resolution (ID-exif$_7$) identified in **Auxiliary data analysis**.

More details on the individual features, their description as well as the categorization in the forensic methods can be found in the middle part of Table I. Although all features can be categorized as *MFDT5*, the individual processing steps are more complex, containing multiple data types. For a more detailed description, the reader is referred to [19].

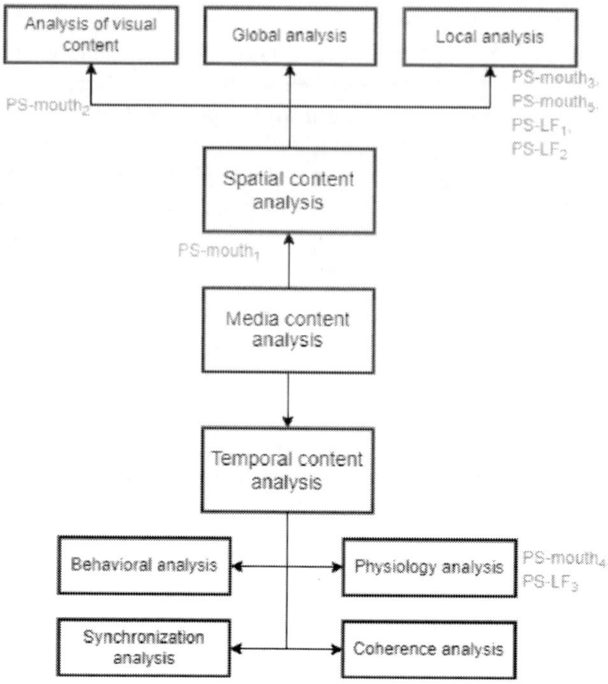


Fig. 3. Processing steps (PS, in red) for ExifTool [4] and the DeepFake detectors DF$_{mouth}$ [5] and LipForensics [6] categorized in the extended BPM-DI [3] for the category Media content analysis.

The second detector LipForensics [6] (herinafter refered to as LF) is included on a theoretical basis. For LF a total of three PS can be identified.

1) In the first step (PS-LF$_1$) the preprocessing occurs. First, a total of 25 frames are extracted from the video. These frames are converted to grayscale images, cropped to the mouth region and scaled to a resolution of 88x88. The resulting image representation can be categorized as *MFDT2*. With the intend of using only the mouth region, the corresponding method is **Local analysis** and the underlying strategy **Context analysis**.
2) In PS-LF$_2$ the feature extraction is done using a pre-trained ResNet-18 architecture trained on lip reading (*MFDT6*). As the result a feature vector of size 512 is generated (*MFDT3*). Again, the corresponding method is **Local analysis** and the underlying strategy **Context analysis**.
3) The resulting feature vector is used for classification purposes (PS-LF$_3$) using a multiscale temporal convolutional network (MS-TCN). The classification result *MFDT5* contains a classification label and the corresponding probability. With the aim of identifying unnatural behavior in mouth movement the corresponding method is **Physiology analysis** and the strategy of **Processing analysis**.

With the introduction of machine learning algorithms in

TABLE I

CATEGORIZATION OF EXIFTOOL [4] (TOP SECTION), $DF_{mouth}$ [5] (MIDDLE SECTION) AND LIPFORENSICS [6] (BOTTOM SECTION) IN THE FORENSIC CONTEXT, BASED ON THE PROPOSED EXTENDED BPM-DI. FOR FEATURE VALUES HIGHLIGHTED IN BOLD HIGHER VALUES INDICATE A DEEPFAKE AND FOR ITALIC LOWER VALUES INDICATE A DEEPFAKE.

| Ext. BPM-DI | | feature | description | value | processing step | analysis | strategy | data type |
|---|---|---|---|---|---|---|---|---|
| Auxiliary data analysis | Analysis of external digital context data | $ID\text{-}exif_1$ | MACtime | timestamp | PS-exif | File system metadata | Processing analysis | MFDT3 |
| | | $ID\text{-}exif_2$ | file size | string | | | | |
| | | $ID\text{-}exif_3$ | system feature flags | | | | | |
| | File structure analysis | $ID\text{-}exif_4$ | file format | string | | File structures | Source & Processing analysis | |
| | | $ID\text{-}exif_5$ | file format version | version number | | | | |
| | | $ID\text{-}exif_6$ | video codec | string | | | | |
| | Embedded meta-data analysis | $ID\text{-}exif_7$ | file resolution | int [0, ∞] | | Additional metadata | Context analysis | |
| | | $ID\text{-}exif_8$ | file frame rate | real [0, ∞] | | | | |
| Media content analysis | Temporal content analysis | $ID\text{-}mouth_1$ | abs max change Y | *real [0, ∞]* | $PS\text{-}mouth_4$ | Physiology analysis | Context analysis | MFDT5 |
| | | $ID\text{-}mouth_2$ | max change Y | *real [0, ∞]* | | | | |
| | | $ID\text{-}mouth_3$ | min change Y | **real [-∞, 0]** | | | | |
| | | $ID\text{-}mouth_4$ | abs max change X | *real [0, ∞]* | | | | |
| | | $ID\text{-}mouth_5$ | max change X | *real [0, ∞]* | | | | |
| | | $ID\text{-}mouth_6$ | min change X | **real [-∞, 0]** | | | | |
| | | $ID\text{-}mouth_7$ | percentage time state 1 | **real [0, 1]** | | | | |
| | | $ID\text{-}mouth_{12}$ | percentage time state 2 | *real [0, 1]* | | | | |
| | Spatial content analysis | $ID\text{-}mouth_8$ | max regions state 1 | *real [0, ∞]* | $PS\text{-}mouth_5$ | Local analysis | Processing analysis | |
| | | $ID\text{-}mouth_9$ | max FAST keypoints state 1 | *real [0, ∞]* | | | | |
| | | $ID\text{-}mouth_{10}$ | max SIFT keypoints state 1 | *real [0, ∞]* | | | | |
| | | $ID\text{-}mouth_{11}$ | max sobel pixel state 1 | *real [0, ∞]* | | | | |
| | | $ID\text{-}mouth_{13}$ | min regions state 2 | **real [0, ∞]** | | | | |
| | | $ID\text{-}mouth_{14}$ | min FAST keypoints state 2 | **real [0, ∞]** | | | | |
| | | $ID\text{-}mouth_{15}$ | min SIFT keypoints state 2 | **real [0, ∞]** | | | | |
| | | $ID\text{-}mouth_{16}$ | max sobel pixel state 2 | **real [0, ∞]** | | | | |
| Media content analysis | Spatial content analysis | $ID\text{-}LF_1$ | extraction of 25 frames, grayscale, crop and align | int [0, 255] | $PS\text{-}LF_1$ | Local analysis | Context analysis | MFDT2 |
| | | $ID\text{-}LF_2$ | feature extraction utilizing ResNet-18 | feature vector of size 512 | $PS\text{-}LF_2$ | Local analysis | Context analysis | MFDT3 |
| | Temporal content analysis | $ID\text{-}LF_3$ | classification of mouth movement based on MS-TCN | label: {real, fake} probability: real [0, 1] | $PS\text{-}LF_3$ | Physiology analysis | Processing analysis | MFDT5 |

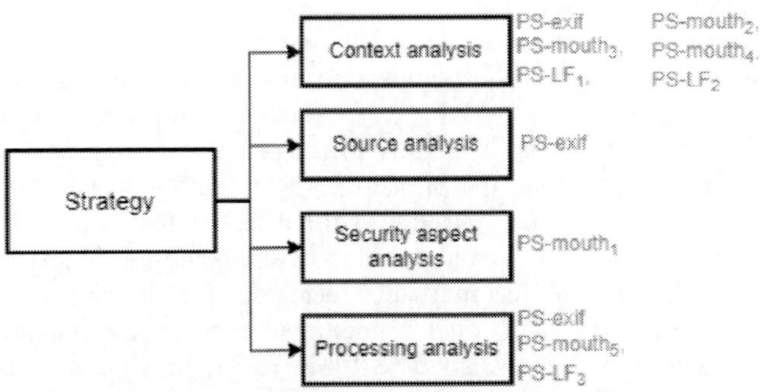


Fig. 4. Processing steps (PS, in red) for ExifTool [4] and the DeepFake detectors $DF_{mouth}$ [5] and LipForensics [6] categorized in the extended BPM-DI [3] for the category Strategy.

combination with previously discussed aspects of human in control and human oversight, the **Peer review** component becomes even more important. Its aim should be to enable the human operator to validate the results of each machine learning step to reduce the potential for error. Figure 5 demonstrates a potential direction to enhance the Method of **Peer review** on the basis of $DF_{mouth}$ and ExifTool [37]. In general, the aim of this visualization is to remove the decision-making from the detector. Instead, the individual features are displayed and evaluated by the human operator. To enable the advanced methodology and the human operator to make a decision, this first conceptual example consists of four segments.

1) A filter for the forensic Methods of analysis (i.e., Auxiliary data analysis and Media content analysis), Strategy, detector and data type (see the top left box of Figure 5). Based on the selected features only suitable features are shown and selectable for further investigation.
2) The second block (see the top right box of Figure 5) acts as media player. It has different views to either visualize the video, individual frames (including potential visualizations for explainability) and the metadata.
3) Based on the selected feature, this element shows its categorization in the forensic Methods and visualizes its value for each frame (see the bottom left box of Figure 5).
4) The last block (see the bottom right box of Figure 5) integrates the human operator in the decision-making process. The operator is provided with questions based on specific features and values to identify potential errors of the algorithm. In addition, the detectors thresholds for classification are provided without the decision itself.

In addition, it should be noted that each step in the pipeline discussed involving machine learning for $DF_{mouth}$ could also have been performed by manually labeling the data to reduce the error susceptibility. However, this would come at the

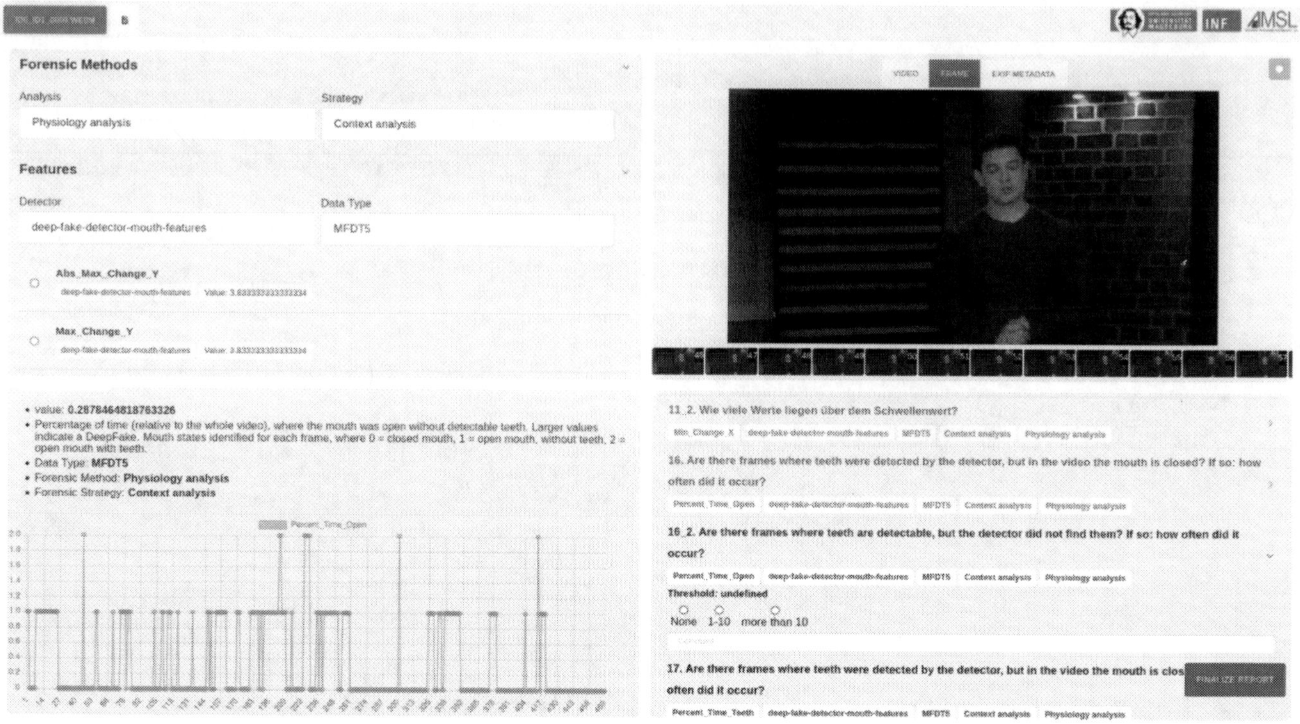


Fig. 5. Demonstration of the extended Methods, exemplified on $\text{DF}_{mouth}$ for video id0_id1_0000 of the Celeb-DF dataset - from a student project in the context of the lecture "Multimedia and Security", 2023 Department of Computer Science, Otto-von-Guericke-University of Magdeburg.

expense of the required review time, especially for long videos with high frame rates.

This potential usage of machine learning indicates the necessity of the *SP* phase within the investigation process. Models have to be benchmarked properly to identify both error rates and potential limitations in their usage, to comply with the Daubert criteria discussed previously [14]. Furthermore, in the context of forensic investigations they have to be certified, so that these are approved for the investigation. These required steps must be performed before the actual investigation in the *SP* phase, which is not considered in the BPM-DI, in contrast to our extended BPM-DI.

## V. Conclusion and Future Work

In this work an extension to the ENFSI BPM for digital image authentication is proposed, utilizing data-driven forensics by adding the eight media forensic data types (MFDT) from DCEA [1], [2] in **Methods** of BPM-DI [3]. In addition, extensions are proposed in the **Media content analysis Methods** using **Spatial** and **Temporal content analysis** to reflect the typical analysis domain of DeepFake detection (and other video authentication methods). Furthermore, the extension of the **Peer review** component to address also **Visualization and explainability** was touched upon. Here, the aspects 'human in the loop' and 'human in control' as well as the topic 'explainable AI' represent important foundations for this component and will be further elaborated in a future paper.

The extended BPM-DI model is applied to the three existing applications ExifTool, the hand-crafted DeepFake detector $\text{DF}_{mouth}$ as well as the deep learning based DeepFake detector LipForensics, showing its applicability to a wide range of approaches. In addition, it was found that the deep learning based features are too complex to achieve the same granularity as the detector $\text{DF}_{mouth}$. Another limitation resulted from the structuring according to the phases, as suggested in DCEA. By omitting the Strategic Preparation (SP) phase, the detection approaches introduced for investigation have to be trained, benchmarked and certified beforehand. On this basis, the suitability of the individual detectors for the respective investigation must be determined, but this is not possible without prior knowledge of SP. Moreover, the interplay of individual **Methods** have been identified. This includes the use of **Auxiliary data analysis** for feature engineering and normalization as shown in PS-mouth$_4$ and PS-mouth$_5$. Furthermore, PS-mouth$_4$ states (see Table I and Figure 3), that spatial traces can be utilized in the temporal context as well.

Beyond that, not all methods of the proposed model could be covered with the selected detectors. This shows that individual tools cannot and should not cover all methods. This indicates that additional tools are needed for integration. Lastly, an even more detailed categorisation of methods can be explored. With regard to the ENFSI "Best Practice Manual for Facial Image Comparison", the method of Local analysis could be split according the facial feature list [10]. It was also discussed that

DeepFakes can occur in audio data, which is not specifically included in the extended model. For this purpose, there is the "Best Practice Manual for Digital Audio Authenticity Analysis" [36], which has to be addressed in the future.

## Author Contributions and Acknowledgments

The work in this paper is funded in part by the German Federal Ministry of Education and Research (BMBF) under grant number FKZ: 13N15736 (project "Fake-ID"). Special thanks to team TraceMap, consisting of Stephan Haussmann, Hannes Hinniger, Tjark Homann and Malte Rathjens (a student project in the context of the lecture "Multimedia and Security", 2023 Department of Computer Science, Otto-von-Guericke-University of Magdeburg) for providing an initial demonstrator used as a basis for Figure 5.

Author Contributions: Initial idea & methodology: Jana Dittmann (JD), Christian Kraetzer (CK); Conceptualization: Dennis Siegel (DS); Modeling & application in the context of DeepFake: DS; Writing – original draft: DS; Writing – review & editing: CK, JD and DS.

## References

[1] S. Kiltz, "Data-centric examination approach (DCEA) for a qualitative determination of error, loss and uncertainty in digital and digitised forensics," *Ph. D. Thesis. Otto-von-Guericke-University Magdeburg, Fakultät für Informatik*, 2020.

[2] D. Siegel, C. Kraetzer, S. Seidlitz, J. Dittmann, "Forensic data model for artificial intelligence based media forensics - illustrated on the example of DeepFake detection," *Electronic Imaging 34*, 2022, pp. 1–6.

[3] European Network of Forensic Science Institutes. "Best practice manual for digital image authentication". *ENFSI-BPM-DI-03*, 2021.

[4] P. Harvey, "Exiftool," https://exiftool.org/, 2016.

[5] D. Siegel, C. Kraetzer, S. Seidlitz, J. Dittmann, "Media forensics considerations on deepfake detection with hand-crafted features," *Journal of Imaging 7, 7*, 2021.

[6] A. Haliassos, K. Vougioukas, S. Petridis, M. Pantic, "Lips don't lie: a generalisable and robust approach to face forgery detection," *Proceedings of the IEEE/CVF Conference on Computer Vision and Pattern Recognition (CVPR)*, 2021, pp. 5039-5049.

[7] C. Kraetzer, D. Siegel, S. Seidlitz, J. Dittmann, "Human-in-control and quality assurance aspects for a benchmarking framework for DeepFake detection models," in Electronic Imaging, 2023, pp. 379–1 - 379-6, https://doi.org/10.2352/EI.2023.35.4.MWSF-379.

[8] M. Reith, C. Carr, G. H. Gunsch, "An examination of digital forensic models," *Int. J. Digit. EVid. 1, 3*, 2002.

[9] R. Böhme, F. C. Freiling, T. Gloe, M. Kirchner, "Multimedia forensics is not computer forensics," *Computational Forensics*, Springer, 2009, pp. 90–103.

[10] European Network of Forensic Science Institutes. "Best practice manual for facial image comparison". *ENFSI-BPM-DI-01*, 2018.

[11] European Network of Forensic Science Institutes. "Best practice manual for forensic image and video enhancement". *ENFSI-BPM-DI-02*, 2018.

[12] R. Altschaffel. "Computer forensics in cyber-physical systems : applying existing forensic knowledge and procedures from classical IT to automation and automotive," *Ph. D. Thesis. Otto-von-Guericke-University Magdeburg, Fakultät für Informatik*, 2020.

[13] Legal Information Institute, "Rule 702. testimony by expert witnesses," 2019.

[14] C. Champod, J. Vuille, "Scientific evidence in europe - admissibility, evaluation and equality of arms," *International Commentary on Evidence 9, 1*, 2011.

[15] European Commission, "Proposal for a regulation of the european parliament and of the council laying down harmonisd rules on artificial intelligence (artificial intelligence act) and amending certain union legislative acts," *COM/2021/206 final*, April,21 2021.

[16] European Parliament, "Amendments adopted by the european parliament on 14 june 2023 on the proposal for a regulation of the european parliament and of the council on laying down harmonised rules on artificial intelligence (artificial intelligence act) and amending certain union legislative acts," *(COM(2021)0206 – C9-0146/2021 – 2021/0106(COD))*, June, 14 2023.

[17] UNICRI, INTERPOL, "Toolkit for responsible AI innovation in law enforcement: principles for responsible AI innovation," June 2023.

[18] National Institute of Standards and Technology (NIST), "Digital and multimedia evidence,", https://www.nist.gov/spo/forensic-science-program/digital-and- multimedia-evidence, 2022.

[19] C. Kraetzer, D. Siegel, S. Seidlitz, and J. Dittmann, "Process-driven modelling of media forensic investigations - considerations on the example of deepfake detection," *Sensors 22, 9*, 2022.

[20] Y. Mirsky, W. Lee, "The creation and detection of deepfakes: a survey," *ACM Comput. Surv. 54, 1, Article 7*, 2021.

[21] B. Lorch, N. Scheler, C. Riess, "Compliance challenges in forensic image analysis under the artificial intelligence act," *30th European Signal Processing Conference (EUSIPCO)*, 2022, pp. 613–617.

[22] S. Agarwal, H. Farid, Y. Gu, M. He, K. Nagano, H. Li, "Protecting world leaders against deep fakes," *IEEE Conference on Computer Vision and Pattern Recognition Workshops*, 2019 pp. 38–45.

[23] V. Conotter, E. Bodnari, G. Boato, H. Farid, "Physiologically-based detection of computer generated faces in video," *IEEE International Conference on Image Processing (ICIP)*, 2014, pp. 248–252.

[24] B. Hosler, D. Salvi, A. Murray, F. Antonacci, P. Bestagini, S. Tubaro, M. C. Stamm, "Do deepfakes feel emotions? a semantic approach to detecting deepfakes via emotional inconsistencies," *IEEE/CVF Conference on Computer Vision and Pattern Recognition (CVPR) Workshops*, 2021, pp. 1013–1022.

[25] S. Agarwal, H. Farid, O. Fried, M. Agrawala, "Detecting deep-fake videos from phoneme-viseme mismatches," *IEEE/CVF Conference on Computer Vision and Pattern Recognition*, 2020, pp. 2814–2822.

[26] F. Matern, C. Riess, M. Stamminger, "Exploiting visual artifacts to expose deepfakes and face manipulations," *IEEE Winter Applications of Computer Vision Workshops (WACVW)*, 2021, pp. 83–92.

[27] A. Elhassan, M. Al-Fawa'reh, M. T. Jafar, M. Ababneh, S. T. Jafar, "DFT-MF: enhanced deepfake detection using mouth movement and transfer learning," *SoftwareX 19*, 2022.

[28] M. A. Hall, E. Frank, G. Holmes, B. Pfahringer, P. Reutemann, I. H. Witten, "The weka data mining software: an update," SIGKDD Explor., 11(1):10–18, 2009.

[29] J. R. Quinlan, "C4.5: programs for machine learning," *Morgan Kaufmann Publishers Inc.*, San Francisco, CA, USA, 1993.

[30] P. Korshunov, S. Marcel, "Deepfakes: a new threat to face recognition? Assessment and detection," *arXiv preprint arXiv:1812.08685*, 2018.

[31] C. Sanderson, B. Lovell, "Multi-region probabilistic histograms for robust and scalable identity inference," *Lecture Notes in Computer Science (LNCS)*, 2009, pp. 199–208.

[32] Y. Li, X. Yang, P. Sun, H. Qi, S. Lyu, "Celeb-df: a large-scage challenging dataset for deepfake forensics," *Conference on Computer Vision and Pattern Recognition (CVPR)*, 2020, pp. 3204–3213, doi:10.1109/CVPR42600.2020.00327.

[33] A. Rössler, D. Cozzolino, L. Verdoliva, C. Riess, J. Thies, M. Nießner, "Faceforensics++: learning to detect manipulated facial images," *International Conference on Computer Vision (ICCV)*, 2019.

[34] Y. Wang, X. Chen, J. Zhu, W. Chu, Y. Tai, C. Wang, J. Li, Y. Wu, F. Huang, R. Ji, "Hififace: 3d shape and semantic prior guided high fidelity face swapping," *Proceedings of the Thirtieth International Joint Conference on Artificial Intelligence, IJCAI-21*, 2021, pp. 1136-1142.

[35] D. E. King, "Dlib-ml: a machine learning toolkit," *J. Mach. Learn. Res. 10*, 2009, pp. 1755–1758.

[36] European Network of Forensic Science Institutes. "Best practice manual for digital audio authenticity analysis". *ENFSI-FSA-BPM-002*, 2018.

[37] D. Siegel, J. Dittmann, "TraceMap", Student project within the lecture of Multimedia and Security [MMSEC], Otto-von-Guericke-University Magdeburg, 2023, unpublished.

[38] German Federal Office for Information Security (BSI), "Leitfaden IT-forensik," https://www.bsi.bund.de/dok/6620610 available in German only, 2011.

# AI-driven Approach for Access Control List Management

Nader Shahata
Center for Strategic Resilience Research and Development
National Institute of Informatics
Tokyo, Japan
e-mail: nader@nii.ac.jp

Hirokazu Hasegawa
Center for Strategic Resilience Research and Development
National Institute of Informatics
Tokyo, Japan
e-mail: hasegawa@nii.ac.jp

Hiroki Takakura
Center for Strategic Resilience Research and Development
National Institute of Informatics
Tokyo, Japan
e-mail: takakura@nii.ac.jp

***Abstract*—With the increasing dependence on digital systems and the pervasive nature of cyber threats, ensuring secure access to information and resources has grown to be a crucial component of our activities online. Access control lists serve as foundational frameworks that govern the authorization and authentication processes within computer systems. This paper examines how access control lists canbe employed effectively in the field of cybersecurity and digs into its important role in protecting sensitive data, mitigating risks, and safeguarding against unauthorized access. Access control lists play a vital role in ensuring the security and confidentiality of sensitive information and resources. Traditionally, access control has relied on predefined rules and policies to determine who has the eligibility in accessing which data. However, the rise of Artificial Intelligence (AI) has introduced new possibilities and challenges in the field of access control. This paper explores the impact of AI on access control lists, examining the benefits and potential concerns associated with the integration of AI technologies. In order to secure the organization's network, we propose an AI-driven ACL management system which generates ACL automatically. By managing the network traffic with the generated ACL, the system supports network analysts to prioritize certain threats that require immediate response. By discussing the effectiveness of the system, we explore the possibility of AI-driven ACL management.**

***Keywords-Access Control; Cyber Security; Network; Artificial Intelligence.***

## I. INTRODUCTION

Access Control models are crucial components in the field of information security, ensuring that only authorized individuals or entities can gain entry to protected resources [1]. Over the years, advancements in technology shifted towards access control systems. One such transformation is the integration of AI and access control models. AI, with its ability to mimic human intelligence and make informed decisions based on a vast amount of data, can revolutionize the way of how access control can be managed which can lead to securing our networks. When applied, AI-powered access control models can offer numerous benefits over traditional rule-based systems. These models can have the ability to strengthen machine learning algorithms [7] to analyze and understand network traffic patterns, behaviors and contextual information to make real-time based access decisions. The shift from static rules to dynamic decision-making can lead to more accurate and adaptive access control mechanisms, strengthening security measures and reducing the risk of unauthorized access. One of the key advantages of AI in access control models is its ability to detect anomalies and identifying potential security threats. By analyzing historical data and learning from past patterns, AI algorithms can establish a baseline of normal behavior for users and systems [7]. Any deviation from this baseline can trigger alerts or generate preventive actions, helping in mitigating risks and preventing security breaches. This proactive approach to access control is particularly crucial in today's ever-evolving threat landscape, where traditional rule-based systems often fall in detecting sophisticated attacks.

Furthermore, AI can significantly improve the user's experience in access control systems. With traditional models, users often face heavy processes, such as repeatedly entering passwords or providing multiple credentials for different systems.

The purpose of our paper is to propose an architecture that can help in increasing the organization's network security when applying AI to generate countermeasures based on ACL rules.

The remaining of this paper is organized as follows: Section II presents the background which discusses the current problems that this paper is aiming to solve. In Section III, we presented our vision on solving the drawbacks that were discussed in the background section through an overflow figure. Section IV illustrates the benefits of AI when it is integrated with detecting anomalies and generating ACLs. Our architecture proposal is presented in section V along with a detailed description of its components. The architecture's assumptions, challenges and limitations are explained in Section VI and Section VII respectively. In Section VIII discusses the importance of AI in generating ACLs. The discussion part in section IX describes how effective our proposed system can be if it is applied when detecting anomalies and generating ACLs. We end our paper with a conclusion in section X.

## II. Background

By controlling user access and privileges, access control models can have a significant part in guaranteeing the security and integrity of digital systems. There is a considerable interest in examining the potential enhancement of access control systems in the light of significant advancements in AI. This background section seeks to give an overview of AI's use in the access control paradigm, as well as its advantages, challenges, and potential future applications. The goal is to obtain an understanding of the evolving status of AI-powered technology and its influence on cybersecurity by studying the existing literature and industry practices [8].

The basis for controlling users' interactions with digital systems and safeguarding sensitive data is access control models. Role-based Access Control (RBAC) and Attribute-Based Access Control (ABAC) are common access control methods. The current Access Control List (ACL) system has some weaknesses even though it works well in many situations.

The existing ACL mechanism has a number of disadvantages that are frequently encountered [13]. For instance, managing an ACL system can be very challenging. The more users, resources, and permissions there are, the harder it is to accurately manage and update ACLs. When the number of users and available resources considerably rises, ACL systems can experience scalability problems. The network administrator in this case will need to maintain a high number of access control entries which could affect the performance of the network [13]. ACL maintenance calls for constant work and modification. The ACL needs to be manually updated if the environment changes, such as when a new user joins a workplace or when resources are added or deleted. This maintenance work can get tedious, especially in complex systems.

In traditional ACL-based systems, ACLs are inefficient because they only support explicitly declared access controls. For example, if a user has access or permissions that are unique because they belong to both the IT department and the management department, that level of access should be explicitly stated rather than inferred on belonging to both. The requirement to explicitly declare these access controls also has an impact on scalability. As the number of users, groups, and resources increases, so does the length of the ACL and the time it takes to determine how much access is granted to a particular user. Also, ACLs lack visibility because user permissions and access levels can be scattered across many independent lists. Auditing, modifying, or revoking access require testing every ACL in the organization's environment to apply the new permissions [14]. Therefore, we need a system that can deal with the previously mentioned current problems as the cyber-attacks are on the rise of being more sophisticated. The promising machine learning algorithms that are used by AI-based ACL can create wise access control decisions. It can help in dynamically determining access privileges which involves examining a number of variables such as users' behaviors, and previous historical data [15]. This strategy can improve security by spotting and identifying anomalies.

Managing alerts from an Intrusion Detection System (IDS) can be a challenging task for a network analyst. These difficulties include the volume of generated alerts, the complexity of the alerts and the need for quick and accurate responses. The reason is most modern IDS systems can generate a large number of alerts, especially in large and complex networks. The volume of these alerts can quickly overwhelm analysts, making it difficult to prioritize genuine threats that require immediate response. Our proposed system will be focusing on managing ACLs for analyzing suspicious traffic and for generating relevant countermeasures. This strategy can improve security by spotting anomalies and abnormal behaviors. Managing ACLs plays a crucial role in doing such tasks. By configuring ACLs properly, suspicious traffic can be filtered out, preventing potentially malicious packets from reaching critical network resources. Therefore, ACLs can help in identifying common attacks that have the ability to compromise the network. Regular analysis of ACLs and their effectiveness in dealing with suspicious traffic can lead to a continuous improvement in the organization's network security posture. Managing ACLs is an essential part of network security because of its efficiency in detecting and preventing suspicious traffic. By analyzing ACLs and adjusting access control rules, network analysts can improve the security of their network infrastructure and protect it from potential threats.

Our proposed system will be relying on machine learning algorithms [6] to assist our AI-based ACL to create wise access control decisions. This strategy can improve security by spotting anomalies. AI-based ACLs will be capable of using related data to determine access decisions and generate countermeasures based on the activities of the users and possible risks that may occur when an incident may happen. By considering these generated countermeasures, the proposed system can have the ability to accurately determine the risk involved with each access request and modify access rights as necessary. The reason behind this accuracy is due to the fact that AI-based ACLs can continuously learn from access patterns and modify their decision-making models as necessary.

## III. System Overflow

We propose a dynamic AI based Access Control system for solving the problems which are explained in Section 2.

Our system involves the integration of AI and generating ACL for improving the network structure in dealing with suspicious traffic analysis [5]. This can lead to generate an efficient countermeasure against future similar attacks. Figure 1 shows an overview of our proposed architecture, it consists of five phases which work in a sequential step-by-step order. We will describe details of each phase below.

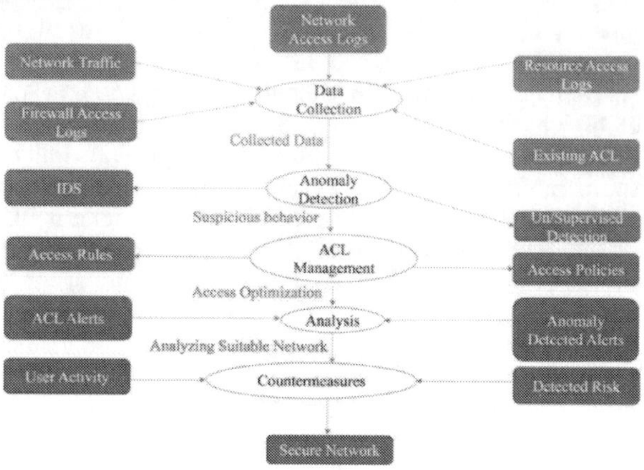


Figure.1 Proposed System Overflow

### *A. Data Collection*

This is the first phase, in which the collection of several attributes of data is required [9]. To be specific, we will be focusing on five attributes. These attributes have an edge over other candidates due to their particular concentration on certain aspects of network security. Organizations can improve their capability to identify, address, and avoid security issues by gathering and analyzing data from these sources.

These attributes include network traffic (which is all the network traffic data that is observed in the organization's network e.g., source IP-address and destination IP-address, protocol, source port, destination port). The second attribute is the firewall access logs (which are obtained and stored in the firewall e.g., rule numbers, protocols that have been used and the action that is taken by the firewall). The third attribute is the network access logs, (which includes the permissions of allowing or denying users from accessing the network e.g., the user name, connection type and connection duration). Then, we have the fourth attribute which is the resource access logs (that determine which resource are allowed or denied for specific users to access with its timestamp e.g., accessing a financial report by a specific user in 3:00 PM). The final attribute is the applied network ACL that already existed in the system, e.g., source IP-address, destination IP-address, protocol, source port, destination port, and the action that has been taken for that rule. These attributes vary depending on the product and configuration, but are basically above formats.

These attributes are all required for the next anomaly detection phase [3].

### *B. Anomaly Detection*

In this phase, the collected data in phase one will be the input to several anomaly detection methods [4]. Currently, a lot of anomaly detection methods exist. With such existing methods, we can detect anomaly behavior from the collected data in phase one. As a typical example, we will consider IDS in detecting anomaly traffic from the network traffic data. Moreover, the applied network ACL and access logs can be used in detecting suspicious activities that are out of the authorized scope access of the network. We chose IDS in our case because it can be adapted to fit into several security configurations and to the needs of organizations as well as its effectiveness when combining it with machine learning methods [7]. They can adjust to various network and system designs because of their flexibility. By inputting these data to AI, it can help in deciding whether the unauthorized activity is due to a user's fault or if it is a suspicious access attempt.

### *C. ACL Management*

In the first and second phases, we used the existing techniques. The third phase is where AI will be applied by controlling ACL configurations to keep track of suspicious activities. Generally, this phase is the core of our architecture and is responsible for managing access rules and access policies. It will also be used to examine historical access logs and permissions data to identify patterns and their relationships. It is important to mention that the patterns and security criteria that are found here will introduce optimization algorithms or reinforcement learning approaches to enhance the ACL policy for later effective countermeasures. This will help in adjusting the ACL rules to make the network more efficient and secure.

### *D. Analysis*

In this phase, the network analyst will evaluate the alert outcomes from the detected anomalies (in the second phase) and from the alerts that are generated from the ACL management (the third phase) to obtain a comprehensive understanding of the system security posture [5]. This posture analysis will be the input for the final countermeasures phase.

### *E. Countermeasures*

After the analyst's evaluation, the countermeasure phase with the help of AI will estimate the seriousness and potential consequences of the detected alerts based on the analysis result.

## IV. THE AI MERGING OF ANOMALY DETECTION AND GENERATING ACCESS CONTROL LISTS

AI helps in access control list (ACL) merging with anomaly identification. ACLs are used to restrict access to resources and systems based on predefined rules, whereas anomaly detection focuses on spotting patterns or behaviors that dramatically depart from the norm [2]. By employing machine learning algorithms [7] to analyze massive volumes of data and spot strange patterns and behaviors, AI can enhance anomaly detection [6].

An AI model may learn what is considered typical behavior and recognize variations that may reveal potential security issues or anomalies by being trained on previous data samples. Identifying unauthorized access attempts and odd system activities will be easier for the network analyst for examining the network's security position. AI can assist in automating the management and enforcement of access restrictions in the context of access control lists. AI algorithms are able to decide what permissions are appropriate for certain users or groups of users by examining user behavior and previous access patterns [5]. This will also simplify the management of ACLs [11], particularly in complicated systems with lots of users and resources. Access control lists and anomaly detection can be used to offer a more complete security solution. AI system's detection of anomalous behavior may result in updates to access control lists (ACLs) to restrict access or notifications for further enquiry. By dynamically modifying permissions based on in-the-moment abnormalities, this integration makes it possible to take a preventative approach to security, lowering the likelihood of unauthorized access and malicious activities. Overall, AI can enhance security posture, automate procedures, and increase the effectiveness of permission management in complicated systems by combining anomaly detection and access control lists.

## V. Proposed Architecture

Before presenting our proposed system in this section, it is important to mention the idea of iteration. Our system is based on the alerts and the generated ACL rules that will be the fundamental concept behind our architecture to work properly. Moreover, it will validate the accuracy and effectiveness when they will be examined by a network analyst. This iterative process helps refine the architecture's performance and will enhance the overall system's output. The proposal of our architecture is as follows.

When matching the discussed overflow in Figure 1 with the system proposed in Figure 2, we will notice that the architecture is emphasizing on generating an AI-based ACL rules (phase 3) depending on the alerts form the Intrusion Detection System IDS (phase 2). The analysist (phase 4) will be responsible for monitoring the results of the IDS (phase 2) and regulating the countermeasures (phase 5) when examining the system. Our architecture's components are presented in Figure 2.

### A. Data Processing

In this step, the preparation of data will be managed to distinguish the data to two types of alerts: old and new alerts. The old alert refers to the alerts that are initially coming from the IDS; while the new alert refers to the alerts that is coming from IDS after applying AI to the managed ACL. In other words, the system will receive concerning alerts previously due to the fact of being IDS always analyzing the traffic and sending alerts accordingly. Therefore, the input data is a combination of both types of alerts (old and new).

### B. Existing ACL

We mean by this a dataset of existing ACLs. These data sets will contain examples of input queries and descriptions along with their corresponding ACL rules. It is worth mentioning that these datasets should cover a wide range of scenarios to train the module effectively.

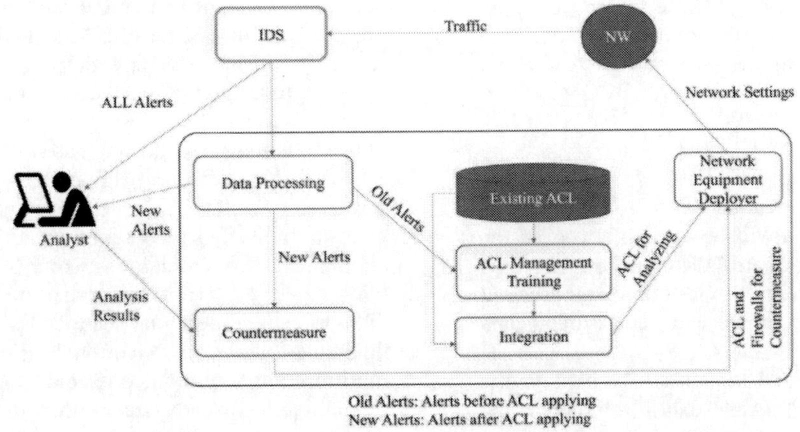


Figure 2. Proposed System

### C. ACL Management Training

In here, the AI system will be adjusted to our processed dataset. The adjustment involves training our module on the ACL rules to make it more knowledgeable and better at generating relevant ACLs. Some machine learning approaches are needed to train the model at this stage.

### *D. Integration*

This step is the result of the combination between the existing ACL and the ACL management training unit. The integration will be beneficial for well training the system to new rules and as a result adapting to newly upcoming permissions. This will also help in optimizing the system's countermeasures.

### *E. Network Equipment Deployer*

The countermeasures (phase 5) that were generated by the alerts of the IDS will be shared with the results of the newly integrated AI-ACL rules. The deployment process will help in generating flexible ACL rules that will be able to deal up with changes that may occur to the network.

### *F. IDS*

Intrusion Detection Systems will include analyzing patterns and behaviors within our system to identify abnormalities from the norm. It will generate alerts when detecting unusual or suspicious actions. These alerts are usually based on pattern recognition techniques but as within our system it will be enhanced with the machine learning approach [6]. In our system, the IDS will be generating alerts when it finds activities that fall outside the predefined threshold.

### *G. Countermeasure*

The role of countermeasures in our case is to respond to the alerts that the network analyst handles to prevent or mitigate the identified threats. These responses may include blocking malicious IP addresses, modifying firewall rules and notifying the network analyst about potential threats.

## VI. ASSUMPTIONS

There are several assumptions to take into consideration when implementing such a system. It is expected that plenty of data will be available to train the AI model for both access control lists and the detected anomalies. To create precise models and comprehend typical patterns and behaviors, we will need enough data samples to begin with.

Our system in which the AI model will be deployed is presumed to be represented by the data used to train the AI model. This presumption guarantees that the model can accurately identify anomalies and decide what the best access control measures are based on actual circumstances. A precise definition of anomalies is necessary [3]. The system must have a clear understanding of what defines an anomaly. This definition could change depending on the system's situation. Therefore, it is crucial to have clear standards for spotting unusual patterns or behaviors.

Access control policies must be in place before AI can be integrated into access control lists. These regulations specify who has access to what resources and how. Rules governing access levels (network administrators), responsibilities (managing alerts), permissions (allowing), and restrictions (denying) are examples of prerequisites that are needed. In real-time applications, AI systems should be scalable to handle any data volumes as well as to the amount of access control requests. We mean by this that traditional anomaly detection methods may struggle with complicated data to handle effectively. To find abnormalities and decide on access restrictions without noticeably affecting performance of the system, our system has to be able to process and analyze data effectively.

AI systems are expected to be able to continuously learn from and modify their behavior to match changing patterns and trends. To enable efficient anomaly detection and access control, The system should be able to update models based on new data and to modify access control policies accordingly.

## VII. CHALLNEGES AND CONSIDERATIONS

The quality and accessibility of the data used for the training purposes have a significant impact on how effective our AI systems will be. To identify deviations from typical patterns and impose the proper access rules, anomaly detection and access control systems need thorough and precise data.

The threat landscape is also rapidly changing, with new attack vectors appearing frequently. In order for models to continuously learn and update for countering new threats, our AI system design must be flexible. It is crucial to routinely update anomaly detection and access control systems based on newly fresh updated information to retain efficacy [12].

False positives and false negatives are also possible [3]. Systems for detecting anomalies can produce false positives (which misinterpret typical behavior as abnormal) and false negatives (which fail to detect actual anomalies). It is crucial to strike a balance between these two types of errors in order to prevent unneeded disruptions and potential security breaches. Adjusting the thresholds and the AI model are both necessary to minimize any likelihood of errors.

Techniques for adversary strength, such as adversary training and input validation, should be taken into consideration to make the AI system more resistant to such attacks [10]. These difficulties and factors are highlighting the complexity in implementing access control lists, anomaly detection, and AI into one system architecture. Carefully addressing these issues will assist in creating a strong and reliable security framework.

## VIII. Improving Access Control Lists with AI

As was stated in our proposal, we can utilize AI to examine patterns and behavior to spot anomalies in network access requests. AI systems can identify suspicious or suspicious access attempts and send notifications and take preventive measures by learning the typical behavior of users [7]. AI can be used to dynamically modify access control policies depending on current information and circumstances. AI algorithms are able to intelligently decide whether to give or refuse access in a more precise and context-aware manner by considering specific user behavior, device attributes, network information, and other related aspects.

ACL rules can be improved over time by AI algorithms that continuously learn from access patterns and security events. This adaptive learning strategy [7] can help in the evolution of ACLs to block unauthorized access more successfully while lowering false positives. AI algorithms can analyze large volumes of data related to user behavior, network traffic, and system logs to identify patterns, anomalies, and potential security risks [8]. This analysis helps in understanding the access requirements and potential threats [5], forming the basis for ACL generation.

Based on historical data and specified risk models, AI algorithms can evaluate the risk related to granting or rejecting particular rights. By taking into account elements like the user's role and potential vulnerabilities, AI systems can provide access control policies that reduce security risks.

Network traffic, user behavior, and security events will be continuously monitored by AI, which may see changes and emerging patterns that can call for ACL adjustments [11]. By constantly modifying ACLs based on current findings, AI systems contribute to the maintenance of an efficient and up-to-date access control architecture.

AI classifies various kinds of network traffic and user behaviors using machine learning algorithms. AI systems can create ACL rules that permit or limit access based on particular categories or traits by comprehending these classifications.

## IX. Discussion

Anomaly detection systems and access control lists (ACLs) are fundamental components for protecting computer networks from unauthorized access and potential threats. An IDS is designed to monitor network traffic and generate alerts when suspicious or malicious activity is detected. AI-based ACLs, on the other hand, use AI techniques to automatically manage and enforce access control policies. Combining AI algorithms for IDS (Intrusion Detection System) alerts with ACL (Access Control List) alerts provides a more complete and intelligent approach to threat detection and response will improve the organization's network security.

Anomaly detection systems are designed to monitor network traffic and detect potential security breaches and malicious activity [2]. It will be used in generating alerts when suspect behavior or patterns are detected. ACLs, on the other hand, are used to regulate access to network resources by creating rules that permit or deny traffic based on predetermined criteria. By combining the AI algorithms of IDS alerts and ACL Alerts, the organizations can harness the power of machine learning and sophisticated analytics to evaluate, classify, and take appropriate actions of incoming alerts.

## X. Conclusion and Future Work

By leveraging the capabilities of AI in conjunction with anomaly detection and access control lists, organizations can achieve proactive threat detection, adaptive access control policies, and efficient countermeasure generation. This paper presented an architecture for managing ACLs for analyzing suspicious traffic and for generating relevant countermeasures. We believe that this will help in creating wise access control decisions by adopting an AI-based ACL. This will help in predicting possible risks that may occur before an incident happen. This research highlights the potential benefits and challenges associated with integrating AI into security systems, along with implementation strategies and performance evaluation metrics. It emphasizes the importance of continually updating and refining AI models to stay ahead of emerging security threats, ultimately strengthening the overall security posture of various domains. Moreover, this will help network analysts in identifying alerts efficiently. In our future work, we will be focusing on managing how ACL can be adapted based on anomalies and policies to create a more secure environment.

## Acknowledgment

This work was partially supported by JSPS KAKENHI Grant Number JP19K20268.

## References

[1] N. Muhammad, U. Shams, B. Mohammad, "Network intrusion prevention by configuring ACLs on the routers, based on snort IDS alerts", IEEE Communications Surveys & Tutorials, vol. 22, no. 2, pp. 1392-1431, October 2010.

[2] C. Lee, J. Kim and S. Kang, "Semi-supervised Anomaly Detection with Reinforcement Learning", Computers and Communications (ITC-CSCC), Phuket, Thailand, 2022, pp. 933-936, July 2022.

[3] C. Varun, B. Arindam, and K. Vipin, "Anomaly detection: A survey". ACM Computing Surveys, vol.41(3), pp.1-58, July 2009.

[4] C. Raghavendra, and C. Sanjay, "Deep learning for anomaly detection: A survey". arXiv:1901.03407, January 2019.

[5] C. Kukjin, Y. Jihun, P. Changhwa, and Y. Sungroh, "Deep Learning for Anomaly Detection in Time-Series Data: Review, Analysis, and Guidelines".IEEE, vol.9, pp. 120043 – 120065, August 2021.

[6] H. Victoria, and A. Jim, "A Survey of Outlier Detection Methodologies". Artificial Intelligence Review 22, Springer, pp.85-126, October 2004.
[7] B. Anna, and G. Erhan, "A Survey of Data Mining and Machine Learning Methods for Cyber Security Intrusion Detection". IEEE Communications Surveys & Tutorials, vol.18 (2), pp. 1153 – 1176, October 2015.
[8] H. Yassine, G. Khalida, A. Abdullah, B. Faycal, and A. Abbes, "Artificial intelligence-based anomaly detection of energy consumption in buildings: A review, current trends and new perspectives, ScienceDirect Applied Energy, vol 287, pp.1-26, April 2021.
[9] Z. Shuai, C. Mayanka, L. Yugyung, and M. Deep, "Real-Time Network Anomaly Detection System Using Machine Learning".IEEE, pp. 267-270, July 2015.
[10] D. Kyle, H. Abdeltawab, and A. Marco, "A Survey of AI-Based Anomaly Detection in IoT and Sensor Networks".Sensors vol.23(3), January 2023.
[11] L. Xiao, H. Brett, and W. Dinghao, "Automated Synthesis of Access Control Lists," International *Conference on Software Security and Assurance (ICSSA)*, Altoona, PA, USA, pp. 104-109, July 2017.
[12] Z. Shakila, A. Khaled, A. Mohammed A, A. Muhammad Raisuddin, K. Risala. Tasin., K. M. Shamim, M. Mahmud, "Security Threats and Artificial Intelligence Based Countermeasures for Internet of Things Networks: A Comprehensive Survey," in IEEE Access, vol. 9, pp. 94668-94690, June 2021.
[13] Twingate, Access Control Lists (ACLs): How They Work & Best Practices. [online]. Available from: https:twingate.com/blog/access-control-list/ 2023/07/25
[14] Dandelife, Understanding the Pros and Cons of Access Control Lists. [online]. Available from: https://dandelife.com/understanding-the-pros-and-cons-of-access-control-lists/ 2023/07/26
[15] I. Muhammad, W. Lei, M. Gabriel-Miro, A. Aamir, S. Nadir, M. K. Razzaq, "PrePass-Flow: A Machine Learning based technique to minimize ACL policy violation due to links failure in hybrid SDN",Computer Networks, vol.184,107706, January 2021.

# Drivers for a Secure Mobile App Development Framework

Christoff Jacobs
Academy of Computer Science and Software Engineering
University of Johannesburg
Johannesburg, South Africa
toffie.cj@gmail.com

Marijke Coetzee
School of Computer Science and Information Systems
North-West University
Potchefstroom, South Africa
marijke.coetzee@nwu.ac.za

***Abstract*—To stay competitive in a fast-evolving landscape, lifestyle, e-commerce, finance, and health sectors use mobile apps to enhance their traditional capabilities with new innovative features to satisfy customer demands. Developing sophisticated and secure mobile apps requires a skilled understanding of software development techniques, protection mechanisms, and mobile security practices to safeguard customers against cyberattacks. Software development teams often apply frameworks and best practices according to their unique experience and knowledge, resulting in vulnerable mobile apps. Numerous software development challenges, a lack of guidelines, and a standardised agile approach for creating secure mobile apps need to be addressed. The primary objective of this research is to initiate the process of delineating mobile application security drivers. This initial step lays the foundation for the subsequent development of a comprehensive, secure software development framework for mobile applications, with an overarching emphasis on security across all stages of development. This framework is designed to be adaptable and customizable to meet the specific security needs of diverse industries. The security drivers can form the foundation for a novel framework to guide the creation of secure mobile apps.**

***Keywords-mobile application; secure software development frameworks, cybersecurity.***

## I. Introduction

The Covid-19 pandemic's uncertainty caused a sharp rise in the usage of mobile apps, particularly in the banking sector, where branches closed worldwide [1] [2]. Mobile app usage has become commonplace across banking, finance, e-commerce and mHealth industries. The Digital.ai Threat Report for 2023 [3] underscores a notable trend wherein over 50% of mobile applications are subjected to at least one cyberattack. Remarkably, these cyberattacks transcend the boundaries of application popularity, affecting both widely recognized and less popular applications. This prevailing threat landscape further intensifies the urgency surrounding the accelerated delivery of mobile applications. Consequently, companies must deploy more advanced mobile protection mechanisms to mitigate the increased risk posed by a larger attack surface. For example, mechanisms, such as the One-Time-Pin (OTP), biometric trait verification, and liveness assessment to authenticate customers digitally are increasingly becoming standard practice across various industries. Unfortunately, individual software development teams continuously reinvent the wheel as no standard approach exists when defining a new sophisticated security mechanism [4] [5]. In addition to the challenges software developers face in keeping up with evolving security threats, the 2021 Global DevSecOps Survey [6] indicates constant friction between security professionals and software developers. More than three-quarters of security teams believe that software developers find errors and bugs too late in the development process. The challenges for mobile app software developers are that they need specialist security knowledge of mobile apps, application frameworks and operating systems and how they can be compromised.

Software developers do not have adequate guidelines when developing secure mobile apps [6]. Historically development teams apply software development best practices in conjunction with their team's expertise and ad-hoc processes developed over many years. Frameworks such as Open Web Application Security Project (OWASP) [7], National Institute of Standards and Technology (NIST) [8] and MITRE ATTACK [9] and approaches, such as DevSecOps [10] are excellent foundations for supporting security within a mobile app. However, a security gap becomes evident when the inner workings of these frameworks are analysed, as the available techniques, tools, and testing requirements do not fully support the need to develop a secure mobile app [11]. Software development frameworks and best practices support the implementation of technical security aspects to safeguard mobile apps against cyber criminals. However, factors, such as resolving issues and new enhancements, sharing security knowledge between various internal teams and collaborating teams between different companies are not addressed [12], [13]. In principle, the secure development of a mobile app should be supported by a secure software development framework tailored to the security requirements of mobile apps. Current mobile app development processes are ad-hoc in nature and do not provide sufficient guidance for companies and development teams [14]–[16]. Research focuses on developing secure mobile apps using various processes and techniques [14] [17] [18] but does not focus on creating a secure software development framework for mobile apps. This research contributes by identifying mobile app security drivers for a secure software development framework as the first step in this direction.

The following section identifies various actors and their roles in mobile app security to understand the complexities of the landscape. Section three briefly reviews relevant software development frameworks to understand methods and approaches commonly used to secure a mobile app. Next, nine security drivers are described by analysing secure mobile app development challenges. Section five evaluates the security drivers against common software development frameworks to identify a research gap. Finally, the paper is concluded in section six.

## II. Mobile app ecosystem

A mobile app ecosystem is a massive integrated network connecting hardware and various systems that communicate securely. Unfortunately, mobile apps open the door to heightened risk and fraud. For example, 693 banking apps across over 80 countries unveiled 2,157 vulnerabilities [19]. Customers, mobile app stores, mobile apps, mobile network operators, security vendors and technologies, such as firewalls, web servers, core systems and various development and security teams exist within the ecosystem [20]. Actors indicate integration points where security controls are required to guarantee a customer transaction's privacy and integrity. Over and above the user interface, software development and security teams, the risk management, anti-money laundering, digital forensics and financial reporting teams aim to establish a trusting relationship between customers, the company and the mobile app [21]. When a mobile app or a new requirement is developed, software teams do not focus on security requirements and mechanisms as they prefer to leave it to experts [22]. Instead, development teams use security vendors to provide mobile security services, such as security controls and app security testing. Once mobile apps are complete and ready for testing, penetration tests are performed by third parties to validate the behaviour of the integrated security mechanisms and mobile security controls [23]. Then the mobile app is submitted to app stores for review. App store reviews include security tests to check for unsolicited application code injection, stealing personally identifiable information, and keeping customers' mobile data safe from cybercriminals. App store reviewers require credentials to access the mobile app, but they are limited and only authorised to access features associated with the intended review. Customers download and install the mobile app onto their mobile device. A firewall filters the mobile app requests to prevent unsolicited access between these entities. The network operator and internet service providers provide the network channel for the mobile app and company to communicate.

Having provided a comprehensive insight into the intricacies of the mobile app ecosystem, it is essential to recognize that organizations may contemplate alternative implementation strategies to develop a secure mobile application. Nevertheless, it is worth noting that these alternative approaches bring forth their unique risks and challenges, which, while relevant, fall beyond the scope of this research inquiry [24].

The mobile app ecosystem has unique security and software development requirements that a unique secure software development framework should address. Therefore, an analysis of current security frameworks used by mobile app developers and the security requirements of mobile apps is needed to determine a research gap, described next.

## III. Secure software development for mobile apps

There is a lack of Software Development Life Cycle (SDLC) models and frameworks for mobile application development [25] [26]. Most works focus on the development of the technical components of a mobile app and not the life cycle. Traditional software development methodologies, such as waterfall or agile, have been implemented over the years but do not directly address security. Generally, software development methodologies address the following activities from a high-level point of view: identification of requirements, architecture and design, coding, testing, production and maintenance of the application. When security is added to traditional SDLC phases, it can result in low-quality insecure apps, as software developers do not conform to SDLC phases and lack training and experience in application and security technologies. Software developers decide how and when various guidelines, standards and practices are applied to the different stages of the development life cycle leading to various ad-hoc approaches.

Searching papers on - a secure software development framework for mobile apps - reveals that no such framework exists. In contrast, generalised software development frameworks are an active field of current research with many approaches addressing security [27]. Recent studies recommend that a secure software development lifecycle should address security considerations in each development phase. Industry standards, such as OWASP, ISO/IEC, MITRE ATT&CK knowledgebase and NIST are recommended to be used, but no guidance is provided on how to include security and when to do it [28]. Other frameworks and standards identified by [29], are Common Criteria (CC), Software Assurance Forum for Excellence in Code (SAFECode), Open Group Architecture Framework, TOGAF, ISO/IEC 41062, Payment Card Industry (PCI), National Information Assurance Partnership (NIAP), ioXt alliance and CREST [29]. Exploring NIST and OWASP frameworks has surfaced myriad distinct security and software development requisites. Notable among these include but are not limited to robust Authentication and Authorization mechanisms, Encryption protocols, diligent Threat Modeling, adherence to Secure Coding Practices, the implementation of Secure Communication protocols, routine Security Testing, and the fortification of Third-party Libraries and Application Programming Interfaces (APIs).

A review of secure software development standards concludes that many do not cover all the security requirements for secure software development when used individually. Instead, a framework to guide the application of relevant standards is required [30].

Next, commonly used industry practice approaches for mobile app security are briefly discussed. The National Institute of Standards and Technology (NIST) and Open Web Application Security Project (OWASP) are described.

The MITRE ATT&CK knowledgebase is also included in the discussion, as MITRE provides many techniques and tools to mitigate mobile app threats. Finally, DevSecOps is discussed as it is a trending practise that brings security into the early stages of software development.

### A. NIST

The National Institute of Standards and Technology (NIST) continually updates and publishes many software development and security regulations, guidelines, and rules. For example, the NIST 800-163, Vetting the Security of Mobile Applications security framework combines various security-focused stages [8]. NIST 800-163 focuses on mobile security and is a generic framework for mobile applications. Mobile app teams use different stages within 800-163 and apply the knowledge gained to improve the security of a mobile app. For example, the App Security Requirements stage identifies general security requirements, organisation-specific requirements and risk tolerance. In addition, each company's development teams use their expertise and skills to identify threats and risks of their mobile app. Development teams execute mobile app security testing cycles using the NIST App Testing and Vulnerability Classifiers. Other security stages are App Vetting System, App Vetting Considerations and App Vetting Process. In addition, NIST 800-218 Secure Software Development Framework (SSDF) [31] provide comprehensive guidelines to mitigate risks.

### B. OWASP

The Open Web Application Security Project is a security standard that contributes to mobile app security by introducing Mobile Security Testing Guide (MSTG) and Mobile Application Security Vetting System (MASVS) security categories [32] [33]. The MSTG and MASVS categories comprise security focus areas for mobile app development. Mobile app teams use various stages within MSTG and MASVS and apply the knowledge gained to improve mobile app development security. For example, the development and testing teams invoke Tampering and Reverse Engineering Code. Teams analyse the application code and web server requests sent and received between the mobile app server to give feedback to the broader team regarding mobile vulnerabilities. Other security focus areas within the MSTG are Data Storage, Authentication mechanisms, Code Quality, and Anti-Reversing techniques. The MASVS stipules eight vulnerability areas that concentrate on mobile app security. Additionally, mobile app teams use the areas as guidelines for vulnerabilities companies should address. Since August 2020, the CREST alliance have introduced the OWASP MASVS as an officially certified standard for mobile app security [34] [35].

### C. MITRE ATT&CK

The MITRE's ATT&CK is a widely known and utilised knowledgebase to understand cyber-attacks or threat actors. The MITRE ATT&CK knowledge base consists of multiple platform-specific security topics to address enterprise and mobile attacks [36]. Mobile app teams use various attacks within MITRE ATT&CK Mobile and apply the knowledge gained to improve developers' mobile app development security expertise. For example, developers can invoke onboot or login initialisation scripts, analyses application code and invoke onboot scripts to bypass mobile device manufacturer security checks. In addition, login initialisation scripts are used to analyse the login web server calls and ultimately manipulate the values to masquerade as a different customer.

### D. DEVSECOPS

DevSecOps [37] is a software development approach that combines development, security, and operations to enable the creation of secure, reliable, and high-quality software products. It is built over DevOps, therefore promoting the integration of security principles and practices through collaboration, communication, and team integration. DevSecOps emphasises secure coding practices to prevent vulnerabilities in the code, requires continuous testing and integration to ensure that the application is secure and reliable using automated testing tools, ensures that new features and updates are released quickly and securely, involves continuous security monitoring and incident response to detect and respond to security threats in real-time. Even though DevSecOps promises much, aspects, such as security or privacy by design, architectural risk analysis, threat modelling, and risk management are complex to implement as substantial human input is required to execute these processes. Silo-based teams are a barrier to secure DevOps that prevent collaboration [38].

Next, nine security drivers are described from an analysis of the mobile app ecosystem and literature to uniquely focus the processes and activities required for secure mobile app development. Both management and technical drivers are identified to provide a more comprehensive approach

## IV. SECURITY DRIVERS FOR AN SECURE MOBILE SOFTWARE DEVELOPMENT FRAMEWORK

The NIST SecureSsoftware Development Framework (SSDF) [39] is a formal approach that embeds secure development activities, such as security requirements elicitation and threat modelling into the software development cycle to address mobile app security requirements, risks, vulnerabilities, development, and a vetting process.

Key security areas or drivers are presented as a first step towards establishing such a framework. Next, the security drivers are identified and described.

### A. Management of software developers for security

Software development teams should be well-managed to ensure that security is a priority. By defining principles that should be followed and ensuring that cross-team collaboration becomes a way of work, a security culture can grow, resulting in motivated teams. Teams should be provided with tools to increase productivity and cut expenditures to increase the return on investment for the company. Development teams require security guidance, job satisfaction and adequate security controls to secure remote work environments [40] [41]. A level of autonomy given to developers can strengthen the symbiosis between management and developers [42]. Agile development processes allow management to break the silos between various development teams [43].

### *B. A structured security approval strategy for security vendors*

Large organisations outsource security functions to security vendors. Security vendors must be managed with care [44] as they may be required to access intricate details and propriety knowledge to reproduce any security compromise and find the cause quickly. While NIST provides comprehensive guidance across multifarious facets of mobile application development, it is prudent to acknowledge a noticeable void in their approach, specifically in the seamless integration of security vendors [39]. This deficiency underscores the challenges of facilitating extensive security approvals for vendors, granting them immediate access to sensitive information. This task presents considerable complexities within the existing secure framework landscape. Customers' confidentiality and privacy are of concern, and trust needs to be ensured. Multiple processes and authorisations are required in order to onboard security providers. Companies should ensure that there is a good motivation for appointing a vendor based on a security gap, and a return on investment (ROI). A legally binding contract needs to identify whether the vendor allows a proof-of-concept trial period, addresses a security gap for the mobile app and whether they will be a long-term partner as these factors influence the company's security posture.

### *C. Integrate security education into secure software development*

In agile software development, there is no phase for security training, but it is assumed that developers have the required knowledge. Developers must be convinced that security is part of their job and trained to add security to their code competently. Unfortunately, adequate mobile app security training is not a focus for development teams [45]. To foster a security-first mobile app, best practices and design techniques must be encouraged [46]. Security education can include specialised security training and certifications of individuals. For those in technical roles, security training should be mandatory. [47] offers a commendable comparative analysis of security certifications accessible to development teams. These certifications serve as valuable resources for mobile developers to refine and authenticate their proficiency in mobile security and other security-related domains. Furthermore, knowledge of security vendors' products and services is another potential gap in the education of developers and security specialists. Integrating a security vendor product with the mobile app and systems requires expertise, extensive documentation and practical experience. In addition, where there is a high staff turnover, a knowledge gap can pose a risk to the company as it may become vague about the vendor's role due to a lack of experience. In such cases, the vendor is responsible for driving the process, which may be to the company's detriment.

### *D. Standardised secure software development practices and coding principles*

A standardised approach to mobile app development is required in the fast-changing mobile app environment. Various secure software development practices and coding principles exist, with development teams having a range of experience and skills gained over the years to create their mobile app. Unfortunately, over time, teams apply several approaches in a non-standard manner, thereby creating the potential for gaps in their security posture. Using the DevOps approach, companies implement security using a layered approach [19] as DevSecOps focuses on implementing software security practices and tools at every stage of the lifecycle. DevSecOps requires an increased focus on collaborations between the development, security, and operations teams to be effective. Unfortunately, different groups may experience intergroup conflicts and may not trust each other.

A mobile app contains various features, performance enhancements, user interface and security, to name a few [48]. Therefore, companies should comply with a standardised level of best practices and coding principles for their mobile apps to keep up with the ever-changing advancements in technology and practices. For example, the OWASP secure coding practices guide can be extended to specifically include mobile app secure coding requirements [7]. In addition, security design patterns help mitigate issues and ensure that trust is established within the mobile ecosystem [7].

### *E. A baseline set of standardised security mechanisms for mobile apps*

Trust within a mobile ecosystem entails app confidentiality, communication integrity between the app and company, app availability, customer authentication and authorisation, and non-repudiation of a financial transaction [49]. Introducing new security mechanisms and altering an existing mechanism require intricate security knowledge of the mobile app, code practices and all mobile ecosystem actors. Developers must implement new security mechanisms without guidance, as no approved library exists. Security mechanisms, such as OTP, Device Registration, Image verification, Passphrase, Digital certificates and Biometrics, and more could fall victim to attackers due to vulnerabilities caused by inexperienced developers. Therefore, companies would benefit from standardised security mechanisms that follow best practices [50]. In conjunction with standardised software development techniques, standardised security mechanisms would support the seamless updating of security mechanisms.

### *F. Standardised threat modelling approach*

Threat modelling is a critical element in integrating security into a mobile app. There are various threat modelling approaches and methodologies that can be employed. Unfortunately, threat modelling for agile development is immature, and few sources are available to consult [51]. Moreover, a specific threat model often limits threats to the mobile app's trust boundaries and communication channels, thereby neglecting potential threats. Threat modelling is a challenging task and is potentially best addressed using a hybrid approach, to combine the best features of different approaches. Currently, no such approach exists for developing a secure mobile app. A potential approach should be informed by the specifics of the environment and software architecture and threats and vulnerabilities specific to the environment.

### G. *Standardise testing schedule*

Software testing is a complex phase that takes time and is very costly. Furthermore, software developers may resist the full scope of required testing, lowering overall software quality. Mobile-specific security testing is often performed only at the end of the development life cycle, just before a release date. As a result, releases may be shipped with a risk. An extensive range of open-source tools and techniques are available for companies to automatically validate security mechanisms and mobile security controls [31]. Penetration tests find vulnerabilities within software systems. While it is recognized that no system can be entirely devoid of flaws, it is imperative to emphasize the significance of adhering to a standardized penetration testing regimen. Such a regimen is obligatory for proactively addressing and mitigating 'low-hanging fruit' vulnerabilities, often exploited by cybercriminals as prime targets [52]. To address all vulnerabilities, security tests need to be conducted by multiple teams within a company. Extensive security testing can only be performed when a formalised threat modelling approach is present and teams are well-trained and knowledgeable.

### H. *Standardised mobile app vetting system for an industry*

App vetting determines whether an app conforms to an organisation's security requirements. Each app store has its unique in-house requirements and vetting processes. A mobile app should be vetted to assure customers that the required security mechanisms are implemented [53]. The mobile app vetting system informs customers of security mechanisms and security controls embodied within the mobile app and the precautions the company took to ensure trust between the mobile app, customer and company. Unfortunately, app stores do not thoroughly examine all security vulnerabilities due to cost constraints. Therefore, each industry requires a more stringent mobile app vetting process to contribute to secure mobile apps.

### I. *Regulated security reporting and collaboration*

A software development framework for secure mobile apps requires interaction between companies, industry custodians, and regulators with authority. Furthermore, reporting incidents and knowledge sharing should be compulsory to ensure a more robust community. For example, a successful attack against a new sophisticated mobile security mechanism must be communicated to safeguard the community. The landscape of security frameworks is abundant, with numerous frameworks catering to diverse regulations and industry sectors [54]. Nonetheless, a conspicuous need arises for a dedicated secure mobile application development framework focusing on security and agile methodologies. Furthermore, while many security controls exist for creating secure mobile applications [55], it becomes evident that various industries must select and extract controls that align with their specific requisites and prioritize their significance. Governance and regulation are essential in safeguarding mobile apps and preventing cybercrime.

Next, the security drivers identified by this research are compared to the software development guidelines, standards, and knowledgebase. The comparison aims to determine to what extent the current frameworks address the identified driver

## V. EVALUATION

This research aims to define a secure software development framework that a software developer or team, who may have limited security knowledge, can use as a guide to secure a mobile app throughout all development life cycle phases. Such a guide can be tailored to an industry, such as banking to reflect its security concerns and best practise.

A research gap is now identified by comparing the various development approaches and guidelines and the identified security drivers. The research gap forms a foundation for developing a secure mobile app development framework. Table 1 compares the security drivers and frameworks, followed by an evaluation. OWASP meets several security drivers. However, managing development teams to develop secure mobile apps and enabling software developers to work remotely from the comfort of their choice is cumbersome and is lacking from all the frameworks. Furthermore, integrating a secure development framework into the various sectors with the structured industry-and-governance process is also missing. NIST guides the validation of security controls within a mobile app by invoking a penetration testing schedule and educating development teams on various security-related topics. Although NIST directs threat modelling, the assistance only applies within the Recommended Standard for Vendor or Developer Verification Code [56]. The MITRE ATT&CK framework educates development teams on various security-related topics from an attacker's perspective, providing in-depth knowledge and relevant tools to attack a mobile app. However, MITRE and NIST lack fundamental security mechanisms for companies to authenticate and authorise customers and ensure integrity, confidentiality and non-repudiation in financial transactions.

DevSecOps provides support for managing teams and collaborations without focusing on security aspects. A focus is on the integration of, e.g., education and testing into all phases. No guidance is provided for a baseline set of security mechanisms and guidelines to follow.

TABLE I. COMPARISON OF SECURE DEVELOPMENT FRAMEWORKS AND SECURITY DRIVERS

| Security drivers | NIST | OWASP | MITRE | DEVSECOPS |
|---|---|---|---|---|
| Management of software developers for security | | | | X |
| A structured security approval strategy | X | | | |
| Integrate security education for secure software development | X | X | X | X |
| Standardised secure software development practices and coding principles | | X | | |
| A baseline set of standardised security mechanisms for mobile apps | | | | |
| Standardised threat modelling approach | | X | | |
| Standardise testing schedule | X | | | X |
| Standardised mobile app vetting system for an industry | | X | | |
| Regulated security reporting and collaboration | | | | |

OWASP supports more security drivers than NIST and MITRE as OWASP assists with testing tools using the Mobile Security Testing Guide and vetting mobile apps using the Mobile Application Security Vetting System. OWASP is an open-source and freely available repository of security controls for applying mobile security controls.

The comparison in Table 1 indicates a need for a secure development framework explicitly tailored to the mobile app space. As this environment is under attack and will be more so in the future, it is worth developing a tailored framework to ensure better security.

## VI. CONCLUSION AND FUTURE WORK

This paper identified the complexities of a mobile ecosystem and the lack of guidance for software developers. Software development teams implement and test new and often sophisticated security mechanisms, as no standard approach currently exists. Additionally, the lack of adequate guidelines and frameworks for secure mobile app development creates challenges for software developers who require specialist security knowledge of mobile apps, application frameworks, and operating systems. While frameworks, such as OWASP, NIST and MITRE ATTACK, and approaches such as DevSecOps are excellent foundations for supporting security within a mobile app, they do not fully support the need to develop a secure mobile app. The research suggests the need for a secure software development framework tailored to the security requirements of mobile apps. The study contributes to this area by identifying nine mobile app security drivers for a secure software development framework as the first step in this direction.

Future work includes an in-depth analysis of the identified security drivers and current software development approaches and frameworks to identify activities and other deliverables that can be used to create a secure software development framework for mobile apps.

## REFERENCES


[1] S. Majumdar and V. Pujari, "Exploring usage of mobile banking apps in the UAE: a categorical regression analysis," *J Financ Serv Mark*, Aug. 2021, doi: 10.1057/s41264-021-00112-1.

[2] Y. W. Prihatiningtias and N. Wipraganang, "The Impact of Mobile Payment on Non-Financial Performance of SMEs During the COVID-19 Pandemic," presented at the Brawijaya International Conference on Economics, Business and Finance 2021 (BICEBF 2021), Atlantis Press, Jan. 2022, pp. 252–258. doi: 10.2991/aebmr.k.220128.033.

[3] Digital.ai, "Digital.ai." 2023. Accessed: Feb. 19, 2023. [Online]. Available: https://digital.ai/

[4] M. Divya and C. Hebbar, "A case study on 'mobile banking is a boon to banking customers during the covid-19 pandemic situation'-with special reference to the sbi customers of mangalore city," *epra*, vol. 8, no. 4, Apr. 2021, [Online]. Available: https://eprajournals.com/jpanel/upload/1243am_2.EPRA%20JOURNALS-6865.pdf

[5] M. Hensher *et al.*, "Scoping review: Development and assessment of evaluation frameworks of mobile health apps for recommendations to consumers," *Journal of the American Medical Informatics Association*, vol. 28, no. 6, pp. 1318–1329, Jun. 2021, doi: 10.1093/jamia/ocab041.

[6] GitLabs, "GitLabDevSecOps," 2022. https://about.gitlab.com/developer-survey (accessed Nov. 01, 2022).

[7] OWASP, "OWASP Secure Coding Practices-Quick Reference Guide | OWASP Foundation," 2022. https://owasp.org/www-project-secure-coding-practices-quick-reference-guide/migrated_content.html (accessed Nov. 01, 2022).

[8] M. Ogata, J. Franklin, J. Voas, V. Sritapan, and S. Quirolgico, "Vetting the security of mobile applications," National Institute of Standards and Technology, Gaithersburg, MD, NIST SP 800-163r1, Apr. 2019. doi: 10.6028/NIST.SP.800-163r1.

[9] W. Xiong, E. Legrand, O. Åberg, and R. Lagerström, "Cyber security threat modeling based on the MITRE Enterprise ATT&CK Matrix," *Softw Syst Model*, Jun. 2021, doi: 10.1007/s10270-021-00898-7.

[10] M. A. Aljohani and S. S. Alqahtani, "A Unified Framework for Automating Software Security Analysis in DevSecOps," in *2023 International Conference on Smart Computing and Application (ICSCA)*, Feb. 2023, pp. 1–6. doi: 10.1109/ICSCA57840.2023.10087568.

[11] Y. Valdés-Rodríguez, J. Hochstetter-Diez, J. Díaz-Arancibia, and R. Cadena-Martínez, "Towards the Integration of Security Practices in Agile Software Development: A Systematic Mapping Review," *Applied Sciences*, vol. 13, no. 7, Art. no. 7, Jan. 2023, doi: 10.3390/app13074578.

[12] B. Reed, "Rethinking the Status Quo of Mobile App Security," *Security Boulevard*, Apr. 19, 2023. https://securityboulevard.com/2023/04/rethinking-the-status-quo-of-mobile-app-security/ (accessed Apr. 28, 2023).

[13] H. Taherdoost, "Understanding Cybersecurity Frameworks and Information Security Standards—A Review and Comprehensive Overview," *Electronics*, vol. 11, no. 14, Art. no. 14, Jan. 2022, doi: 10.3390/electronics11142181.

[14] D. Ghelani, T. K. Hua, and S. K. R. Koduru, "Cyber Security Threats, Vulnerabilities, and Security Solutions Models in

Banking," Preprints, preprint, Sep. 2022. doi: 10.22541/au.166385206.63311335/v1.

[15] J. R. Kala Kamdjoug, S.-L. Wamba-Taguimdje, S. F. Wamba, and I. B. Kake, "Determining factors and impacts of the intention to adopt mobile banking app in Cameroon: Case of SARA by afriland First Bank," *Journal of Retailing and Consumer Services*, vol. 61, p. 102509, Jul. 2021, doi: 10.1016/j.jretconser.2021.102509.

[16] Y. Liu, Z. Liang, C. Li, J. Guo, and G. Zhao, "An Investigation into the Adoption Behavior of mHealth Users: From the Perspective of the Push-Pull-Mooring Framework," *Sustainability*, vol. 14, no. 21, Art. no. 21, Jan. 2022, doi: 10.3390/su142114372.

[17] Y. Huang and C. Chen, "Smart App Attack: Hacking Deep Learning Models in Android Apps." arXiv, Apr. 23, 2022. Accessed: Apr. 29, 2023. [Online]. Available: http://arxiv.org/abs/2204.11075

[18] S. A. Butt, T. Jamal, M. A. Azad, A. Ali, and N. S. Safa, "A multivariant secure framework for smart mobile health application," *Trans Emerging Tel Tech*, vol. 33, no. 8, Aug. 2022, doi: 10.1002/ett.3684.

[19] R. T. Yarlagadda and M. Sabri, "An exploratory study of devops & it's future in usa," *SSRN Electronic Journal*, vol. 8, pp. 82–92, Jan. 2021.

[20] N. T. Msweli and T. Mawela, "Financial Inclusion of the Elderly: Exploring the Role of Mobile Banking Adoption," *AIP*, vol. 10, no. 1, pp. 1–21, Jun. 2021, doi: 10.18267/j.aip.143.

[21] A. Mahalle, J. Yong, and X. Tao, "Challenges and Mitigation for Application Deployment over SaaS Platform in Banking and Financial Services Industry," in *2021 IEEE 24th International Conference on Computer Supported Cooperative Work in Design (CSCWD)*, Dalian, China: IEEE, May 2021, pp. 288–296. doi: 10.1109/CSCWD49262.2021.9437798.

[22] M. Tahaei, K. Vaniea, K. (Kosta) Beznosov, and M. K. Wolters, "Security Notifications in Static Analysis Tools: Developers' Attitudes, Comprehension, and Ability to Act on Them," in *Proceedings of the 2021 CHI Conference on Human Factors in Computing Systems*, Yokohama Japan: ACM, May 2021, pp. 1–17. doi: 10.1145/3411764.3445616.

[23] B. Yankson, J. V. K, P. C. K. Hung, F. Iqbal, and L. Ali, "Security Assessment for Zenbo Robot Using Drozer and mobSF Frameworks," in *2021 11th IFIP International Conference on New Technologies, Mobility and Security (NTMS)*, Apr. 2021, pp. 1–7. doi: 10.1109/NTMS49979.2021.9432666.

[24] A. S. George and S. Sagayarajan, "Securing Cloud Application Infrastructure: Understanding the Penetration Testing Challenges of IaaS, PaaS, and SaaS Environments," *Partners Universal International Research Journal*, vol. 2, no. 1, pp. 24–34, 2023.

[25] R. Nataraj and S. Jagatheesan, "Lack of SDLC Models and Frameworks in Mobile Application Development - A Systematic Literature Review and Study," *Journal of Xi'an University of Architecture & Technology*, vol. 13, no. 8, pp. 250–258, Oct. 2021.

[26] C. Catal, A. Ozcan, E. Donmez, and A. Kasif, "Analysis of cyber security knowledge gaps based on cyber security body of knowledge," *Education and Information Technologies*, vol. 28, pp. 1809–1831, 2022.

[27] A. Kudriavtseva and O. Gadyatskaya, "Secure Software Development Methodologies: A Multivocal Literature Review." arXiv, Nov. 29, 2022. Accessed: May 08, 2023. [Online]. Available: http://arxiv.org/abs/2211.16987

[28] R. Fujdiak *et al.*, "Managing the Secure Software Development," in *2019 10th IFIP International Conference on New Technologies, Mobility and Security (NTMS)*, CANARY ISLANDS, Spain: IEEE, Jun. 2019, pp. 1–4. doi: 10.1109/NTMS.2019.8763845.

[29] M. Naeem, W. Ozuem, and P. Ward, "Understanding the accessibility of retail mobile banking during the COVID-19 pandemic," *IJRDM*, vol. 50, no. 7, pp. 860–879, Jun. 2022, doi: 10.1108/IJRDM-02-2021-0064.

[30] A. Ramirez, A. Aiello, and S. J. Lincke, "A Survey and Comparison of Secure Software Development Standards," in *2020 13th CMI Conference on Cybersecurity and Privacy (CMI) - Digital Transformation - Potentials and Challenges(51275)*, Nov. 2020, pp. 1–6. doi: 10.1109/CMI51275.2020.9322704.

[31] M. Hassan, Z. Shukur, and M. Mohd, "A Penetration Testing on Malaysia Popular e-Wallets and m-Banking Apps," *International Journal of Advanced Computer Science and Applications*, vol. 13, Jun. 2022, doi: 10.14569/IJACSA.2022.0130580.

[32] E. B. Blancaflor, G. A. J. Anson, A. M. V. Encinas, M. A. V. Marin, and S. L. G. Zamora, "A Vulnerability Assessment on the Parental Control Mobile Applications' Security: Status based on the OWASP Security Requirements," p. 10, 2021.

[33] A. Pradeep *et al.*, "A comparative analysis of certificate pinning in Android & iOS," in *Proceedings of the 22nd ACM Internet Measurement Conference*, Nice France: ACM, Oct. 2022, pp. 605–618. doi: 10.1145/3517745.3561439.

[34] CREST, "CREST OVS Web Application Programme," *CREST*, 2022. https://www.crest-approved.org/membership/crest-ovs-programme/ (accessed May 08, 2023).

[35] H. Al-Shaikh *et al.*, "SHarPen: SoC Security Verification by Hardware Penetration Test," in *Proceedings of the 28th Asia and South Pacific Design Automation Conference*, Tokyo Japan: ACM, Jan. 2023, pp. 579–584. doi: 10.1145/3566097.3567918.

[36] R. Al-Shaer, J. M. Spring, and E. Christou, "Learning the Associations of MITRE ATT&CK Adversarial Techniques," *arXiv:2005.01654 [cs]*, May 2020, Accessed: Dec. 08, 2021. [Online]. Available: http://arxiv.org/abs/2005.01654

[37] H. Myrbakken and R. Colomo-Palacios, *DevSecOps: A Multivocal Literature Review*. 2017, p. 29. doi: 10.1007/978-3-319-67383-7_2.

[38] R. N. Rajapakse, M. Zahedi, M. A. Babar, and H. Shen, "Challenges and solutions when adopting DevSecOps: A systematic review." arXiv, Jul. 29, 2021. Accessed: Dec. 12, 2022. [Online]. Available: http://arxiv.org/abs/2103.08266

[39] M. Souppaya, K. Scarfone, and D. Dodson, "Secure Software Development Framework (SSDF) Version 1.1: (Draft): Recommendations for Mitigating the Risk of Software Vulnerabilities," National Institute of Standards and Technology, Gaithersburg, MD, NIST 800-218, Feb. 2022. doi: 10.6028/NIST.SP.800-218.

[40] D. Russo, P. P. H. Hanel, S. Altnickel, and N. van Berkel, "The Daily Life of Software Engineers during the COVID19 Pandemic." arXiv, Jan. 12, 2021. Accessed: Aug. 19, 2022. [Online]. Available: http://arxiv.org/abs/2101.04363

[41] S. Mandal and D. Khan, *A Study of Security Threats in Cloud: Passive Impact of COVID-19 Pandemic*. 2020. doi: 10.1109/ICOSEC49089.2020.9215374.

[42] S. Fraser and D. Mancl, "Engineering for Chaos: Lessons Learned from COVID-19," vol. 46, no. 2, p. 3, 2021.

[43] C. NicCanna, M. A. Razzak, J. Noll, and S. Beecham, "Globally Distributed Development during COVID19." arXiv, Mar. 31, 2021. Accessed: Aug. 19, 2022. [Online]. Available: http://arxiv.org/abs/2103.17181

[44] S. Viveka, "Lessons learnt from COVID-19 for business continuity management in banking sector," in *Building Resilient Organizations: Predicaments & Prospects*, 2022, pp. 241–251. Accessed: Aug. 25, 2023. [Online]. Available: https://books.google.co.za/books?hl=en&lr=&id=XrOGEAAAQBAJ&oi=fnd&pg=PA241&dq=Covid+vendors+challenge+banking+&ots=ezXw5xnOpC&sig=NZGqRg_5QFae5I_B2LLNIlpY5Nc&redir_esc=y#v=onepage&q&f=false

[45] E.-L. Nawa, M. Chitauro, and F. B. Shava, "Assessing Patterns of Cybercrimes Associated with Online Transactions in Namibia Banking Institutions' Cyberspace," in *2021 3rd International Multidisciplinary Information Technology and Engineering*

*Conference (IMITEC)*, Nov. 2021, pp. 1–6. doi: 10.1109/IMITEC52926.2021.9714697.

[46] A. "bunnie" Huang, "Betrusted: Improving Security Through Physical Partitioning," *IEEE Pervasive Computing*, vol. 19, no. 2, pp. 13–20, Apr. 2020, doi: 10.1109/MPRV.2020.2966190.

[47] E.-C. Davri *et al.*, "Cyber Security Certification Programmes," in *2021 IEEE International Conference on Cyber Security and Resilience (CSR)*, Rhodes, Greece: IEEE, Jul. 2021, pp. 428–435. doi: 10.1109/CSR51186.2021.9527974.

[48] A. Patidar and U. Suman, "Towards Analyzing Mobile App Characteristics for Mobile Software Development," in *2021 8th International Conference on Computing for Sustainable Global Development (INDIACom)*, Mar. 2021, pp. 786–790.

[49] Q. Hammouri, T. Majali, D. Almajali, A. Aloqool, and J. A. AlGasawneh, "Explore the Relationship between Security Mechanisms and Trust in E-Banking," vol. 26, no. 6, pp. 17083–17093, 2021.

[50] F. Alt and S. Schneegass, "Beyond Passwords—Challenges and Opportunities of Future Authentication," *IEEE Secur. Privacy*, vol. 20, no. 1, pp. 82–86, Jan. 2022, doi: 10.1109/MSEC.2021.3127459.

[51] K. Bernsmed, D. S. Cruzes, M. G. Jaatun, and M. Iovan, "Adopting threat modelling in agile software development projects," *Journal of Systems and Software*, vol. 183, p. 111090, Jan. 2022, doi: 10.1016/j.jss.2021.111090.

[52] N. Kshetri, "Cybercrime and Cybersecurity in Africa," *Journal of Global Information Technology Management*, vol. 22, no. 2, pp. 77–81, Apr. 2019, doi: 10.1080/1097198X.2019.1603527.

[53] T. L. Andarzian, "SANT: Static Analysis of Native Threads for Security Vetting of Android Applications," vol. 14, no. 1, p. 13, 2022.

[54] CISecurity, "3 Ways We've Made the CIS Controls More Automation-Friendly," *CIS*, 2023. https://www.cisecurity.org/insights/blog/3-ways-weve-made-the-cis-controls-more-automation-friendly (accessed Aug. 25, 2023).

[55] D. Miessler, "The Consumer Authentication Strength Maturity Model (CASMM) V6," 2023. https://danielmiessler.com/p/casmm-consumer-authentication-security-maturity-model/ (accessed Aug. 25, 2023).

[56] A. Shostack, "NIST Brings Threat Modeling into the Spotlight," *Dark Reading*, Sep. 23, 2021. https://www.darkreading.com/threat-intelligence/nist-brings-threat-modeling-into-the-spotlight (accessed Oct. 25, 2022).

# Quantum Threats to the TLS 1.3 Protocol

Luiz Filipi Anderson de Sousa Moura
*Informatics and Statistics Institute*
*Federal University of Santa Catarina*
Florianópolis-SC, Brazil
e-mail: luiz.f.s.m@posgrad.ufsc.br

Alexandre Augusto Giron
*Computer Engineering Department*
*Federal University of Technology-Paraná*
Toledo-PR, Brazil
e-mail: alexandregiron@utfpr.edu.br

Ricardo Felipe Custódio
*Informatics and Statistics Institute*
*Federal University of Santa Catarina*
Florianópolis-SC, Brazil
e-mail: ricardo.custodio@ufsc.br

*Abstract*—**Transport Layer Security 1.3 is the latest version available. This protocol is widely used in Internet security, present in more than 60% of all Internet connections based on HTTPS. Quantum computers are a new computational paradigm that threatens information security as we know it, solving mathematical problems used in current cryptography in polynomial time or providing quadratic acceleration for brute force attacks. This paper highlights the quantum threat to Transport Layer Security, focusing on public key cryptography, exposes threat scenarios, propose a detailed attack model to the protocol, shows expected storage requirements to store-now-decrypt-later attacks, and explores ways to mitigate these quantum threats.**

***Index Terms*—Quantum Computing; Transport Layer Security (TLS) 1.3; Store-Now-Decrypt-Later.**

## I. INTRODUCTION

Transport Layer Security (TLS) 1.3 is a notorious Internet security protocol, present in more than 60% of all Internet connections based on HTTPS [1][2]. TLS is the de-facto standard for securing applications like web servers, browsers, e-mails, messaging, and Voice over Internet Protocol (VoIP), providing end-to-end secure channels with confidentiality, integrity protection, peer authentication, Forward Secrecy (FS), and other [3] guarantees. TLS, like many security protocols, uses Public Key Cryptography (PKC) in its design, for example, for peer authentication and Key Exchange (KEX).

Quantum Computers (QCs) are a threat to PKC since 1994, when Shor's algorithm [4] presented ways to solve the integer factorization problem and Discrete Logarithm Problem (DLP) with an exponential speedup [5]. For symmetric cryptography, the threat is also present with Grover's 1996 [6] search algorithm, capable to perform a brute force attack on a size $n$ list with only $n^{1/2}$ steps, while a classical computer needs about $n/2$ steps for the same task [7].

It is difficult to say when QCs will be ready to break the cryptographic systems we know today. A good guess is about 15 years or less [8]. However, even if the QCs are not yet available, we cannot ignore their threat, as the encrypted data can be stored now and decrypted when the QCs are ready. This process is called "Store-Now-Decrypt-Later" (SNDL) [9].

It is, then, strikingly important to understand the threat to TLS before the arrival of QCs. For this reason, this paper:

- exposes the quantum threat specifically on TLS 1.3, modeling the steps necessary to perform an attack on the PKC;
- predicts the storage requirements for a SNDL attack;
- explores possible threat actors, their capabilities, and post-quantum stages; and
- presents mitigation techniques.

This paper is organized as follows: Section II presents the TLS 1.3 protocol; Section III explores quantum computers and algorithms relevant to perform an attack on PKC; Section IV models the quantum threat on TLS; Section V presents approximate resources for a SNDL attack; Section VI discuss ways to mitigate the threat; and Section VII is a conclusion.

## II. TLS 1.3 PROTOCOL

TLS is a secure communication protocol, developed throughout the years, with the current version (1.3) defined in RFC 8446 [3]. The protocol is divided in three parts: the handshake protocol, where most of the PKC operations are employed; the record protocol, securing the application data with symmetric encryption; and the alert protocol, responsible for triggering error messages and counter actions. We focus on the TLS 1.3 handshake messages in this section, since this part is vulnerable to attacks on PKC, except for the Post-Handshake Authentication mode. They are detailed below.

- `ClientHello`: the first message, sent by the client, to start the TLS handshake. It includes a random nonce, protocol versions, list of supported cryptographic algorithms, and extensions. Example extensions are: the `keyshare`, used to carry an Eliptic-Curve Diffie-Hellman Exchange (ECDHE) public key, and the `pre_shared_key`, carrying Pre-Shared Key (PSK) labels.
- `ServerHello`: This message contains a random nonce, the negotiated algorithms, and extensions. Depending on the extensions that the client has sent in the `ClientHello`, the server replies accordingly. Again, examples include a `keyshare` containing an ECDHE public key, and the selected PSK label, depending on what the client demanded. After the `ServerHello` is received, the client and server can derive symmetric keys for encrypting their application data.
- Authentication messages: The most common use case is server authentication (see Figure 1), but client authentication, although optional, can be used (see Figure 2). The messages used for certificate-based authentication are:
  - `Certificate`: this message comprises a set of certificate(s) that identifies one TLS peer. Servers

send this message if not authenticating by PSK. Clients can authenticate as well and in the mutual authentication scenarios they also send their certificate with this message type;
  - `CertificateVerify`: this message comprises a digital signature on the TLS handshake transcript. The transcript is a hash of the handshake messages. `CertificateVerify` is sent only if not authenticating by PSK; and
  - `Finished`: concludes the handshake. Both peers send this message for two purposes: integrity check and key confirmation. A `Finished` is an HMAC of the handshake transcript, using keys derived after the KEX (`ClientHello`, `ServerHello`) so that each peer can verify that they have established symmetric keys correctly.
- `EncryptedExtensions`: this message carries additional server parameters as extensions that are not appended to the `ServerHello` because they are sent encrypted to the client.
- `NewSessionTicket`: this optional message is sent by the server for the Session Resumption feature. After establishing a handshake, the server can optionally send this message, which contains the information required to derive a new PSK. The new PSK can be used for resuming the TLS connection (called Session Resumption), avoiding a complete handshake.

It is worthy to note that all handshake messages are encrypted using keys derived from the ECDHE (or PSK) process, except `ClientHello` and `ServerHello`. Depending on the scenario, some messages are used in contrast to others. The scenarios of Authentication in TLS 1.3 handshakes are [3]: Certificate-based, in which either Server-only or Mutual Authentication types are offered; and Pre-shared-key (PSK), either by Session Resumption or Out-Of-Band (OOB) PSK which authenticates the parties for the session.

Figure 1 shows two types of handshake authentication: Certificate-based and PSK-mode (in a session resumption). The first type is more commonly used, such as in a first-time interaction between the peers. In the PSK-mode, no certificates are sent. Normally, the PSK-mode saves communication bandwidth, but it requires a previous handshake to establish the PSK (or an OOB method). Additionally, a PSK allows sending Zero Round Trip Time Resumption (0-RTT) data, which means that application data is sent together with the `ClientHello` but encrypted using a PSK established in a previous handshake (or by OOB). Note that PSK can be used in conjunction to ECDHE, allowing Forward Secrecy (RFC 8446, Section E.1 [3]).

Figure 2 shows the scenarios for client authentication. The server can request the client certificate and corresponding signature within the handshake (Mutual Authentication) or after the handshake, depending on the desired policy. For example, the server can establish the handshake, at its discretion, without client authentication, or abort the connection.

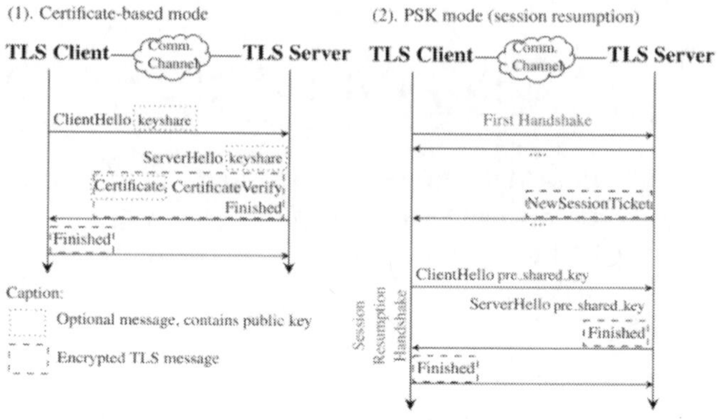


Fig. 1. TLS 1.3 Handshake Authentication types.

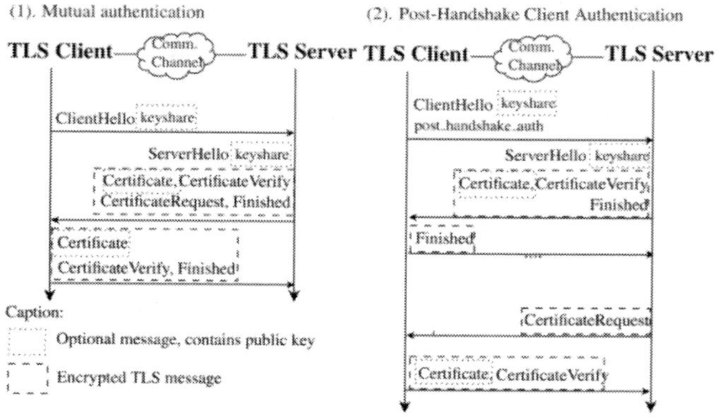


Fig. 2. TLS 1.3 Client Authentication types.

TLS 1.3 implements a key-derivation method called Key Schedule, responsible for deriving and updating encryption keys, and based on the OPTLS protocol [10]. Basically, it takes as input a shared secret after the KEX process and uses a key derivation method to derive new secrets that will then be derived into keying material for encryption. Each type is used for a particular purpose and has different input labels. For example, the keys for encrypting client-to-server are different from the keys used to server-to-client application messages.

## III. Quantum Computer and Algorithms

In general, a QC is a computer that takes advantage of quantum mechanics for its computation. A quantum bit (qubit) is a linear combination of two states — ground and excited, hence represented by $|\psi\rangle = a|0\rangle + b|1\rangle$, being on state 0, on state 1, or in a superposition of both states in its quantum state. After measurement, the qubit's wave function collapses to one of the two states [7][11]. When measuring a qubit, the probabilities of it to collapse to state 0 or state 1 must sum 1, so we say it is normalized, $|a|^2 + |b|^2 = 1$. A quantum register is a physical system containing a set of qubits in sequence. The state of a quantum register is a tensor product of the states of each qubit within: $|q\rangle = |q_1\rangle \otimes |q_0\rangle = c_{00}|00\rangle + c_{01}|01\rangle + c_{10}|10\rangle + c_{11}|11\rangle$ [11].

A circuit model QC uses the initial state of a quantum register as the input (usually a sequence of qubits in the ground state). Then, a number of gates (G) are applied to the quantum register to perform a computational step. After a sequence of computational steps is finished, the result is measured as the output. When the last gate is applied, the quantum register goes to state $|q_n\rangle = G^n |q_{n-1}\rangle$ [11].

Another model of quantum computation is quantum annealing or adiabatic quantum computing. This type of computation is very suitable for optimization (minimization) problems of a cost function. It functions by preparing an initial quantum register in equal superposition of all configurations. Then an adiabatically slow time evolution of the state is applied, changing the system to a final Hamiltonian, from which the solution can be extracted [12][13].

In quantum cryptanalysis, the most discussed algorithm is Shor's algorithm. A period finding algorithm that provides an exponential speedup for solving factorization and DLP based problems [7][14] with some newer implementations extending its usability to ECDLP [15][16]. However, there are some challenges in implementing it. The most economic implementation of Shor's algorithm requires $2n + 1$ qubits and roughly $n^3 \log n$ gates to factorize an n-bits long number [17]. It means the most economic implementation of Shor's algorithm in terms of the number of qubits will require 4097 stable qubits and billions of gates to break a 2048-bits Rivest-Shamir-Adleman (RSA) key, still far beyond the current IBM's 433-qubits universal QC Osprey. And even the 4158-qubits QC IBM has plans to release in 2025 [18] will not be enough due to errors, what can be mitigated executing the calculations multiple times or combining circa 1568 noisy qubits into each perfect logical qubit [19]. Another thing to consider is the gate time, which depends on the technology used. On average, a superconductor QC has a gate time of 25 ns, one built on neutral atoms has a gate time of 19 $\mu$s, and one built on trapped ions has a gate time of 32 $\mu$s [20]. It is clear that the key length to decrypt does change the final execution time by raising the number of gates. If the execution time is longer than the coherence time of the qubits, it will not be able to complete the algorithm.

There are also implementations of factoring algorithms using adiabatic QC that presented good results [21][22][23], and implementations to solve the discrete logarithm problem using adiabatic QC as well [24]. Table I, adapted from [14][17][25], shows some of the best achievements in factoring RSA public keys for quantum computers.

TABLE I. Achievements in factoring RSA public keys.

| Year | Key Length | Algorithm |
|---|---|---|
| 2001 | 4 bits | Shor |
| 2012 | 5 bits | Shor |
| 2012 | 16 bits | Adiabatic |
| 2016 | 18 bits | Adiabatic |
| 2018 | 19 bits | Adiabatic |
| 2019 | 20 bits | Adiabatic |
| 2020 | 41 bits | Adiabatic |

## IV. Threat Model and Attack Scenarios

We hereby use the terms "pre-quantum era" for the era we are now, when quantum computers are still not powerful enough for an effective break on cryptography, and "post-quantum era" for the time after t, when the quantum computers will be already an effective threat. Following the idea of [25], it is possible to name a few quantum threat actors. For a better modeling, it is necessary to subdivide the post-quantum era in three:

- **Initial post-quantum era**: QCs are slow, gate times are high, and coherence times are low. Only a few qubits are available. The cost to perform an attack is high, and the skill level necessary is also high.
- **Intermediate post-quantum era**: The quantum hardware, price, and skill level to perform an attack are at an intermediate stage.
- **Advanced post-quantum era**: The QC is fully established and available. The cost to perform and attack is low and the wide range of algorithms, frameworks, and libraries available make the skill level necessary for an attack much lower.

The threat actors can also be further divided according to the total resources available for an attack, in terms of money and number of personnel. Governments and large organizations play the biggest threat here, followed by hacker groups and small organizations, and an individual playing the smallest threat. Each one of the threat actors also have a certain skill level (3, 2, 1, or no threat) on applying quantum algorithms on cryptographic scheme and other skills relevant for a security attack. Table II correlates threat actors and skill levels to the respective post-quantum era at which they become a threat. From the table, it is clear to see that threat actors with more available resources and skill level become a threat earlier.

TABLE II. Correlating threat actors and its skills to post-quantum era.

| Available Resources | Skill Level | Becomes a Threat at Which Post-Quantum Era? |
|---|---|---|
| Governments and Large Organizations | 3 | Initial |
| | 2 | Intermediate |
| | 1 | Advanced |
| Hacker Groups and Small Organizations | 3 | Intermediate |
| | 2 | Advanced |
| | 1 | $\infty$ |
| Individuals | 3 | Advanced |
| | 2 | $\infty$ |
| | 1 | $\infty$ |

For a prediction of the time t, which is the threshold from the pre-quantum to the post-quantum era, a big number of the respondents in [8] came up with 15 years or less as the time we have left within the pre-quantum era. So, it is plausible to think that the post-quantum era will begin before 2038.

Two main capabilities of a quantum attacker on TLS are impersonation and breaking confidentiality. Impersonation is the capability a threat actor has to authenticate as another client or as another server; and breaking confidentiality means the threat actor is able to read confidential messages. The attacker can also perform the attack in two different ways: passive, listening to the network channel; and active, modifying the communication. With this in mind, impersonation will always be an active attack, whilst breaking confidentiality can be both.

A quantum attack on TLS 1.3 should follow these steps to break confidentiality, on each one of the handshake types (Figures 1 and 2):

- **Certificate-based (server)**:
  1) collect `Client` and `ServerHello` (CH and SH, respectively), extracting the public keys $epk_{CH}$ and $epk_{SH}$ present in `keyshare` messages;
  2) use Shor's algorithm for ECDLP to break the KEX: it computes the private key from $epk_{ch}$ or $epk_{sh}$ in order to recover the ephemeral private key; and
  3) use the recovered ephemeral key to derive the symmetrical keys, using the TLS Key Schedule [3] (Section 7), allowing to decrypt the whole communication.
- **Mutual Authentication**: same as previous.
- **Post-Handshake Auth.**: same as previous.
- **PSK-based resumption**:
  1) use the steps 1-3 above on the First Handshake (right part of Figure 2);
  2) use the recovered ephemeral key to derive the symmetrical keys used throughout the communication;
  3) decrypt the `NewSessionTicket` message, recovering the ticket information (such as nonces and labels);
  4) use the recovered information to derive the resumption PSK; and
  5) use the PSK to derive the second handshake's (Session Resumption) symmetrical keys, allowing to violate confidentiality of the resumed connection.

To achieve impersonation, a quantum attacker has to follow these steps:

- **Certificate-Based (server)**:
  1) collect `Client` and `ServerHello`, extracting the public keys $epk_{CH}$ and $epk_{SH}$ present in `keyshare` messages;
  2) use Shor's algorithm for ECDLP to break the KEX: it computes the private key from $epk_{ch}$ or $epk_{sh}$ in order to recover the ephemeral private key;
  3) use one of the recovered private keys to derive the symmetrical keys, using the TLS Key Schedule [3] (Section 7), and then decrypt the authentication messages (which contains `Certificate`, `CertificateVerify`, and `Finished`); and
  4) use one of the alternatives to attack the `Certificate` message and return the certificate private key:
     - use Shor's algorithm or adiabatic QC to solve the factorization problem on the RSA public key; or
     - use Shor for ECDLP on the public key based on elliptic curves.
- **Mutual Authentication**: same as for server authentication mode, but the attacker can choose to impersonate server or client. The main difference is the target `Certificate` message (from the server or client).
- **Post-Handshake Auth.**: impersonate the server is similar to the previous modes, but to impersonate client:
  1) check the presence of `post_handshake_auth` extension;
  2) use the steps 1-2 of the Certificate-based authentication (server);
  3) decrypt the communication using the recovered symmetric keys, searching for the `CertificateRequest` message; and
  4) use one of the alternatives to attack the client's `Certificate` message and return the private key:
     - solve the factorization problem with Shor's algorithm or adiabatic QC; or
     - use Shor for ECDLP instead.
- **PSK-based resumption**: similar steps as used for server authentication mode, but the steps should be applied to the First Handshake. Having the PSK information, the attacker can impersonate both peers. However, PSKs duration time can be limited up to 7 days [3], so, the attack window is limited.

Applying these methods to impersonate a client, the threat actor can pretend to be another person to the server, getting access to confidential information. Impersonating the server makes a client or a set of clients think they are sending data to a trustworthy server, who is receiving confidential data from the users. When the threat actor applies these methods to break confidentiality, it is possible that the attacker only listens to the communication channel or actively communicate to the other side, in both ways, causing harm to the victim.

## V. Resources for a SNDL Attack

If the threat actor decides to store packets now to decrypt in the post-quantum era, the attacker will face the problem of storing days, weeks, months, or years of information. Table III brings expected storage cost for SNDL attacks against some of the most accesses websites worldwide. The packets were collected with Wireshark using the URL's IP address as a filter, filtering all the connection between a logged user and the server, simulating a man in the middle attack.

TABLE III. Estimating the SNDL storage requirements.

| Site | 1 h of captured packets (MB) | Expected Storage Cost for 24 h (GB) | Expected Storage Cost for 1 y (TB) |
|---|---|---|---|
| instagram.com | 835.4 | 19.6 | 7 |
| youtube.com | 723.7 | 17 | 6 |
| amazon.com | 272.6 | 6.4 | 2.3 |
| gmail.com | 124.8 | 2.9 | 1 |

As it is possible to infer, SNDL attacks require a large amount of storage, depending on the nature of the content to be captured, the timespan of the capture, and the number of victims. Table III considers the attack against a single victim, for more victims the expected value is multiplied by the number of victims. E.g., to store 1 y of packets from 200 GMail users the necessary storage would be $200 \times 1$ TB =

200 TB; and from Amazon users the storage would be 200 × 2.3 TB = 460 TB. Of course this number cannot be exact, due to different navigation profiles, but it is approximate.

## VI. Mitigation and Discussion

Quantum cryptography is the use of quantum physics to create a different class of cryptography. The simplest example is the use of quantum superposition in order to provide a perfectly random number, but the most common example in this class is the Quantum Key Distribution (QKD) [25][26]. The most known QKD protocol is BB84 [27], but there are many others, as can be found on [28].

- **Pros of implementing QKD**:
  - the mathematics of quantum mechanics guarantees the key exchange is perfectly secure; and
  - the no-copy property of quantum mechanics ensures there will be no man-in-the-middle attack, because a measurement of the system would modify it.
- **Cons of implementing QKD**:
  - the no-copy property makes it impossible to re-rout or broadcast a qubit, making it necessary to develop special network channels and hardware for QKD;
  - it is affected by decoherence and longer travels might be impossible. Most of the current QKD systems do not allow travels further than 200 km [28]; and
  - implementation cost immensely for large networks. Making it a viable solution only for limited use cases.

Post-Quantum Cryptography (PQC) rely on mathematics running on classical devices that are not easily solvable by a QC. NIST announced in 2022 four PQC algorithms promised to be quantum-safe: CRYSTALS-Kyber [29], a key-encapsulation mechanism that can be used to establish symmetric keys for TLS or other protocols; CRYSTALS-Dilithium [30], a digital signature algorithm; Falcon [31], another method for digital signatures; and SPHINCS+ [32], a hash-based digital signature algorithm. There is also the Open Quantum Safe Project, an open-source project created to evaluate PQC candidates and to prototype their use in protocols like TLS 1.3 [33].

- **Pros of implementing PQC**:
  - a more viable solution for KEX than QKD; and
  - there are also implementations for digital signatures.
- **Cons of implementing PQC**:
  - PQC algorithms have been tested for years, but it is still impossible to tell for how long they will remain unbreakable [28]; and
  - most of the existent PQC algorithms are slower or require larger keys than the most common classical algorithms for KEX or digital signature, impacting in slower page loads and a risk of packet loss.

There are also hybrid implementations that combine a pre-quantum cryptography with a post-quantum one. To exemplify, a hybrid KEX scheme can be achieved by combining the output of a pre-quantum algorithm and a post-quantum one with an XOR operation. An example of how it could be applied in TLS 1.3 can be found at [34]. For the case of a hybrid digital signature, it is possible to create two signatures, one with a pre-quantum algorithm and another with a post-quantum one [35].

Some newer implementations also tackle the problem by using Post-Quantum Key-Encapsulation Mechanisms (PQKEM) [36] or lattice-based cryptography [37].

Other than the previous presented alternatives, there are approaches that are not a definitive solution, but can make the attacker give up on the attack by diminishing the return or raising the investment. From Section 3, it is possible to infer that the key length influences both the number of gates and the number of qubits needed for decryption, also, each gate consumes a certain amount of processing time. The number of qubits and the processing time can raise the attack cost, and further, a very long key may make the attack time longer than the coherence time, turning the attack impractical. E.g., using a QC to break RSA would be impractical if the key length is 8 KB [38].

The Extended Triple Diffie-Hellman (X3DH) key agreement protocol [39], present in the Signal protocol, provide multiple key exchanges in parallel, what can drive up the attack requirements, since the QC ought to be used for each encryption layer. Other algorithms like this, that add new encryption layers, might be a good idea, or tunneling a TLS connection to another encrypted Virtual Private Network (VPN) [25].

Diminishing the attack return can be achieved by diminishing the amount of data recovered on each attack, making it necessary to perform the same attack multiple times or conforming to have limited information extracted. Security controls such as Perfect Forward Secrecy (PFS) and Post Compromise Security (PCS) can limit the attacker's access to information [25]. Other examples are the Double Ratchet key management algorithm [40] also present in the Signal protocol, and short-term certificates like the one present in the ACME protocol [41]. Short-term certificates are a good mitigation due to the short attack window available to both break the certificate's algorithm and, consequently, impersonate.

SNDL attacks are more urgent, since malicious individuals might be storing information now to decrypt later. A way for an organization to decide a good moment to migrate to quantum safe cryptography is given by [8]. Also, the company has to be aware of social engineering attacks, because, as Table III portrayed, the amount of storage necessary for SNDL attacks is huge, and the threat actor may use social engineering to better filter which packets on which specific date to collect.

## VII. Conclusion and Future Work

This paper exposed the threat of QC on TLS 1.3, presenting: existing quantum algorithms for an attack against PKC, and achievements on practical implementations of these algorithms; detailed steps to perform a quantum attack against the PKC in different TLS 1.3 handshake modes; approximate storage requirements for a practical SNDL attack; existing and new mitigation methods to avoid such attacks.

Section III brought different implementations of Shor's algorithm and adiabatic alternatives, but no adiabatic implementation for the ECDLP were found. As showed in Section III, the adiabatic implementations are outperforming on the factorization, and not having an adiabatic alternative for the ECDLP can delay the threat to TLS in some years.

Section IV exposed threat actors and the steps necessary to attack PKC in TLS 1.3. From Section VI, KEX can be done securely with QKD, at the cost of a large investment and research, making PQC and hybrid solutions a more viable way to achieve KEX and digital signatures, however, at the cost of losing performance. Section VI also presented more immediate forms of mitigation that can be implemented before changing drastically the TLS 1.3 infrastructure.

SNDL attacks are a more immediate threat, but, as Section V showed, they require a huge amount of storage. As a sidenote: it is important to notice SNDL is a threat not limited to the advent of QC, since technology naturally evolves.

Future work to complement this one can be done by studying different attacks against TLS 1.3.

## References


[1] C.-I. Chan, R. Fontugne, K. Cho, and S. Goto, "Monitoring tls adoption using backbone and edge traffic," in: IEEE INFOCOM 2018-IEEE Conference on Computer Communications Workshops (INFOCOM WKSHPS), IEEE, 2018, pp. 208–213.

[2] D. Sikeridis, P. Kampanakis, and M. Devetsikiotis, "Post-quantum authentication in tls 1.3: a performance study," Proceedings of the Network and Distributed Systems Security (NDSS) Symposium, 2020.

[3] E. Rescorla, "The transport layer security (tls) protocol version 1.3," RFC 8446, August 2018.

[4] P. W. Shor, "Algorithms for quantum computation: discrete logarithms and factoring," in: Proceedings 35th annual symposium on foundations of computer science, IEEE, pp. 124–134, 1994.

[5] J.-P. Aumasson, "The impact of quantum computing on cryptography," Computer Fraud & Security, 2017.

[6] L. K. Grover, "A fast quantum mechanical algorithm for database search," in: Proceedings of the twenty-eighth annual ACM symposium on Theory of computing, pp. 212–219, 1996.

[7] V. Mavroeidis, K. Vishi, M. D. Zych, and A. Jøsang, "The impact of quantum computing on present cryptography," unpublished.

[8] M. Mosca and M. Piani, "Quantum threat timeline report 2022," Global Risk Institute, Toronto, ON.

[9] G. Mone, "The quantum threat," Communications of the ACM, 2020.

[10] H. Krawczyk and H. Wee, "The optls protocol and tls 1.3," in: 2016 IEEE European Symposium on Security and Privacy (EuroS&P), IEEE, pp. 81–96, 2016.

[11] P. I. Hagouel and I. G. Karafyllidis, "Quantum computers: Registers, gates and algorithms," in: 2012 28th International Conference on Microelectronics Proceedings, IEEE, pp. 15–21, 2012.

[12] C. R. Laumann, R. Moessner, A. Scardicchio, and S. L. Sondhi, "Quantum annealing: The fastest route to quantum computation?," The European Physical Journal Special Topics, 2015.

[13] S. Yarkoni, E. Raponi, T. Bäck, and S. Schmitt, "Quantum annealing for industry applications: Introduction and review," Reports on Progress in Physics, 2022.

[14] A. Petrenko, Applied Quantum Cryptanalysis, CRC Press, 2023.

[15] J. Proos and C. Zalka, "Shor's discrete logarithm quantum algorithm for elliptic curves," unpublished.

[16] D. Maslov, J. Mathew, D. Cheung, and D. K. Pradhan, "An O($m^2$)-depth quantum algorithm for the elliptic curve discrete logarithm problem over gf $(2^m)^a$," Quantum Information & Computation, 2009.

[17] J. Suo, L. Wang, S. Yang, W. Zheng, and J. Zhang, "Quantum algorithms for typical hard problems: a perspective of cryptanalysis," Quantum Information Processing, 2020.

[18] C. Q. Choi, "Ibm's quantum leap: The company will take quantum tech past the 1,000-qubit mark in 2023," IEEE Spectrum, 2023.

[19] C. Gidney and M. Ekerå, "How to factor 2048 bit rsa integers in 8 hours using 20 million noisy qubits," Quantum, 2021.

[20] M. Suchara, A. Faruque, C.-Y. Lai, G. Paz, F. T. Chong, and J. Kubiatowicz, "Comparing the overhead of topological and concatenated quantum error correction," unpublished.

[21] Z. Li, N. S. Dattani, X. Chen, X. Liu, H. Wang, R. Tanburn, H. Chen, X. Peng, and J. Du, "High-fidelity adiabatic quantum computation using the intrinsic hamiltonian of a spin system: Application to the experimental factorization of 291311," unpublished.

[22] S. Jiang, K. A. Britt, A. J. McCaskey, T. S. Humble, and S. Kais, "Quantum annealing for prime factorization," Scientific reports, 2018.

[23] W. Peng, B. Wang, F. Hu, Y. Wang, X. Fang, X. Chen, and C. Wang, "Factoring larger integers with fewer qubits via quantum annealing with optimized parameters," SCIENCE CHINA Physics, Mechanics & Astronomy, 2019.

[24] M. Wroński, "Practical solving of discrete logarithm problem over prime fields using quantum annealing," in: Computational Science–ICCS 2022: 22nd International Conference, London, UK, June 21–23, 2022, Proceedings, Part IV, Springer, pp. 93–106, 2022.

[25] T. Runge, "Dismantling the quantum threat," Ph.D. thesis, Technische Hochschule Brandenburg, 2023.

[26] V. Padamvathi, B. V. Vardhan, and A. Krishna, "Quantum cryptography and quantum key distribution protocols: a survey," in: 2016 IEEE 6th International Conference on Advanced Computing (IACC), IEEE, pp. 556–56, 20162.

[27] G. Brassard and C. H. Bennett, "Quantum cryptography: Public key distribution and coin tossing," in: International conference on computers, systems and signal processing, pp. 175–179, 1984.

[28] G. Xu, J. Mao, E. Sakk, and S. P. Wang, "An overview of quantum-safe approaches: Quantum key distribution and post-quantum cryptography," in: 2023 57th Annual Conference on Information Sciences and Systems (CISS), IEEE, pp. 1–6, 2023.

[29] J. Bos, L. Ducas, E. Kiltz, T. Lepoint, V. Lyubashevsky, J. M. Schanck, P. Schwabe, G. Seiler, and D. Stehlé, "Crystals-kyber: a cca-secure module-lattice-based kem," in: 2018 IEEE European Symposium on Security and Privacy (EuroS&P), IEEE, pp. 353–367, 2018.

[30] L. Ducas, E. Kiltz, T. Lepoint, V. Lyubashevsky, P. Schwabe, G. Seiler, and D. Stehlé, "Crystals-dilithium: A lattice-based digital signature scheme, IACR Transactions on Cryptographic Hardware and Embedded Systems," 2018.

[31] P.-A. Fouque, J. Hoffstein, P. Kirchner, V. Lyubashevsky, T. Pornin, T. Prest, T. Ricosset, G. Seiler, W. Whyte, Z. Zhang, et al., "Falcon: Fast-fourier lattice-based compact signatures over ntru," Submission to the NIST's post-quantum cryptography standardization process, 2019.

[32] D. J. Bernstein, A. Hülsing, S. Kölbl, R. Niederhagen, J. Rijneveld, and P. Schwabe, "The sphincs+ signature framework," in: Proceedings of the 2019 ACM SIGSAC conference on computer and communications security, pp. 2129–2146, 2019.

[33] D. Stebila and M. Mosca, "Post-quantum key exchange for the internet and the open quantum safe project," in: International Conference on Selected Areas in Cryptography, Springer, pp. 14–37, 2016.

[34] D. Stebila, S. Fluhrer, and S. Gueron, "Hybrid key exchange in TLS 1.3," Internet-Draft draft-ietf-tls-hybrid-design-06, Internet Engineering Task Force, work in progress, February 2023.

[35] W. Beullens, J.-P. D'Anvers, A. T. Hülsing, T. Lange, L. Panny, C. de Saint Guilhem, and N. P. Smart, "Post-quantum cryptography: Current state and quantum mitigation," Tech. rep., Eindhoven University of Technology, 2021.

[36] P. Schwabe, D. Stebila, and T. Wiggers, "Post-quantum tls without handshake signatures," in: Proceedings of the 2020 ACM SIGSAC Conference on Computer and Communications Security, p. 1461–1480, 2020.

[37] J. W. Bos, C. Costello, M. Naehrig, and D. Stebila, "Post-quantum key exchange for the tls protocol from the ring learning with errors problem," in: 2015 IEEE Symposium on Security and Privacy, pp. 553–570, 2015.

[38] K. Li and Q.-y. Cai, "Practical security of rsa against ntc-architecture quantum computing attacks," International Journal of Theoretical Physics, 2021.

[39] M. Marlinspike and T. Perrin, "The x3dh key agreement protocol," Open Whisper Systems, 2016.

[40] T. Perrin and M. Marlinspike, "The double ratchet algorithm," GitHub wiki, 2016.

[41] Y. Sheffer, D. Lopez, O. G. de Dios, A. Pastor, and T. Fossati, "Support for short-term, automatically renewed (star) certificates in the automated certificate management environment (acme)," RFC 8739.

# Long-Distance Remote Diagnostics for Cyber-Physical System Security

## A Preliminary Investigation into Remote Security Assessments for Maintenance Testing

Kazutaka Matsuzaki
Faculty of Global Informatics
Chuo University
Tokyo, Japan
email: matsuzaki@tamacc.chuo-u.ac.jp

Masatoshi Enomoto
Faculty of Commerce
Yokohama College of Commerce
Kanagawa, Japan
email: masatoshi-e@shodai.ac.jp

Kenji Sawada
iPERC
The University of Electro-Communications
Tokyo, Japan
email: knj.sawada@uec.ac.jp

***Abstract*— This extended abstract introduces an initial application of long-distance remote security diagnostics for Cyber-Physical Systems (CPS), focusing on Industrial Control Systems (ICS) during maintenance testing. Through the Internet, a distance of 350 kilometers was bridged to conduct a preliminary security assessment of a building automation system. Emphasizing the importance of monitoring essential functions of ICS, such as digital outputs and serial communication, we utilized a pair of devices designed to encapsulate digital outputs using TCP/IP, enabling remote monitoring at the test device over a temporally configured site-to-site Virtual Private Network (VPN). Despite an average network latency of 33 milliseconds and an approximate delay of around 3 seconds for digital outputs, the system was able to effectively communicate changes in the essential services of the control systems to the test device. Preliminary results underline the feasibility of this long-distance approach, setting the stage for future work on comprehensive real-world demonstrations using diverse simulated control systems, namely factory automation and gas plant control systems. The goal is to advance the field of remote security diagnostics during maintenance testing, providing reliable and effective security evaluation of CPS.**

***Keywordss-Industrial Control Systems (ICS); Remote Security Diagnostics; Maintenance Testing.***

## I. INTRODUCTION

As society increasingly relies on Cyber-Physical Systems (CPS) in sectors such as distributed solar power plants, cloud-based building management, and smart factories, the inherent cyber risks and potential disruptions multiply. A successful cyberattack on CPS can cause significant damage in both digital and physical realms, rendering critical infrastructures like pipelines, water treatment facilities, and power grids vulnerable to shutdowns and disruptions.

In an environment where new vulnerabilities are continuously discovered and cyber attackers' tactics constantly evolve, it is crucial to persistently assess cybersecurity measures. Existing security evaluation frameworks include certification tests for control systems and embedded devices, focusing on known vulnerabilities and communication robustness. However, executing such tests on systems under operation is fraught with challenges due to time, workforce, and cost constraints [1].

This extended abstract discusses the potential of remote, network-based testing as an alternative strategy for enhancing cybersecurity in CPS. We delve into a cloud-based diagnostic approach designed to minimize on-site testing while providing a practical assessment of the security posture of these systems [2].

The primary focus of this extended abstract is to establish whether the distance between testing and target sites impacts the efficacy of remote security diagnostics during the maintenance testing of Industrial Control Systems (ICS), according to IEC 62443 standards. A key challenge we seek to address is determining how remote testing conditions can simulate Local Area Network (LAN) testing conditions, despite significant physical distances between systems.

The rest of the extended abstract is organized as follows: Section 2 provides an overview of the proposed methodology for remote security diagnostics, while Section 3 presents an analysis of our initial findings. Section 4 discusses potential implications, and Section 5 concludes.

## II. METHODOLOGY

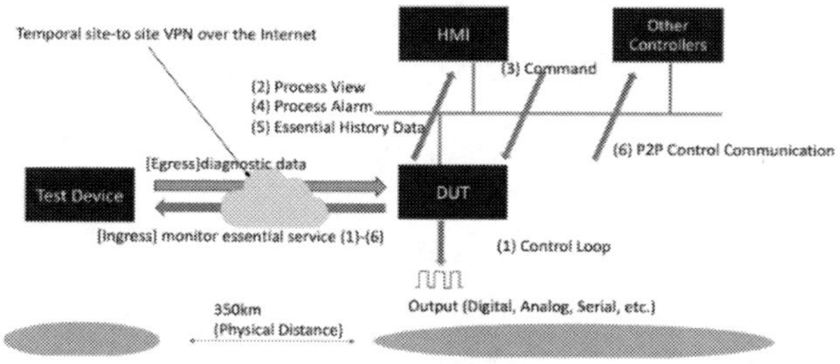


Figure 1. Whole Picture of Remote Security Diagnosis for ICS.

In our study, we designed and executed a series of tests utilizing a practical testbed with the following characteristics (Figure 1):

**Physical distance from the Test Device:** The target systems were located 350 kilometers away from the Test Device. This considerable physical distance provides a realistic scenario for assessing the capability of remote diagnostics during the maintenance of ICS.

**Temporal site-to-site VPN over the Internet**: The test environment temporally utilized an Internet-based Virtual

Private Network (VPN) for communication between the Test Device and the target systems.

**Diverse Simulated Control Systems:** The subjects of our security diagnostics were different types of simulated control systems, each using varied control protocols and implemented using different control devices. These systems were:

- Building Automation System: This system controls elements such as air conditioning, lighting, and electricity reception in a building.
- Factory Automation System: This system simulates a section of a robotic arm in an automobile assembly factory, specifically one that sorts parts.
- Gas Plant Control System: This system controls the pressure in gas tanks to maintain consistency.

The diversity of these systems provides a comprehensive testing ground to evaluate our remote diagnostic approach across various operational conditions and requirements. The results from these tests provide insights into the efficacy of remote security diagnostics during maintenance testing and can inform future development in this field.

## III. Implementation and Preliminary Results

In the implementation phase of our study, we first set up the necessary equipment for our testing environment. This included a pair of devices designed to encapsulate digital outputs using TCP/IP and enable Ethernet-based remote monitoring of distant equipment, bridging the physical gap of 350 kilometers (Figure 2) [3]. These devices were placed at both the test device and the Device Under Test (DUT), a Programmable Logic Controller (PLC) of the building automation system, in our preliminary testing.

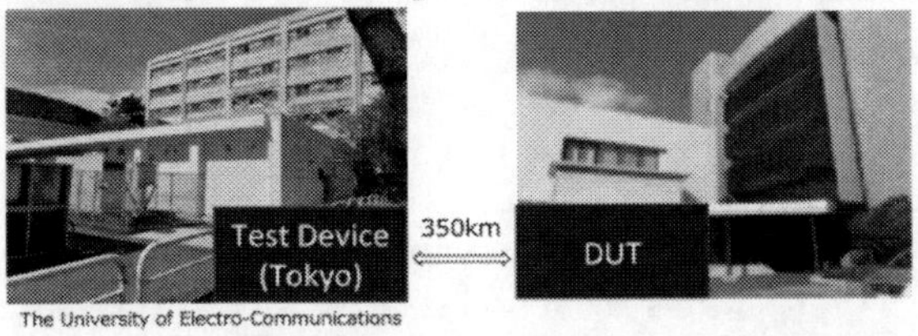


Figure 2. Two buildings to run long-distance remote diagnostics trials.

Once the setup was complete, we conducted preliminary testing by sending diagnostic data from the test device to the DUT and remotely monitoring the state of the building automation system's essential services from the test device as closely as possible. Notably, this was achieved despite the inherent latency in our network setup, characterized by an average network latency of 33 milliseconds (ICMP: Internet Control Message Protocol) and a delay of around 3 seconds for digital outputs (DO over TCP/IP).

Our preliminary results showed that the proposed system effectively conveyed changes in the essential services of the control systems to the test device, even in the presence of notable network latency and digital output delay. The tests demonstrated that the method could consistently deliver changes to the test device from the remote building automation system, fulfilling its goal of reliable remote security diagnostics.

## IV. Future Work

We will extend the remote diagnostic methodology developed and tested preliminarily on a building automation system to other control systems, specifically factory automation and gas plant control systems. This diversity will provide a more comprehensive view of the applicability and efficacy of our methodology across different industrial scenarios.

Firstly, we will refine our approach to remote monitoring of essential services. Essential services, which include communication between DUT, Human-Machine Interfaces (HMI), and other controllers, are integral to the functioning of control systems. It is, therefore, crucial to ensure the reliability and accuracy of their remote monitoring, despite the inherent challenges posed by the physical distance and consequent latency. To achieve this, we will continue optimizing the systems for encapsulating digital outputs and transferring data over temporal site-to-site VPN.

Furthermore, we will investigate the impact of the 350 kilometers distance, particularly the associated network latency and digital output delay, on the quality of the remote diagnostics. Our preliminary results have shown that the proposed methodology can reliably deliver changes in the essential services to the test device from a remote building automation system. However, a more in-depth understanding of how the inherent latency affects the quality of diagnostics is crucial. This analysis will aid in refining the methodology for optimal performance even over long distances.

## V. Conclusion

In this extended abstract, we have presented an initial application of remote diagnostics over a long-distance network for the security evaluation of CPS. Our preliminary results, based on a building automation system situated 350 kilometers away, demonstrate the feasibility of this approach. We have highlighted the importance of reliable data transfer and effective monitoring of essential services, even in the presence of inherent network latency. The future research will continue to refine this methodology, exploring the impacts of long distance on diagnostic quality across different control systems.

## References

[1] K. Matsuzaki and S. Honiden, "Enhancing ICS Security Diagnostics with Pseudo-Greybox Fuzzing During Maintenance Testing," in Proceedings of the 18th International Conference on Software Technologies (ICSOFT 2023) pp. 660-667.

[2] M. Enomoto, K. Sawada, S. Hosokawa, and K. Matsuzaki, "Prototype Experimental Environment Using Actual Equipment for Remote Control Security Verification," IEEE 12th Global Conference on Consumer Electronics (GCCE 2023).

[3] K. Matsuzaki, K. Sawada, and S. Honiden, "Remote Security Assessment for Cyber-Physical Systems: Adapting Design Patterns for Enhanced Diagnosis," in Proceedings of the 20th International Conference on Security and Cryptography (SECRYPT 2023) pp. 805-812

# Coordination of Controllers and Switches in Software Defined Networks (SDN) for Multiple Controllers

Stavroula Lalou
*Department of Digital Systems*
*University of Piraeus*
Piraeus, Greece
slalou@unipi.gr

Georgios Spathoulas
*Dept. of Inform. Sec. and Comm. Techn.*
*NTNU*
Gjøvik, Norway
georgios.spathoulas@ntnu.no

Sokratis Katsikas
*Dept. of Inform. Sec. and Comm. Techn.*
*NTNU*
Gjøvik, Norway
sokratis.katsikas@ntnu.no

***Abstract*—Coordination of the workload among distributed SDN controllers is critical role for both the network performance and the control plane scalability. Therefore, various load balancing techniques were proposed for SDN to efficiently utilize the control plane's resources. However, such techniques suffer from increased latency and packet loss that come as the result of load migration requirements and intensive communication between the SDN controllers. The proposed system adopts OpenFlow mechanism and introduces a new system that offers coordination, synchronization and stable performance.**

***Index Terms*—*Software Defined Networks, multiple controllers, coordination, load balancing.***

## I. Introduction

SDN aims to offer easier management and faster through dynamically customizing the operation of a network through the use of the combination of a centralized controller and programmable network devices. When SDN is deployed in large-scale networks, they may consist of multiple controllers or different administrative vendors. Hence, how multiple controllers and switches coordinate is a critical issue. OpenFlow [1], is one of the mostly representative protocol for SDN, carries the message between an SDN controller and the underlying network infrastructure. One of the most fundamental features of the OpenFlow protocol is the "packet-in" message. If a packet arrived at a OpenFlow based switch does not match any forwarding rule, the packet can be configured as the "packet-in" message to be forwarded to the controller for corresponding policing processing. The use of multiple controllers is an approach that offers greater availability but it also introduces a new problem regarding the coordination between multiple controllers and switches. Insufficient coordination may result in sub optimal network performance. In large data centers, the traffic patterns are usually unpredictable due to elastic resources and flexible services. For example, if the switch to controller map-ping configuration is static, some switches can generate a larger number of packet-in messages than other switches of the network. This condition implies that the corresponding controller, which these switches are mapped to will become overloaded, while other controllers will remain under-utilized. On the other hand, in multi-controller SDN [7] each controller is responsible for a set of switches (domain). A controller can be master, equal, or slave, where the first two types can process the flow requests from the switches and install the forwarding rules in the switches. A slave controller can only read the switch flow table, but cannot update it. Each switch can have multiple equal and slave controllers, but only one master controller. Furthermore, a master controller for a specific switch can be slave controller for another one, and whenever a master controller fails, a slave or local controller can request (via OpenFlow role-request message) to become the new master of the affected switches. The multi-controller paradigm is shown to improve many aspects of SDN, but it presents many challenges, especially for controllers' utilization when switch-controller assignments are static. The load of a controller is mainly caused by the processing of the packet-in messages sent from the switches, and due to network dynamics, the number of these messages vary both regionally and temporally. As a result of these variations, some controllers will be over committed , while some others will be underutilized. This leads to domain failure (and multi-domain failure), or network under utilization. The coordination among controllers is a major issue with several protocols proposed thus far [2]. OpenDaylight [3] [4] and ONOS, two state-of-the-art controller implementations, rely on RAFT and Anti-entropy protocols for disseminating coordination messages among controllers. Each controller is responsible fora part of the network only, commonly referred to as the controller's domain. The messages disseminated by a controller to the other controllers convey its view on the state of its domain (e.g., available links and installed flows). The composition of these messages allows the controllers to synchronize and agree on the state of the entire network. Also the authors of [5] proposed a load re balancing method based on switch migration mechanism for clustered controllers. They also using the OpenFlow 1. 3.. The multiple controllers use JGroups to coordinate actions for switch migration. The whole network is divided into several groups and each group has a controller cluster set up. In this paper we will discuss the available mechanisms that offer multiple controller coordination and network synchronization. To address this problem, we propose a scalable and crash-tolerant load balancing based on controller switch connection for multiple OpenFlow controllers. The contribution of this paper is:

- A dynamic coordination and synchronization system among SDN controllers and switches that focus particularly on the impact of the rate of synchronization on the performance of network.
- A system that can dynamically shift the load across multiple controllers through switches.
- A controller fail-over without switch disconnection avoiding the single point of failure problem.

The remaining of the paper is structured as follows: In Section II, we briefly review necessary background knowledge on SDN and on the RAFT consensus algorithm. In Section III, we discuss related work. In Section IV, we present our proposal for coordination of the workload among distributed SDN controllers. In Section V, we present the experimental setup that we used for evaluating the performance of the proposal and we discuss the results. Finally, section VI summarizes our conclusions.

## II. BACKGROUND

### A. OpenFlow Protocol

The OpenFlow architecture consists of numerous pieces of OpenFlow-enabled switching equipment which are managed by one or more OpenFlow controllers, as shown in Figure 1. It depicts the fundamental concept of the SDN architecture [2]. Network traffic can be partitioned into flows, where a flow could be a Transmission Control Protocol (TCP) connection, packets with the same MAC address or IP address, packets with the same Virtual Local Area Network (VLAN) tag, or packets arriving from the same switch port [6].

An OpenFlow switch contains multiple flow and group tables. Each flow table consists of many flow entries. These are specific to a particular flow and are used to perform packet look-up and forwarding. The flow entries can be manipulated as desired through OpenFlow messages exchanged between the switch and the controller on a secure channel. By maintaining a flow table, the switch can make forwarding decisions for incoming packets by a simple look-up on its flow- table entries. Open-Flow switches perform an exact match check on specific fields of the incoming packets. For every incoming packet, the switch goes through its flow table to find a matching entry. The flow tables are sequentially numbered. The packet-processing pipeline always starts at the first flow table. The packet is first matched against the entries of a flow table. If the packet matches a flow entry in a flow table, the corresponding instruction set is executed. Instructions associated with each flow entry describe packet forwarding, packet modification, group table processing, and pipeline processing [6].

Pipeline-processing instructions enable packets to be sent to subsequent tables for further processing and enable aggregated information (metadata) to be communicated between tables. Flow entries may also forward to a port. This is usually a physical port, but may also be a virtual port [6]. Flow entries may also point to a group, which specifies additional processing. A group table consisting of group entries offers additional methods of forwarding (multicast, broadcast, fast reroute, link aggregation, etc.). A group entry consists of a group identifier, a group type, counters, and a list of action buckets, where each action bucket contains a set of actions to be executed and associated parameters. Groups also enable multiple flows to be forwarded to a single identifier, e.g., IP forwarding to a common next hop. [6].

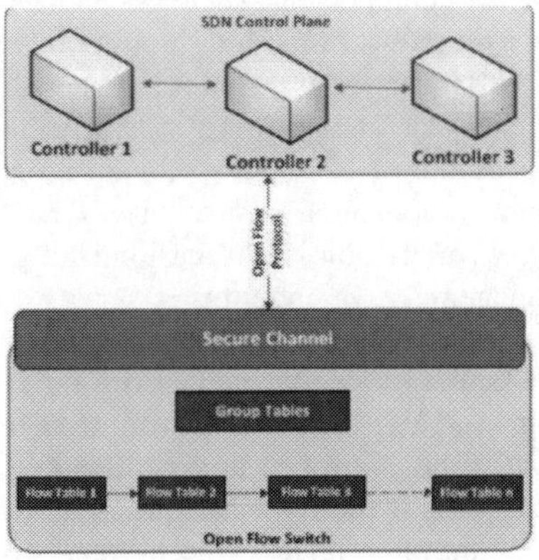


Fig. 1. Software Defined Networking.

### B. Connection Strategy

The first issue is to address the switch-to-controller connection strategy and how switches are connected to SDN controllers. In early OpenFlow version, switches can only attach to one controller. Furthermore, that link is static, meaning that operators have to configure the switch manually when it needs to attach to a new controller. A distributed SDN controllers setup, on the other hand, requires a dynamic connection between switches to controllers. The dynamic connection enables to move a switch from one controller to another controller during a fail-over or load balancing process. Fortunately, there are two options to deploy such flexible switch to controller connection, using the IP alias connection or OpenFlow Master/Slave connection.

In the Master state, the controller has full access to the switch as in the Equal role. When the controller changes its role to Master, the switch changes the other controller in the Master role to have the Slave role. The role change does not affect controllers with the Equal role. The controller receives from switch asynchronous Port- status messages. The controller can send Asynchronous- Configuration messages to set the asynchronous message types it wants to receive. An OpenFlow instance can connect to one or more controllers, depending on the controller connection mode the OpenFlow instance uses ether Single instance in which the OpenFlow instance connects to only one controller at a time. When communication with the current controller fails, the OpenFlow instance uses another controller, or the Multiple instances so it can simultaneously connect to multiple controllers. When communication with any controller fails, the OpenFlow instance attempts to reconnect to the controller after a reconnection interval [6].

## III. Related Work

Distributed SDN controller deployments require a coordination protocol among controllers. To address the coordination, synchronization and performance challenge different systems and approaches have been introduced. ONOS [4] stands for Open Network Operating System, uses RAFT, and provides the control plane for a software-defined network (SDN). It manages network components, such as switches and links, and runs software programs or modules to provide communication services to end hosts and neighboring networks. The most important benefit of an operating system is that it provides a useful and usable platform for software programs designed for a particular application or use case. ONOS applications and use cases often consist of customized communication routing, management, or monitoring services for soft-ware-defined networks. Some examples of things which you can do with ONOS, and software written to run on ONOS, may be found in Apps and Use Cases [4]. Devoflow [7] actually reduce the overhead of the control plane by offloading the controller by delegating some work to the forwarding devices and enable a cluster of controller nodes to achieve distributed control plane. Onix [9], Kandoo [10], and HyperFlow [11] use this approach to achieve a control planewith high scalability and reliability. ElastiCon [12] supports for elasticbehaviorwhichincreases or decreases the number of controllers based on load estimates of control plane. The "Doing It Fast And Easy" (DIFANE) [13] approach examines the scalability issues that arise with OpenFlow in large networks and with many fine-grained flow entries. Scalability concerns can be classified by (1) the number of flow entries inside the switches and (2) the load on the controller that is caused whenmany flows have tobe installed simultaneously. DIFANE installs all forwarding information in the fast path, i.e., in TCAM, in a few selected switches, called "authority switches". This is achieved by wildcard match fields and the intelligent distribution of flow table entries on the authority switches. The other switches forward traffic that cannot be resolved by their own flow table towards authority switches. The authors show the applicability of DIFANE in large networks by evaluating their proposal on various metrics, such as the number of required TCAM entries, packet loss caused by failures, etc.

Some recent works propose to reduce the overhead of control traffic by strategically placing the controllers in the network [14] or by finding the appropriate forwarding paths for loadbalancing on control traffic. Eventual consistency, where the controllers coordinate periodically rather than on demand basis, is another way to reduce control overheads. Levin et al. [15] showed that certain network applications, like load-balancers, can work around eventual consistency and still deliver acceptable performance. This would require some additional effort to be made to ensure that conflicts such as for-warding loops, black holes and reachability violation are avoided. The authors [14] studied the problem of finding the optimal synchronization rates among controllers in a distributed eventually-consistent SDN system. They considered two different objectives, namely, (i) the maximization of the number of controller pairs that are consistent, and (ii) the maximization of the performance of applications which may be affected by the synchronization decisions, as highlighted by emulations on a commercial SDN controller.

## IV. Our proposal

The proposed system implements a novel network of multiple controllers using RAFT consensus algorithm to maintain stability, scalability, and consistency, it was presented in a prior work [18]. In this paper we extend our approach using features from Open-Flow connection methods. It is based in Master/ Slave connection between controllers and switches. It supports the connection and coordination of multiple distributed SDN controllers to serve as backup controllers in case of a failure. According to our experiments the load conditions of controllers, our proposed method can dynamically shift the load across the multiple controllers. Moreover, multiple controllers allow data load sharing when a single controller is overwhelmed with numerous flow requests. In general, our approach can reduce latency, increase scalability, and fault tolerance, and provide enhanced availability in SDN deployments.

### A. Implementation

The proposed mechanism, consists of multiple SDN controllers that collaborate to manage the network. Each controller is responsible for a subset of switches in the network. Controllers communicate with each other using a coordination and synchronization mechanism. Controllers exchange their load information with other controllers in the network. We use a consensus-based coordination and synchronization mechanism. Each controller registers with the coordination service and participates in the distributed coordination protocol. The coordination service maintains a shared state, such as network topology information and controller assignments.

Controllers periodically synchronize their local state with the shared state in the coordination service. This synchronization is achieved by employing a combination of data replication, using flow tables. When a controller joins or leaves the system, the coordination service notifies other controllers to update their view of the network and redistribute the load if necessary.

Load balancing across controllers can be achieved through dynamic redistribution of switches and their associated flows. Controllers use load balancing algorithms based on factors like controller workload, switch capacity, and network traffic patterns. When load balancing decisions are made, controllers negotiate and transfer the ownership of switches and their flows based on the new load distribution. To handle controller failures, a fail-over mechanism is necessary. When a controller fails, the coordination service detects the failure and triggers a fail-over process. The fail-over process involves selecting a new controller to take over the responsibilities of the failed controller. The new controller establishes connections with the switches managed by the failed controller, ensuring a seamless transition without disrupting network operations.

Controllers use a standard protocol, the OpenFlow, to communicate with the switches and exchange network control messages. The coordination and synchronization mechanism discussed above enables controllers to exchange coordination messages to maintain consistency and distribute control responsibilities.

### B. Load Balancing

Controllers exchange their load information with other controllers in the network. The Controller Election Process is been implemented in the controller election process using the OpenFlow protocol. The controllers negotiate and decide which controller will be the master and which will be the backup using protocols, such as OpenFlow's Role Request message.

Each controller monitors its own load using metrics such as CPU utilization, memory usage, or the number of active flows. The load information is periodically updated and maintained by each controller, its record. Each controller compares its load metric with the load metrics received from other controllers. The comparison helps identify the least loaded controller among the available options. If the controller determines that it is the least loaded based on the load comparison, it continues to handle incoming traffic as usual. If the controller determines that another controller has a lower load, it takes appropriate actions for load balancing. The load balancing decisions can be implemented by modifying the flow table entries in the switches, redirecting traffic to the appropriate controllers based on the load balancing algorithm. The SDN controllers use the OpenFlow protocol to install, update, or remove flow rules dynamically to achieve load balancing.

When a new request arrives at a switch, the switch forwards the request to its designated controller. The OpenFlow protocol allows switches to direct incoming packets to a specific controller based on rules defined in the flow tables. Configure the flow tables in the switches to match and forward the incoming requests to the appropriate controller based on load balancing policies.

Each switch maintains the load information received from the controllers it is connected to. The switch compares the load information of the connected controllers. Based on the comparison, the switch selects the least loaded controller as the destination for incoming requests.By leveraging the capabilities of the OpenFlow protocol, the switch can make informed decisions about which controller to forward incoming requests to, ensuring load balancing among the controllers in the SDN system.

To implement load balancing, packet fields, such as source IP address, destination IP address, transport protocol are record in the flow table entries to direct packets to the desired controller. We use the OpenFlow protocol to set the flow action in the flow rules of the switches:

- output action: Specify the output port of the switch to forward the traffic to the desired controller.
- controller action: Direct the traffic to the controller by specifying the action to send the packet to the controller's port.

Load information from the controllers can be periodically collected and used to determine the least loaded controller. Based on this dynamic load information, the flow tables are updated to reflect the current load balancing requirements. Depending on the dynamic nature of the load balancing, the flow rules may need to be updated periodically or in response to load changes. The SDN controller can monitor the load, collect load information, and make appropriate updates to the flow rules as needed.This can be done by sending OpenFlow messages to the switches to modify or add flow rules.

## V. Performance Evaluation

### A. Experimental Setup

A simulation has been conducted to assess the performance of the proposed scheme. The system on which the simulation was executed was based on an VM with Ubuntu 22.04 OS, 16 GB of memory and OpenFlow Switches. We evaluated the performance of our system in terms of load balancing in terms of response time, throughput, packet lost, delay and the time overhead imposed by the controllers and switches to coordinate. The coordination performance and scalability between controllers, switches and hosts also have been depicted according to the scenario of routing several packets that are successfully routed (without traversing any failed link) to their destinations. We emulate the performance using Mininet and Ryu [17]component-based software defined networking framework. Ryu [17] provides software components with well defined API that make it easy for developers to create new network management and control applications. and created a topology of 10 SDN controllers, consisting of one master controller and nine SDN controllers, along with 20 switches.

- Master Controller:Controller M
- SDN Controllers: Controller C1, Controller C2, Controller C3, Controller C4, Controller C5, Controller C6, Controller C7, Controller C8, Controller C9
- Switches 1-20: S1, S2, S3, S4, S5, S6, S7, S8, S9, S10, S11, S12, S13, S14, S15, S16, S17, S18, S19, S20

Initially, it distributes switches evenly among the client controllers. Master Controller M does not handle any switches directly. Each controller can handle up to three switches. We have assigned an initial load distribution of switches to controllers. Controller C1: S1, S2, S3; Controller C2: S4, S5, S6; and so on. We have set initial metric values for each controller ( CPU utilization, memory usage, number of active flows) based on the simulation scenarios.Periodically collect metrics from each controller and switch and update the metric values based on the simulated workload and network conditions.

Calculates a score for each controller based on the weighted metrics. Assigns appropriate weights to each metric based on their importance and impact on load balancing decisions. Computes the score for each controller using the weighted sum of the metrics. Then identifies the controller with the highest score as the "over loaded" controller and the one with the lowest score as the "under loaded" controller. Defines a threshold value to determine when a controller is considered overloaded or under loaded. If the score difference between the overloaded and under loaded controllers exceeds the threshold, initiate load redistribution. Determines a subset of switches to be transferred from the overloaded controller to the underloaded controller. For example, if Controller C1 is overloaded and Controller C2 is under loaded, it can transfer S1 and S2 from Controller C1 to Controller C2. It updates the flow tables of the affected switches to redirect traffic to the under loaded controller. The under loaded controller assumes control of the transferred switches and their associated flows. According to the Master/slave constraint the switch can be controlled by more than one SDN controllers but only one master controller at time. Therefore, we chose Mininet, which emulates a network of software-based virtual OpenFlow switch as our experimental testbed. Each controller is connected to the other controllers and the available switches. Each controller can handle up to 3 switches, which are used as the traffic generator to initiate UDP flows to any other host in the network. The performance of routing application is determined by the number of packets that are successfully routed to their destinations. We emulate the performance for three different scenarios of workload to test the controllers coordination and the management of the switch. Our system shifts dynamically the load across the switches and the controllers. We simulated three different workloads to stress controllers through adjusting the flow rate. For the first scenario we sent 1000 packets in a time of 100ms, for the second 2000pps and for the third we flood the network to see how it performs and how the nodes coordinate under heavy load. The simulation results are shown in Table 1 and Figure 2.

TABLE I
NETWORK PERFORMANCE PACKETS SEND PER SECOND

| packets | Average Time in ms | Packet loss |
|---|---|---|
| Workload A- 1000 | 0.041 | 1.2 % |
| Workload B- 2000 | 0.049 | 3 % |
| Workload C-5000 | 0.060 | 3.5 % |

Also, we tested the communication between all nodes of the network for a time duration of 100 sec, as in a OpenFlow network the controller response time directly affects the flow completion times. We evaluated the average response time at 0.041 ms, for sending packets throughout the network. The performance of routing application is determined by the number of packets that are successfully routed (without traversing any failed link) to their destinations. To analyze the load balancing algorithm, we simulated different network scenarios and workload conditions. Vary the weights assigned to different metrics and observed the resulting load distribution among controllers.

We emulate the performance for three different scenarios where all the controller synchronize at the same rate equal to (i) 0.041ms (ii)0.049 ms, (iii)0.060 ms, (messages per second) and the results are depicted in Figure 4.

We used iperf [16] to evaluate and plot the mean throughput with varying workloads as illustrated in Figure 2. We perform additional emulations to test the performance of a load balancing application. The switches generate flows uniformly at random. The flows can be routed and queued to any of the 10 controllers. Each controller is aware of the load of each one of them manages. We can ensure that this is the least loaded server, since the controllers are synchronized at all times.

### B. Results

During the tests we compared the proposed system to another system that is also based on OpenFlow switch connections [5], in terms of response time and throughput. Our approach exhibits shorter response times when transferring packets over the network comparing to the system that was previously introduced in [5]. To evaluate and plot the mean throughput of the proposed system we compared it with [5] with varying workloads as illustrated in Figure 4. In proposed method, as the figure shows, when the system is under heavy load it is steady and it needs 0.041 ms of average time to send all the packets, while in [5] it needs 0.3 ms for the first workload test and increases as the the packet requests increase.

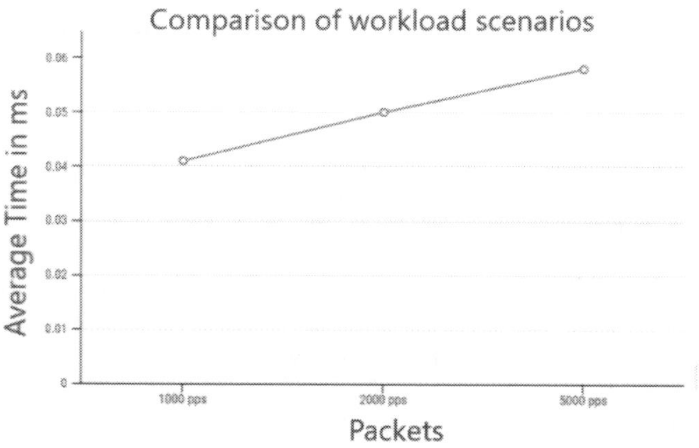


Fig. 2. Basic packet forwarding with OpenFlow in a switch.

In a OpenFlow network where flow entry setup is performed reactively, the controller response time directly affects the flow completion times. We evaluate the response time of the systems by hping command. As Figure 4 shows, the workload significantly affected response time. Comparing the response time in [5], it increases marginally up under workload B and goes up higher under workload C. That is because once the packet interval rate exceeded the capacity of the controller, queuing causes response time to shoot up. Finally, we measure the the time overhead caused by assigning roles to the switches

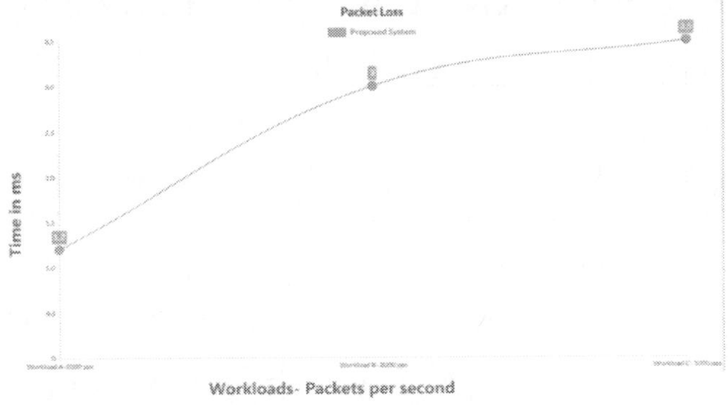


Fig. 3. Packet loss

and the cost of switch migration process in the compared system [5]. We observe the migration process takes about 2ms under workload A and increases as the. The failover process takes about an average of 20ms, which mostly affected by the failure detection based on heartbeat messages provided by JGroups. In our proposed system, the average required time for assigning Master role to a controller node is 10,06 ms.

We also tested the packet loss. We define the delay to have a normal distribution, which provides a more realistic emulation of networks. As a result, all packets leaving the controller C1 on its interface C1-eth0 will experience delay time which is normally distributed between the range of 10ms ± 20ms, we have consider this delay due to the master election. Also NETEM permits user to specify a distribution that describes how delays vary in the network.

Usually delays are not uniform, so it may be convenient to use a non-uniform distribution such as normal. For this test, we specified a normal distribution for the delay in the emulated network. In a network, packets may be lost during transmission due to factors such as bit errors and network congestion. The rate of packets that are lost is often measured as a percentage of lost packets with respect to the number of sent packets. The results indicated that there was a small and stable packet loss starting with 1.2% up to 3.5 % and almost all packets were received successfully.

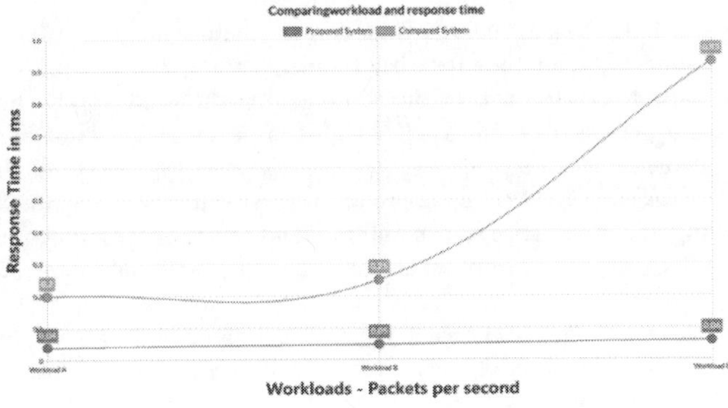


Fig. 4. Comparingworkload and response time.

## VI. Conclusion

SDN aims to simplify network architecture and makes it possible to build programmable and agile flexible networks. According to the experimental results that were presented, the proposed system can efficiently coordinate and synchronize the controllers and switches of the network in stable and low time, thus ensuring good performance at all times irrespective of the traffic dynamics. Also, it supports high- throughput, fault-tolerance, and controller synchronization. The result of evaluation showed that our method can improve the communication of all network nodes and improve the throughput and response time of control plane. It can maintain system coordination and network stability and the average response time in all workload tests are low.

## Acknowledgement

This work has been partly supported by the University of Piraeus Research Center.

## References

[1] "Open Networking Foundation." , https://opennetworking.org (Retrieved July 2023).
[2] Y. E. Oktian, S. Lee, H. Lee, and J. Lam, "Distributed SDN controller system: A survey on design choice," Computer Networks, vol. 121, no. 5, pp. 100–111, Jul. 2017, doi: https://doi.org/10.1016/j.comnet.2017.04.038.
[3] "OpenDayLight", https://www.opendaylight.org (Retrieved July 2023).
[4] P. Berde et al., "ONOS," Proceedings of the third workshop on Hot topics in software defined networking, Aug. 2014, doi: https://doi.org/10.1145/2620728.2620744.
[5] L. Chu, et al. "Scalable and Crash-Tolerant Load Balancing Based on Switch Migration for Multiple," 2014.
[6] OpenFlow Switch Consortium, https://opennetworking.org/?s=openflow (Retrieved July 2023).
[7] A. R. Curtis, et al., "DevoFlow," ACM SIGCOMM Computer Communication Review, vol. 41, no. 4, pp. 254–265, Oct. 2011, doi: https://doi.org/10.1145/2043164.2018466.
[8] V. Yazici, M. S. "Controlling a software-defined network via distributed controllers", 2014.
[9] R. Y. Shtykh and T. Suzuki, "Distributed Data Stream Processing with Onix," in IEEE International Conference on Big Data and Cloud Computing (BdCloud), IEEE, 2014.
[10] S. Yeganeh and Y. Ganjali, "Kandoo: a framework for efficient and scalable offloading of control applications," Semantic Scholar, 2012.
[11] A. Tootoonchian and Y. Ganjali, "HyperFlow: a distributed control plane for OpenFlow", in Proceedings of the 2010 internet network management conference on Research on enterprise networking (INM/WREN'10), USENIX Association, USA, 2010.
[12] A. Dixit, F. Hao, S. Mukherjee, T. V. Lakshman, and R. Kompella, "Towards an elastic distributed SDN controller," ACM SIGCOMM Computer Communication Review, vol. 43, no. 4, pp. 7–12, Aug. 2013, doi: https://doi.org/10.1145/2534169.2491193.
[13] M. Yu, J. Rexford, et al. "Scalable Flow-Based Networking with DIFANE," ACM SIGCOMM Comput. Commun. Rev., pp. 351–362, 2010.
[14] K. Poularakis, et al. Learning the Optimal Synchronization Rates in. arXiv:1901.08936v1 [cs.NI], 2019.
[15] D. Levin, A. Wundsam, B. Heller, N. Handigol, and A. Feldmann, "Logically centralized?," Proceedings of the first workshop on Hot topics in software defined networks, Aug. 2012, doi: https://doi.org/10.1145/2342441.2342443.
[16] "Iperf." http://iperf.sourceforge.net (Retrieved July 2023).
[17] "Ryu omponent-based software,"https://ryu-sdn.org/ (Retrieved July 2023).
[18] S. Lalou, et al. "Efficient Consensus Between Multiple Controllers in Software Defined Networks (SDN)," in The Sixteenth International Conference on Emerging Security Information, Systems and Technologies, IARIA, pp. 35–40, 2022.

# Leveraging Attack Graphs in Automotive Threat Analysis and Risk Assessment

Mera Nizam-Edden Saulaiman
*BioTech Research Center, EKIK,*
*Óbuda University*
Budapest, Hungary
Email:Mera.Abbassi@stud.uni-obuda.hu

Miklos Kozlovszky
*BioTech Research Center, EKIK,*
*Óbuda University*
Budapest, Hungary
Email:kozlovszky.Miklos@nik.uni-obuda.hu

Ákos Csilling
*Academic Relations*
*Robert Bosch Kft.*
Budapest, Hungary
Email:Akos.Csilling@hu.bosch.com

***Abstract*—With the increase in complexity of automotive network systems and the shift towards connected vehicles, cyber threats are constantly evolving, creating the need for advanced methodologies to assess and mitigate these threats and ensure the security of these systems. The ISO/SAE 21434 standard defines the Threat Analysis and Risk Assessment (TARA) methodology as a key activity for analyzing and assessing cybersecurity risks for a defined automotive system. In this paper, we introduce a Graph-based Attack Path Prioritization Tool (GAPP), which aims to introduce the concept of automation and address the limitations of manual TARA. GAPP automates the generation of attack paths, calculates the feasibility of each path, and identifies the most feasible attack paths within automotive networks. By providing a more dynamic, comprehensive, and automated means of analyzing network security, our approach aims to enhance TARA and offers a promising avenue for future research and development in the field of automotive cybersecurity.**

***Index Terms*—TARA, threat and risk analysis, automotive network, connected vehicles**

## I. INTRODUCTION

In recent years, the automotive industry has witnessed a significant technological shift towards smart and connected vehicles that connect multiple embedded computers to form a complex advanced network [12].

The ISO/SAE 21434 standard [1] provides the technical basis for the cybersecurity engineering process of Electrical and Electronic (E \E) road vehicles and the requirements for cybersecurity management in the automotive industry. TARA is a core part of the security engineering process, which involves executing a comprehensive analysis, entailing the calculation of impact and attack feasibility values, leading to the derivation of the associated risk metrics. By implementing TARA, the automotive industry can proactively predict and identify potential security threats and vulnerabilities during the design phase, prioritize security measures, and ensure the safety and integrity of modern vehicles in the face of evolving cyber threats.

In our previous paper [8], we reviewed open-source attack analysis methodologies and frameworks from the IT domain and mapped their concepts to the automotive domain, highlighting that TARA is presently executed through manual effort by cybersecurity experts, a practice that has several inherent limitations and requires a significant amount of time and effort [9]. In [2] we proposed a generic model for automating the analysis and generation of attack paths within the TARA process. The objective is to seamlessly integrate this model into the TARA process, enhancing its efficacy in identifying potential threats.

In this study, we introduce the Graph-based Attack Path Prioritization Tool (GAPP), a tailored approach based on graphical modeling, leveraging the TARA methodology in alignment with the ISO/SAE 21434 standard. GAPP is designed to address security challenges specific to automotive systems with the primary objective of automating the generation of attack paths within a predefined network. By automating the analysis of attack paths and feasibility ratings, we utilize input data defined manually and employ an algorithm to calculate attack paths and their associated feasibility. Consequently, GAPP aims to provide an efficient means of assessing the security of modern automotive systems, capturing correlations between security events, and enabling quantitative reasoning for enhanced risk management in the ever-evolving landscape of automotive networks and connected vehicles.

The remainder of this paper is organized as follows. First, we provide a brief overview of modeling in security analysis in Section II. In Section III, the architecture and components of the GAPP tool are introduced. In Section IV, we conduct a comparative analysis between GAPP's results and the ISO TARA analysis to assess its effectiveness and efficiency. Finally, we conclude the paper and offer insights into future work in Section V.

## II. MODELLING IN SECURITY ANALYSIS

Model-based security assessment methodologies offer a range of techniques for visual understanding and mapping of most likely threats. In threat modeling, different approaches and perspectives are used, which can be classified into three main categories:

**Attacker-based:** This approach revolves around understanding the motivations, capabilities, and strategies of potential attackers. This emphasizes how an attacker might target a system.

**Asset based:** Asset-based threat modeling begins with a focus on the critical assets or resources within a system. It aims to protect these assets by identifying threats that could target them. This is the approach used in TARA.

**Vulnerability-based:** This approach focuses on identifying and addressing vulnerabilities within a system, with a primary focus on weaknesses that could be exploited by attackers.

Furthermore, in terms of the structure, there are two main modelling categories: attack trees, and attack graphs.

**Attack Trees** provide a formal representation of potential attacks within a system [7]. In a hierarchical tree structure, the root represents the ultimate objective of the attacker. The branching paths from the leaves to the root symbolize the diverse strategies that an attacker might employ. [3].

In contrast to the tree structure, **Attack Graphs** are typically represented as Directed Acyclic Graphs (DAG) [6], and focus on vulnerabilities identified within a system. These graphs illustrate the interdependencies among the vulnerabilities of a system, providing a different perspective on system security [4].

With the GAPP methodology, we address a specific situation that often arises in automotive attack modeling. Each attack starts with an initial attack vector, which is one of several external interfaces to the system and continues through any number of internal interfaces connecting various internal subsystems, most often Electrical Control Units (ECUs), or even smaller components, such as firmware or data storage. The ultimate target is one of multiple security assets that require protection. The traditional methodology invites the analyst to draw up a list of all possible attack paths from all possible initial attack vectors to all assets and select those with the highest evaluated feasibility. However, for realistically complex systems, the number of possible combinations makes it practically impossible to perform a thorough analysis, and experts must rely on their expertise to find the most relevant attack paths. In the GAPP approach, the analyst only evaluates the direct attack steps from one subsystem to the next, and needs to consider only those directly connected to an internal interface. We assume that an attacker can combine multiple attacks in any sequence. Therefore, we evaluate all possible combinations that constitute an attack path. Fortunately, this part can be automated, so the construction of the actual paths, the evaluation of their feasibility, and ultimately, the ranking are fully automated using the GAPP tool.

## III. GAPP Structure

The GAPP framework is designed to be easily defined and extendable, accommodating additional aspects that may emerge from various systems or scenarios. We followed the TARA process in ISO/SAE 21434, as discussed in our previous work [2]. The TARA process involves seven steps, each with a defined input and output, as shown in Fig. 1. In our current implementation in this study, GAPP addresses the attack path analysis and the attack feasibility rating steps of TARA, while the risk assessment and defense graph generation are currently out of scope.

The main inputs of GAPP are the list of assets, which become the nodes in the graph, their reachability via direct attack steps from one node to another, which become the edges on the graph, and the feasibility rating for each of these

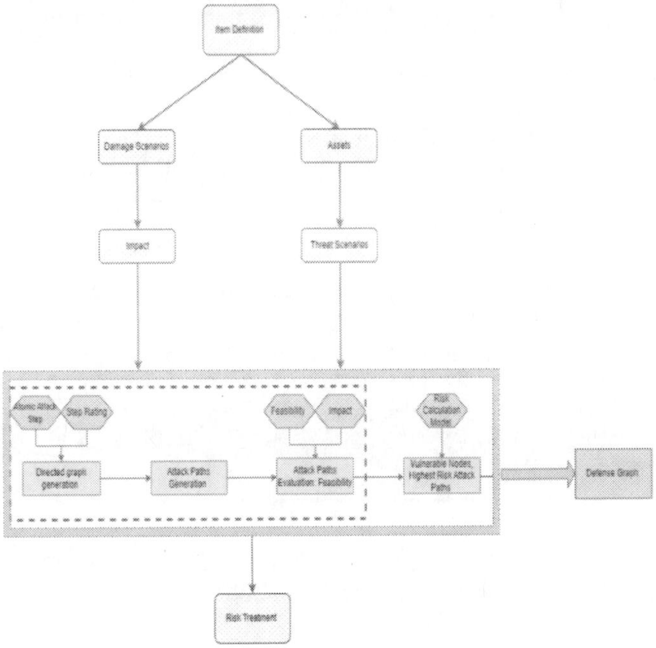


Fig. 1. Integration of the GAPP methodology into the TARA process, our current implementation is highlighted in the red rectangle.

steps, which become weights on the edges. The main output of GAPP is the list of attack paths ranked by the combined feasibility of all steps along the path.

In this section, we explain the essential concepts that serve as the foundation of GAPP and offer insights into the core principles of our methodology.

### A. Attack steps

In the input layer, The GAPP tool primarily relies on the assets, network reachability, and attack steps. Assets are the output of the asset identification step in TARA, and include entities such as functions, data, and components that can affect the system and take part in a damage scenario. These assets are identified in the GAPP as nodes. These nodes are subsequently classified into distinct types: *Input nodes* represent external interfaces or attack entry points. *Internal nodes* are subsystems and components that might get compromised by the attacker. The *end nodes* represent the potentially targeted assets or vehicle functions.

*Reachability* refers to the potential ability of an attacker to traverse from one node to another with a single step. These atomic steps establish the pathways an attacker can take from an entry point (input node) to reach and potentially compromise the targeted assets (end nodes) within the system. The aggregation of these atomic steps from the input nodes to the end nodes signifies the potential routes that an attacker may take to gain control of individual assets.

### B. Feasibility rating

The feasibility calculation is based on the attack potential method from the ISO/IEC 18045 [5], and includes these criteria:

- **Elapsed time:** The duration required for an attacker to exploit the asset.
- **Specialist expertise:** The level of expertise an attacker would need to exploit the asset.
- **Knowledge of the item or component:** The amount of information an attacker would need about the asset to exploit it.
- **Window of opportunity:**The time frame during which an attacker could exploit the asset
- **Equipment:** The tools or resources an attacker would need to exploit the asset.

The ISO/SAE 21434 [1] defines the associated numeric values to the factors discussed previously, as shown in Fig. 2. The attack potential values are mapped to the Attack feasibility rating as shown in Fig. 3.

| Elapsed time | | Specialist expertise | | Knowledge of the item or component | | Window of opportunity | | Equipment | |
|---|---|---|---|---|---|---|---|---|---|
| Enumerate | Value | Enumerate | Value | Enumerate | Value | Enumerate | Value | Enumerate | Value |
| ≤1 day | 0 | Layman | 0 | Public | 0 | Unlimited | 0 | Standard | 0 |
| ≤1 week | 1 | Proficient | 3 | Restricted | 3 | Easy | 1 | Specialized | 4 |
| ≤1 month | 4 | Expert | 6 | Confidential | 7 | Moderate | 4 | Bespoke | 7 |
| ≤6 months | 17 | Multiple experts | 8 | Strictly confidential | 11 | Difficult/ none | 10 | Multiple bespoke | 9 |
| >6 months | 19 | | | | | | | | |

Fig. 2. Attack potential values

| Attack feasibility rating | Values |
|---|---|
| High | 0 - 9 |
| | 10 - 13 |
| Medium | 14 - 19 |
| Low | 20 - 24 |
| Very low | ≥ 25 |

Fig. 3. Attack potential rating

In GAPP, a feasibility assessment is performed at the level of individual attack steps, rather than evaluating the entire attack path in a single assessment. This approach involves a granular examination of feasibility, in which each atomic attack step is individually assessed using a potential-based approach. Subsequently, these individual assessments are used to determine the overall feasibility of the complete attack path.

To calculate the overall feasibility of a path, we followed the maximum approach discussed in [10], in which we selected the maximum value per attack potential along the attack path. This concept has been partially used in the model described in [11].

In the context of the GAPP tool, let $R$ denote the set of all tuples of attack feasibility factors. Function affmax : $R^* \rightarrow R$ represents a function that takes an arbitrary count $k \in \mathbb{N}$ of tuples of attack feasibility factors $r_1, \ldots, r_k$ as input and computes the maximum value for each attack feasibility factor. Specifically, employing an approach based on attack potentials as the attack feasibility factors in GAPP, the computation of affmax$[r_1, \ldots, r_k]$ is expressed as follows:

$$\text{affmax}[r_1, \ldots, r_k] :=$$

$$(\max[v_{1,1}, \ldots, v_{k,1}], \ldots, \max[v_{1,f}, \ldots, v_{k,f}])$$

where $\max[v_{i,j}]$ refers to the maximum value of each attack feasibility factor $j$ across the tuples $r_1, \ldots, r_k$.

### C. Automated attack path generation

By automating this process, GAPP combines the defined atomic steps to construct comprehensive attack paths encompassing all possible communication routes that an attacker may follow. The primary objective of this automation is to eliminate the need for the manual enumeration of attack paths.

The GAPP tool performs two key tasks in its current process:

1) Enumeration of Attack Paths: The tool systematically enumerates all possible combinations of paths that lead from an input node to an asset or compromised function within the system.
2) Feasibility Calculation: GAPP calculates the combined feasibility along each enumerated path. This involves evaluating the feasibility of the individual attack steps and determining their cumulative impact on the overall path.

GAPP is currently implemented in python using standard libraries. So far no integration with other tool frameworks has been done. The principle of operation is described here.

- Directed Weighted Graph Generation: The GAPP tool creates a directed graph by connecting atomic attack steps, representing all possible paths. Entry points accessible to attackers are linked to starting nodes, and assets vulnerable to damage are the end nodes. Edges, including the virtual starting node, are weighted using feasibility ratings.
- Attack Path Analysis: The generated directed weighted graph is further analyzed to calculate the feasibility of each path by considering the weighted attack steps. These paths are computed starting from the starting nodes, leading to a comprehensive set of attack paths throughout the directed attack graph.

## IV. EVALUATION

In this section we present the results of the evaluation of GAPP on the example system delineated in ISO 21434 [1], as this is a publicly available, well known basic example.

### A. The system

The example contains a headlamp system designed to control the headlamp's operation based on the driver's input. In the high-beam mode, the system automatically switches to a low beam when it detects an oncoming vehicle and reverts to a high beam once the vehicle has passed. The system is connected to the gateway ECU, which in turn is linked to the navigation ECU through data communication. The navigation ECU has Bluetooth and cellular external communication interfaces, whereas the gateway ECU has an OBD-II interface. Fig. 4 shows a functional overview of the headlight system. It is assumed that both ECUs have security measures to prevent unauthorized data communication.

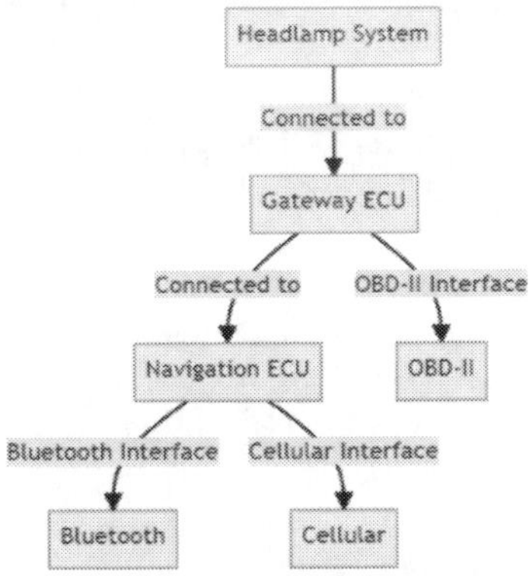


Fig. 4. Functional overview of the headlight system

### B. Assets and damage scenarios

As shown in Fig. 1, the TARA process begins by identifying the assets and their damage scenarios. Assets in this system include data communication for lamp requests and oncoming car information as well as the firmware of the ECUs. Each asset is associated with its respective damage scenario and impact rating, which are out of scope in this study. These assets were then evaluated for the potential threat scenarios.

In the GAPP model, the external interfaces, assets and damage scenarios become the nodes of the graph, as shown in Table I.

TABLE I
GRAPH NODES IN GAPP

| Nodes | Asset | Node type |
|---|---|---|
| Node 1 | Physical access | Input node |
| Nodes 2 | Bluetooth interface | Input node |
| Nodes 3 | Cellular interface | Input node |
| Nodes 4 | OBD port | Input node |
| Nodes 5 | Navigation ECU | Internal Node |
| Nodes 6 | GW ECU | Internal Node |
| Nodes 7 | Data: DOS attack | End Node |
| Nodes 8 | Data: spoofing the signal | End Node |
| Nodes 9 | extract FW | End Node |

### C. Threat scenario and attack path analysis

The threat scenarios were identified for each damage scenario. As seen in Fig. 5 from the ISO standard [1], for each threat scenario, an attack path analysis is conducted to deduce all the possible paths that can lead to realizing the attack scenario.

| Threat scenario | Attack path |
|---|---|
| Spoofing of a signal leads to loss of integrity of the data communication of the "Lamp Request" signal to the power switch actuator ECU, potentially causing the headlamp to turn off unintentionally | i. Attacker compromises navigation ECU from cellular interface.<br>ii. Compromised navigation ECU transmits malicious control signals.<br>iii. Gateway ECU forwards malicious signals to power switch actuator.<br>iv. Malicious signals spoof the lamp request (OFF). |
| | i. Attacker compromises navigation ECU from Bluetooth interface.<br>ii. Compromised navigation ECU transmits malicious control signals.<br>iii. Gateway ECU forwards malicious signals to power switch actuator.<br>iv. Malicious signals spoof the lamp request (OFF). |
| | i. Attacker gets local (see Table G.9) access to OBD connector.<br>ii. Attacker sends malicious control signals from OBD connector.<br>iii. Gateway ECU forwards malicious signals to power switch actuator.<br>iv. Malicious signals spoof the lamp request (OFF). |
| Denial of service of oncoming car information | i. Attacker compromises navigation ECU from cellular interface.<br>ii. Compromised navigation ECU transmits malicious control signals.<br>iii. Gateway ECU forwards malicious signals to power switch actuator.<br>iv. Attacker floods the communication bus with a large number of messages. |
| | i. Attacker attaches a Bluetooth-enabled OBD dongle to OBD connector when vehicle is parking unlocked.<br>ii. Attacker compromises driver's smartphone with Bluetooth interface.<br>iii. Attacker sends message via smartphone and Bluetooth dongle to Gateway ECU.<br>iv. Gateway ECU forwards malicious signals to power switch actuator.<br>v. Attacker floods the communication bus with a large number of messages. |

Fig. 5. ISO Example attack paths for threat scenarios

With the GAPP approach, we only need to identify the individual steps that lead from one node to an other, leading to the attack steps discussed in the next subsection.

### D. Attack steps and feasibility

We have applied the attack potential-based method to assess the feasibility of each atomic step in our attack paths. Table II presents the specific attack steps and their corresponding attack potential. Although this approach may not fully reflect the realistic risk and feasibility, it serves our research purposes and provides a more granular understanding of attack scenarios.

### E. Attack Graph

GAPP generates the directed attack graph as shown in Fig. 6, representing all the possible paths from the attacker entry points that represent the start nodes.

### F. Attack paths

In 7, GAPP utilizes system interconnections to generate distinct attack paths, resulting in 4 paths for the first attack scenario and 4 paths for the second attack scenario. Interactions between steps are considered, and each path is color-coded from start to end, enabling visualization and analysis.

TABLE II
ATTACK STEPS AND ATTACK POTENTIAL IN GAPP

| Attack step | Edge | Attack potential | | | | |
|---|---|---|---|---|---|---|
| | | ET | SE | KoIC | WoO | EQ |
| Compromise OBD through physical access | 1→4 | 1 | 6 | 7 | 10 | 4 |
| Compromise navigation ECU from BLE Interface | 2→5 | 1 | 6 | 5 | 4 | 4 |
| Compromise navigation ECU from cellular interface | 3→5 | 1 | 6 | 5 | 4 | 4 |
| Compromise navigation ECU from OBD Interface | 4→5 | 1 | 6 | 5 | 4 | 4 |
| Compromise the GW to send malicious messages | 5→6 | 1 | 6 | 7 | 4 | 4 |
| Extract FW from GW | 6→9 | 1 | 6 | 11 | 7 | 4 |
| DOS of oncoming car information | 6→7 | 1 | 3 | 7 | 4 | 4 |
| Signal spoof of Headlamp data | 6→8 | 1 | 3 | 7 | 4 | 4 |

TABLE III
ATTACK PATH GAPP

| Attack Path | Max Attack potential | | | | | |
|---|---|---|---|---|---|---|
| | ET | SE | KoIC | WoO | EQ | Rating |
| [1→4→5→6→9] | 1 | 6 | 11 | 10 | 4 | low |
| [1→4→5→6→8] | 1 | 6 | 7 | 10 | 4 | low |
| [1→4→5→6→7] | 1 | 6 | 7 | 10 | 4 | low |
| [2→5 →6 →9] | 1 | 6 | 7 | 4 | 4 | Medium |
| [2→5→6 →8] | 1 | 6 | 7 | 4 | 4 | Medium |
| [2→5 →6 →7] | 1 | 6 | 7 | 4 | 4 | Medium |
| [3→5→6→9] | 1 | 6 | 7 | 4 | 4 | Medium |
| [3→5→6→8] | 1 | 6 | 7 | 4 | 4 | Medium |
| [3→5→6→7] | 1 | 6 | 7 | 4 | 4 | Medium |

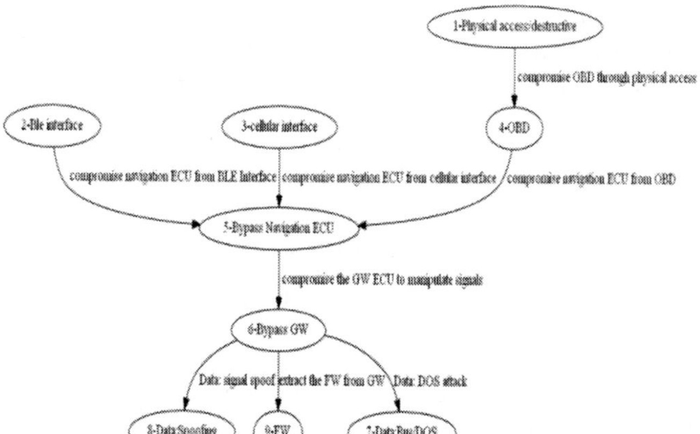


Fig. 6. GAPP Attack graph

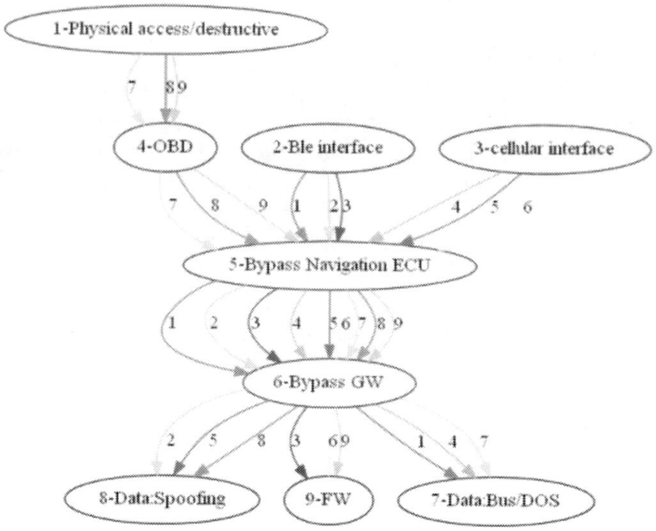


Fig. 7. GAPP attack graph highlighted path

## G. Assessment

Table IV compares the attack paths generated by ISO and GAPP.

The evaluation of the GAPP tool in comparison with the ISO/SAE 21434 [1] standard involves assessing three main categories: attack path identification, feasibility assessment, and coverage and completeness.

In the attack path identification category, we compared the attack paths identified by GAPP to those mentioned in the ISO standard. We analyzed the sequence of steps and nodes involved and identified variations in the attack scenarios or paths in both analyses. GAPP provided more attack paths for each scenario, indicating its ability to capture a more comprehensive range of potential attack routes.

Next, in the feasibility assessment category, we compared the feasibility ratings assigned to the attack paths in GAPP with those provided in the ISO standard. Using averaging for each attack step and the same additional method as in the potential approach, GAPP yielded more accurate data. However, there is room for improvement to further enhance the accuracy. Finally, in the coverage and completeness category, we evaluated the coverage of attack scenarios and paths in GAPP compared to the ISO standard. We found that GAPP successfully covered the entire attack path and scenario, demonstrating its ability to encompass all relevant attack vectors and scenarios mentioned in the standard.

## V. CONCLUSION & FUTURE WORK

The main benefit of our approach and the GAPP tool is to provide scalability for the identification of the most relevant attack paths in large systems. Instead of manually constructing and evaluating all possible paths, the tool only requires the manual evaluation of individual steps. The combination and ranking of these paths is performed by the tool, which provides a list of the highest-ranking attack paths. Security engineers can concentrate on these issues in their TARA.

This is a small step in the full TARA process; nevertheless, the GAPP tool lays the foundation for further advancements in automotive cybersecurity. As an automated and efficient approach to attack path analysis, GAPP opens possibilities for future research and development. Here are some areas of future work to consider.

The current approach uses a crude combination of the feasibility rating of each individual step into a rating for the full path. Future work can focus on refining the feasibility assessment in GAPP by exploring alternative methods for calculating the feasibility values and considering more factors in the assessment process. Today, we recommend to set a wide cut-off value, and evaluate the edge cases in detail. A more refined formula could increase confidence in the evaluation and save effort.

The tool can be enhanced by integrating real-world data and real attack scenarios to provide more accurate and realistic results. In this study we used the publicly available ISO example to provide a comparison with an accepted standard evaluation. While similar studies on real products are surely confidential, a more extensive study could construct a larger imaginary example and provide more data for comparison.

In an industrial environment the GAPP tool would be integrated into the existing TARA framework, and reuse already evaluated attack steps from previous projects.

Enhanced Visualization: Improving the visualization capabilities of GAPP can help users better understand and interpret the generated attack paths and feasibility ratings.

TABLE IV
COMPARISON OF ATTACK PATHS BETWEEN THE MANUAL ANALYSIS IN [1] AND THE AUTOMATIC ANALYSIS WITH THE GAPP MODEL.

| GAPP Attack Path | Feasibility | ISO attack Path | Feasibility |
|---|---|---|---|
| [ 1→4→5→6→8 ] | Low | [ 1→4→5→6→8 ] | Low |
| [ 2→5→6 →8] | Medium | [ 2→5→6 →8] | Medium |
| [ 3→5→6→8] | High | [ 3→5→6→8] | Medium |
| [ 1→4→5→6→7 | Low | [ 1→4→5→6→7] | Low |
| [ 3→5→6→7] | Low | [ 3→5→6→7] | Medium |
| [ 2→5 →6 →7 ] | Medium | none | - |

## REFERENCES


[1] *Road vehicles – Cybersecurity engineering*, ISO/SAE 21434, 2021

[2] M. N. -E. Saulaiman, M. Kozlovszky, A. Banati and Á. Csilling, "Use Cases of Attack Graph in Threat Analysis And Risk Assessment for The Automotive Domain," 2022 IEEE 1st International Conference on Cognitive Mobility (CogMob), Budapest, Hungary, 2022, pp. 000085-000092, doi: 10.1109/CogMob55547.2022.10118297.

[3] V. Saini, Q. Duan, and V. Paruchuri, 'Threat Modeling Using Attack Trees', Journal of Computing Sciences in Colleges, vol. 23, 04 2008.

[4] A. Bánáti, E. Rigó, R. Fleiner and E. Kail, "Use cases of attack graph for SOC optimization purpose," 2022 IEEE 26th International Conference on Intelligent Engineering Systems (INES), Georgioupolis Chania, Greece, 2022, pp. 000143-000148, doi: 10.1109/INES56734.2022.9922617.

[5] Information security, cybersecurity and privacy protection — Evaluation criteria for IT security — Methodology for IT security evaluation, ISO/IEC 18045, 2022, Available: https://standards.iso.org/ittf/PubliclyAvailableStandards/index.html

[6] J. B. Hong, D. S. Kim, C.-J. Chung, and D. Huang, 'A survey on the usability and practical applications of Graphical Security Models', Computer Science Review, vol. 26, pp. 1–16, 2017.

[7] K. Edge, 'A Framework For Analyzing And Mitigating The Vulnerabilities Of Complex Systems Via Attack And Protection Trees', p. 219, 07 2007.

[8] M. N.-E. Saulaiman, M. Kozlovszky, Á. Csilling, A. Banati and A. Benhamida, "Overview of Attack Graph Generation For Automotive Systems," 2022 IEEE 10th Jubilee International Conference on Computational Cybernetics and Cyber-Medical Systems (ICCC), Reykjavík, Iceland, 2022, pp. 000135-000142, doi: 10.1109/ICCC202255925.2022.9922866.

[9] D. Zelle, C. Plappert, R. Rieke, D. Scheuermann, and C. Krauß, 'ThreatSurf: A method for automated Threat Surface assessment in automotive cybersecurity engineering', Microprocessors and Microsystems, vol. 90, p. 104461, 2022.

[10] C. Plappert, D. Zelle, H. Gadacz, R. Rieke, D. Scheuermann, and C. Krauß, 'Attack Surface Assessment for Cybersecurity Engineering in the Automotive Domain', in 2021 29th Euromicro International Conference on Parallel, Distributed and Network-Based Processing (PDP), 2021, pp. 266–275.

[11] D. Angermeier, H. Wester, K. Beilke, G. Hansch, and J. Eichler, 'Security Risk Assessments: Modeling and Risk Level Propagation', ACM Trans. Cyber-Phys. Syst., vol. 7, no. 1, Feb. 2023

[12] Mundhenk, P. "Security for Automotive Electrical/Electronic (E/E) Architectures;" Technical University of Munich: Munich, Germany, 2017.

# Science-Tracker Fingerprinting with Uncertainty: Selected Common Characteristics of Publishers from Network to Application Trackers on the Example of Web, App and Email

Stefan Kiltz, Robert Altschaffel, Jana Dittmann
Faculty of Computer Science.
Otto-von-Guericke University
Magdeburg, Germany
*e-mail: sec-by-design <at> iti.cs.uni-magdeburg.de*

***Abstract*—Science tracking in information systems provided by publishers is a common pattern in today's scientific world. Besides impacting on the privacy of researchers, science tracking can have potentially adverse or even grave consequences for researchers. The comparison of tracking mechanisms employed by publishers can lead to interesting findings about their popularity over time and to better fine-tuned countermeasures. Publisher could also be identified according to the tracking mechanisms employed. Studies concerning user tracking in general and in particular science tracking exist. The approaches considered therein are concerned with detecting whether tracking is employed on the example of Web, App and email. Our goals are to allow a better comparison of publisher tracking as a privacy measurement by also including results from different forensic tools and to get hints/leads to individualize (attribute) science trackers. Towards our goals we introduce a BNF-style expression based Science-Tracking Fingerprint (STF) as semantics to support individualizing a publisher and for privacy measurements generally. Syntactically, a vector consisting of element-value pairs is created. We propose a certainty category as a metric in support of privacy measurement to rank privacy measurements as plausible, uncertain, or non-match. We investigate intra- and inter-application matches per publisher on URL and tracker information of existing and adapted static tools (of-/on-premises). We analyze 4 exemplary chosen science publishers in 3 selected application areas (web, app, email) with 4 known tools for web, 3 known tools for apps and 2 known tools for email. For the latter, we also introduce a self-implemented tool. We show that the STF is, according to our first tests, fit for the purpose of comparing of publisher tracking and to provide hints/leads for individualization of publishers employing science tracking.**

***Keywords-Security, trust and privacy metrics; IT forensics; Attribution.***

## I. Introduction

Science tracking is a common practice [1], [2] impacting the privacy and transparency of data processing of users when working with literature information systems. Apart from the obvious privacy violations, as stated in [3], tracking can put scientists at concrete and grave risk. At least it potentially encourages data misuse and academic espionage and can result in personal discrimination against researchers [1]. To have reliable information on the extent of this impact, techniques from IT-forensics are used [4], mainly because of its carefully designed, measured and systematic approaches. Important for IT-forensics is to have at least an estimate on the levels of error, loss and in particular uncertainty [5], [6]. One of the goals of forensics is to individualize the traces and being able to attribute an entity with a given course of action [7] and thus to extract a characteristic fingerprint (quite literally in the case of crime scene forensics). In related work, other user data tracking studies are concerned with detecting science tracking, in this article, however, the individualization of the tracker (attribution) is addressed to allow also a better comparison of publisher tracking. Also, as a result of the individualization, specific and more effective countermeasures against the specific form of science tracking employed by a publisher can be devised.

Our main contributions in this article are:

- the proposition of a Science-Tracking Fingerprint (STF) as semantics based on a BNF expression with a element-value vector description as syntax to individualize science-trackers in support of attribution and improve comparison of publisher tracking as well as the forensic tools results and generally for privacy measurements,
- the certainty category as a metric in support of privacy measurements describing matches between tools as being plausible, uncertain or non-existent.
- intra- and inter-application area (web, app, email) matching of results of existing tools based for URL and tracker detection,
- inclusion of DNS response based A-Record and CNAME evaluation as part of a dynamic network data stream examination involving 1st and 3rd parties,
- implementation of RA_email_forensic toolbox for a semi-automated email forensic examinations,
- practical privacy measurements on 4 selected publishers on all 3 application areas (web, app, email) totaling 191 comparisons
- both our self implemented open source software RA_email_forensics and our material, which is available as open data, can be requested via email-request towards sec-by-design <at> iti.cs.uni-magdeburg.de.

This article is structured as follows: In Section II the state of the state regarding previous work is discussed. In Section III, the fundamentals regarding the employed forensic model, the existing tools and data sources, and uncertainty in forensic examinations is described.

In Section IV we describe our concept of the semantics and syntax of the Science-Tracking Fingerprint (STF) followed by a tool property comparison. Next we discuss the intra- and inter-application area tool comparison and provide a system landscape analysis. In Section V we describe the implementation of the Science-Tracking Fingerprint (STF) followed by a selected intra-application area matching (web) on the example of one publisher. We provide a Science-Tracking Fingerprint (STF) for 4 selected publishers. In Section VI we perform an evaluation of the findings. The article closes with an conclusion and an outlook on future work in Section VII.

## II. State of the Art

There a number of studies looking into data tracking in general (e.g., [8], [9]). The study done by Hanson [10] looks into the extent of science tracking. These existing studies share the fact that they try to determine to what extent tracking exist on various application fields and elaborate on the consequences of user tracking. One study [4] already employs forensic techniques for the detection of tracking. However, according to our knowledge, no study devised forensically motivated systematic means to give hints/leads to individualize (attribute) tracking to identify an originator. The approach outlined in Section IV is a first attempt at fingerprinting originators of science tracking also for the task of comparing different originators. The authors are fully aware that the suggested approach alone will not suffice for individualization and thus attribution but believe that it can give hints/leads towards further investigation.

## III. Fundamentals

In this section, we provide the prerequisites to comprehend our approach and discuss the need for their advancement. We start with a selection of a specific model of the forensic process, which does not only order steps to be taken during an investigation as many others do, but also locates and describes the data within the examined system and its transformation process.

### A. DCEA forensic process model

To examine science tracking in a systematic way, an accepted course of action is to follow a model-based approach that describes a forensic examination. The model from [6] provides the notion of data streams and forensic data types, which together with forensic methods (represented by capabilities of forensic tools) supports a detailed description of the provenance of the data from the beginning of the examination to its end. This is a seen by the authors as an aid to attribution. The model from [6] distinguishes 3 data streams:

- Mass storage data stream $DS_T$ (time-discrete, low volatility, long-term data retention),
- Main memory data stream $DS_M$ (time-discrete, high volatility, short-term data retention),
- Network data stream $DS_T$ (time-continuous, high volatility, short-term data retention).

Throughout article we will use $DS_T$ and $DS_N$ during our examinations. Those data streams can be further divided into 8 forensic data types with the assumption that data of a specific data type is created, processed, stored and used similarly by a given IT system and thus can be acquired, investigated, analyzed and documented similarly in a forensic examination [6]. For our article we use $DT_3$ (details about data) and $DT_5$ (communication protocol data) in the context of the network data stream and its representation in mass storage.

Of importance is the system landscape analysis as part of a forensic examination [6]. The spatial and temporal intricacies of tool placement and operation define what can be obtained and analyzed. As stated in [4], the usage of on-premises tools allows for finer control over the tool operation and external data (e.g., lists used for comparison against known tracker URLs) and better data access (e.g., regarding intermediate results). In our research we will use both on- and off-premises tools for two way corroboration of the tool results. In Section IV.E we discuss the properties of both approaches with our system landscape analysis.

The existing model-based approach of the forensic examination as described in [6] alone is not sufficient for the individualization (attribution). However, provides us with the elementary building blocks for the fingerprint (e.g., data streams, forensic data types).

### B. Selected tools and data sources for URL and Tracker examination

We select mostly existing tools for the examination of science tracking based on URL and tracker information. These are forensic tools in the sense that they provide relevant forensic information during their operation (similar to the class of methods of the IT-Application, see [6]) but leave the comprehensive documentation and the integrity preservation of the results to the examiner. One exception is the self-implemented *RA_email_forensics* toolbox, which covers the integrity checksum creation and an extensive logging for forensic documentation. This software is available as Open Source per email-request towards sec-by-design <at> iti.cs.uni-magdeburg.de.

Tools can be hosted by a 3rd party (*off-premises*) or operated by the examiners (*on-premises*) and tools can capture a discrete snapshot (*static operation S*) or allow for continuous examinations (*dynamic operation D*). The latter is used to gather DNS information (A-Record, CNAMEs) based on the requests from the local name services and its responses.

For website-based 3rd party URL information ($DT_5$ according to [6]) on the network data stream $DS_N$ we select the *static, off-premises* tools privacyscore [11] and webbkoll [12] and the *static, on-premises* tool website-evidence-collector [13]. Additionally, we use wireshark [14] for the dynamic part of the examination.

For website-based *static* tracker information ($DT_3$ according to [6]) on the network data stream $DS_N$ we use the information also offered by privacyscore [11] and webbkoll [12]. Their results are based on *external data* typically available as lists (e.g., disconnect [15] for webbkoll) and their accuracy thus depends on the accuracy of that list. Naturally, those lists are dynamic in nature (new tracker sites, sites disappearing, etc.). Thus, for repeatability, the date of the respective list and the list itself need to be conserved, otherwise e.g., a tracker might get reported at $t_{i+1}$ but not at $t_i$ (see also [6]).

For Android app-based 3rd party static URL information ($DT_5$ according to [6]) we rely on the mass storage data stream $DS_T$ since as the chosen *on-premises* tools of exodus-standalone [16] and appchecker [17] operate on the apk file based representation of an Android app. Those tools provide only a the subset of URL information that also contains a detected tracker. For appchecker this information is readily available, for exodus we perform a manual lookup using the tracker name at the online list provided by the developers [18] For the *dynamic*, *on-premises* investigation we rely on the network data stream $DS_N$. We use an environment where Android x86 [19] is executed as guest OS on VirtualBox [20] which is running a bridged network with Debian Linux [21] as the host OS. We download the app into the virtualized Android x86 and monitor the connection attempts of the app during startup and idling for 5 minutes using wireshark running on the host and capturing the bridged network. For app-based *static* tracker information ($DT_3$ according to [6]) we again rely on the mass storage data stream $DS_T$ since this information is made automatically available alongside the URL information by exodus-standalone and appchecker.

For email-based *static* 3rd party URL information ($DT_5$ according to [6]) on the mass storage data stream $DS_T$ we examine the emails *on-premises* as a file using the existing emlAnalyzer [22] and the self-implemented RA_email_forensics (see also Section IV.C). For a *dynamic*, *on-premises* URL examination we use wireshark whilst starting the ungoogled chromium browser [23] on a Debian system, both of which are configured for being passive on the network. Simulating an email-client's reaction, we paste the extracted URLs from the static examination and record DNS communication and potential redirections.

For email-based *static* tracker information ($DT_3$ according to [6]) on the storage data stream $DS_T$ we use the RA_email_forensics tool on-premises, which automatically compares the URLs contained in an email against the disconnect list [15]. For email-based *dynamic* tracker information we feed the URLs identified by emlAnalyzer and RA_email_forensics into the ungoogled chromium browser and manually look for phenomena typically employed by trackers (e.g., 1x1 white tracking pixel, mismatch of downloading a gif but returning a webpage, etc.).

The following Table I shows our data sources together with the date and additional information for our 4 selected publishers and 3 application areas (web, app, email). This material is available as Open Data per email-request towards sec-by-design <at> iti.cs.uni-magdeburg.de.

TABLE I. OUR DATA SOURCES WITH DATE AND ADDITIONAL INFORMATION FOR 4 SELECTED PUBLISHERS AND 3 APPLICATION AREAS (WEB, APP, EMAIL)

| Application area | Publisher | Data source | Date | Additional information |
|---|---|---|---|---|
| Web | ACM | https://dl.acm.org | 06/06/23 | due to unavailable 3rd party and tracker detection re-run for privacyscore on 16/06/2023 |
| | Elsevier | https://www.elsevier.com | 06/06/23 | due to unavailable 3rd party and tracker detection re-run for privacyscore on 16/06/2023 |
| | IEEE | https://www.ieee.org | 06/06/23 | due to unavailable 3rd party and tracker detection re-run for privacyscore on 16/06/2023 |
| | SN-MME | https:// www.springernature.com/de/ macmillaneducation | 06/06/23 | due to unavailable 3rd party and tracker detection re-run for privacyscore on 16/06/2023 |
| App | ACM | ACM TechNews V1.4.6 | 31/05/23 12:53 | Store URL: https://play.google.com/store/search?q=ACM%20Technews&c=apps |
| | Elsevier | eReader V8.0.0 | 31/05/23 11:08 | Store URL: https://play.google.com/store/apps/details?id=com.impelsys.elsapac.android.ebookstore |
| | IEEE | MyXplore V4.0.4 | 31/05/23 15:21 | Store URL: https://play.google.com/store/apps/details?id=org.ieee.mobile.pubs.myxplore |
| | SN-MME | Macmillan Education eReader V1.0.8.18 | 01/06/23 09:22 | Store URL: https://play.google.com/store/apps/details?id=com.macmillaneducation.ereader |
| Email | ACM | Subject: Publish Your Work in the ACM Journal on Responsible Computing (JRC) | 29/09/22 16:00 | Sender: "Kenneth R. Fleischmann, ACM JRC Editor-in-Chief (do not reply)" <call-for-papers@hq.acm.org> |
| | Elsevier | Subject: Programme announced \| Register now to join our expert speakers | 27/10/22 18:42 | Sender: AI in Aging and Age-related Diseases 2022 <conferences@author.email.elsevier.com> |
| | IEEE | Subject: July 2022 Issue of IEEE Signal Processing w/Content Gazette is Now Available | 09/08/22 17:00 | Sender: IEEE Signal Processing Magazine <ieee-pubs@deliver.ieee.org> |
| | SN-MME | Subject: Springer Nature Editorial Newsletter May 2022 | 12/05/22 13:11 | Sender: Springer Nature <springernature@newsletter.springernature.com> |

## C. *Uncertainty in forensic examinations*

According to [5], all digital evidence comes with some degree of uncertainty. A forensic expert should be capable of determining the level of certainty (and thus having uncertainty to certain extent) given to a piece of evidence. Corroboration is a common mechanism used to raise the level of certainty, where multiple sources of evidence are taken into account. However, if inconsistencies exist, the level of certainty is reduced [5]. A source of inconsistencies is, if one or more forensic tools return different results in repeated runs [6]. In the absence of a ground truth to weight the results against, this results in uncertainty regarding the returned results. In our research presented in this article, we will encounter many instances of uncertainty especially regarding URL information and the tracker detection capabilities of tools.

## D. *Variations of URL information based on A-Records and CNAMEs*

The domain name system (DNS) is used to provide a consistent name space to map resources [24]. Domain names are used to identify a node. Resource information associated with a (domain) name form a resource record (RR). For usage in our paper, two distinct records can be distinguished: A-Record and CNAME. An A-Record describes a host address whereas the CNAME-Record describes a canonical name of an alias to this host [24]. As we will encounter in our research, IP addresses can point towards multiple A-Records, multiple CNAMEs can point towards the same A-Record and possibly further combinations of those three items exist. This adds uncertainty in interpreting tool results, e.g., when trying to associate URLs to entities that could act as 1st or 3rd parties in science tracking research.

CNAMEs can be used for benign purposes, e.g., not having to alter A-Records in a changing environment. But they can also used to disguise a 3rd party using this DNS mechanism (CNAME cloaking, see e.g., [25]).

## IV. Concept of Science-Tracking-Fingerprint (STF) with an intra- and inter-application assessment using URL and tracking Similarities

In this section the semantics and syntax of the concept of a Science-Tracking Fingerprint (STF) is introduced. We look and tools properties and describe intra- and inter-application area comparisons and provide a system landscape analysis.

### A. *Semantics of Science-Tracking Fingerprint (STF)*

The individualization [7] and attribution of science tracking on the application areas of web, app and email is the result of an orchestrated usage of tools following the model-based approach from [6]. The result is a (according to our first, preliminary results) distinct Science-Tracking Fingerprint (STF) that can provide hints/leads towards the publisher's system that is conducting the science tracking whilst also generally supporting privacy measurements. We assume that tool results characteristic and the mode of operation is stable for a given amount of time.

The fingerprint semantics are formed as an evaluation of the tool results when:

- accessing the publisher's website,
- opening an app available from the publisher,
- processing an email from the publisher.

The main challenge is define metrics for ordering the tool results to form the semantics of the Science-Tracking Fingerprint. Since we do not have a ground truth, generally, uncertainty (see also Section III.C) will remain. We propose the notion of Certainty as a metric (also in support of privacy measurements), which uses 3 result categories when matching the set of the individual tool results as being:

- plausible (pl): all tools return the same or comparable result,
- uncertain (unc): at least one tool returns a diverging result,
- none (-): no tool returns a meaningful result.

For URL information ($DT_5$, see Section III.A), the last category of none (-) is omitted since in our scenario there is no tracker detection ($DT_3$, see Section III.A) without an URL. URLs from 1st or 3rd party, however, can come with no associated tracker detection.

For the Science-Tracking Fingerprint (STF) we created a notation in the style of the Backus-Nauer Form (BNF) as depicted in Figure 1. A matrix is formed consisting of cells. Each cells carry the semantics of:

- Counter: Number of occurrences,
- Certainty: plausible, uncertain or none,
- Data stream: Mass storage (T) or Network (N),
- Data type: $DT_5$ (URL) or $DT_3$ (Tracker),
- Discovery mode: list-based (L) and/or manual (M).

```
<MATRIX> ::= <ROW> && <MATRIX>

<ROW> ::= <CELL> | /0/ <CELL> | /0/ <CELL> | /0/ <CELL> | /0/

<CELL> ::= <Counter> <EXPR>

<EXPR> ::= <EXPR1> | <EXPR>; <EXPR1>

<EXPR1> ::= <CERTAINTY>,<DATASTREAM>,<DATATYPE> |
<CERTAINTY>,<DATASTREAM>,<DATATYPE>,<DISCOVERYMODE>
```

Figure 1: BNF-style representation of the Science-Tracking Fingerprint (STF)

This does not only help avoiding uncertainties when comparing tool results. This information is also vital for forming the Science-Tracking Fingerprint (STF). The presence of a particular arrangement of CNAME usage can be characteristic for a given publisher and its embedded 3rd party content.

With those elements we can describe quantifiable and qualitative differences between the science-tracking employed by the publishers. The Science-Tracking Fingerprint (STF) obviously changes if the provision of the application area (web, app, email) by a publisher is altered (e.g., embedded 3rd party content and tracker in the web/app application, number of included items in campaign emails, etc.). We treat the Science-Tracking Fingerprint (STF) as a similarity measure.

### B. *Syntax of Science-Tracking Fingerprint (STF)*

With the BNF-style description of the Science-Tracking fingerprint (STF) we capture its semantics. Syntactically, we create a vector consisting of an element and a value. The concatenation of the vector/element pairs leads to the matrix described in Section III.A as depicted in Figure 2.

| | **A-Record 1st Party** | **CNAME 1st Party** | **A-Record 3rd Party** | **CNAME 3rd Party** |
|---|---|---|---|---|
| **Web** | BNF cell | BNF cell | BNF cell | BNF cell |
| | BNF cell | BNF cell | BNF cell | BNF cell |
| **App** | BNF cell | BNF cell | BNF cell | BNF cell |
| | BNF cell | BNF cell | BNF cell | BNF cell |
| **Email** | BNF cell | BNF cell | BNF cell | BNF cell |
| | BNF cell | BNF cell | BNF cell | BNF cell |

BNF Cell: 0 | Counter<pl | unc | none>, <N | T>, <DT5 | DT3>, <M | L>

Figure 2: Syntactical matrix representation of the Science-Tracking Fingerprint (STF)

Each row contains one or more BNF-style Cells where the counter records the number of occurrences if the following conditions are met:

- matching certainty per cell,
- tracker certainty is either plausible or uncertain.

If a row contains entries where the DNS response provided URL information containing CNAMEs for the 1st and/or 3rd party, we duplicate the cell entries from the A-Record to the CNAME. The value of the counter, however, remains unchanged and will only be evaluated once per row since technically this row describes the same examination step.

### C. Tool property comparison

The tools used for our experiments represent methods of the forensic process (see Section III.A). In the following Table II we compare the properties of the tools.

TABLE II. TOOL COMPARISON WITH THE PROPERTIES OF LOCATION, INPUT DATA STREAM, INPUT FORENSIC DATA TYPE, OUTPUT DATA STREAM, OUTPUT DATA TYPE, URL OUTPUT, IP OUTPUT, TRACKER DETECTION AND RELIANCE ON EXTERNAL DATA

| Application | Tool | Location | Input data stream | Input data type | Output data stream | URL output ($DT_5$) | IP output ($DT_5$) | Tracker Output ($DT_3$) based on external data | external data |
|---|---|---|---|---|---|---|---|---|---|
| Web | Privacyscore | Off-premises | $DS_N$ | ($DT_1$) | $DS_T$ | x | N/A | x | easlist to |
| | Webbkoll | Off-premises | $DS_N$ | ($DT_1$) | $DS_T$ | x | x | x | disconnect |
| | Website Evidence Collector | On-premises | $DS_N$ | $DT_1$ | $DS_T$ | x | N/A | N/A | N/A |
| | Wireshark | On-premises | $DS_N$ | $DT_1$ | $DS_T$ | x | x | N/A | N/A |
| App | Exodus-Standalone | On-premises | $DS_T$ | $DT_1$ | $DS_T$ | x | N/A | x | exodus |
| | AppChecker | On-premises | $DS_T$ | $DT_1$ | $DS_T$ | x | N/A | x | AppAuthor's list |
| | Wireshark | On-premises | $DS_N$ | $DT_1$ | $DS_T$ | x | x | N/A | N/A |
| Email | emlAnalyze | On-premises | $DS_T$ | $DT_1$ | $DS_T$ | x | N/A | x | N/A |
| | RA_email_forensics | On-premises | $DS_T$ | $DT_1$ | $DS_T$ | x | N/A | x | N/A |
| | Wireshark | On-premises | $DS_N$ | $DT_1$ | $DS_T$ | x | x | N/A | N/A |

All tools internally operate on raw data ($DT_1$ according to [6]). This also applies to our self-implemented RA_email_forensics (see also Section III.B), which is available per email-request towards sec-by-design <at> iti.cs.uni-magdeburg.de. However, in the case of *off-premises* tools (privacyscore [11] and webbkoll [12]) this data is inaccessible to us. Some tools operate on the network data stream $DS_N$, however, in our examination we require all tools to produce output data on the mass storage stream $DS_T$. In the case of the *off-premises* tools this is achieved by saving the results as the html archive using the web browser's export function. CNAME information as part of URL data $DT_5$ can only be obtained from the *dynamic* examination using wireshark [14]. Wireshark and webbkoll also acquire the IP, which can help finding matches but in times of load balancing and other mechanisms, it is not reliable in case of a mismatch. List-based tracker detection requires external data. Since those lists change over time, *off-premises* tools have a lower repeatability since old lists cannot be supplied easily.

### D. Intra- / Inter-Application (Web, App, Mail) comparison to gather semantics

During the tool result comparison as part of our examinations we evaluate intra-application and inter-application matches per publisher. We look for URL data $DT_5$ and tracker detection data $DT_3$ intra-application matches between the tools used for examining the application area and maintain the two separately. To detect intra-application matches we aggregate the URL data results of the dynamic examination (e.g., multiple A-Record or CNAME data) using a best-fit approach. Of course the detailed information is kept for further use. Table III shows an exemplary table header for the web intra-application matching.

TABLE III. EXEMPLARY TABLE HEADER FOR INTRA-APPLICATION MATCHING (WEB)

| Static examination | | | | | | Dynamic examination | | | |
|---|---|---|---|---|---|---|---|---|---|
| Off-Premesis | | | | | On-Premesis | | | | |
| *Privacyscore Web_S: Off Premesis ($DS_N$; $DT_5$, $DT_3$)* | | *Webbkoll Web_S: Off Premesis ($DS_N$; $DT_5$, $DT_3$)* | | | *Website Evidence Collector_S: On Premesis ($DS_N$; $DT_5$)* | *Wireshark Web_D: On Premesis ($DS_N$; $DT_5$, $DT_3$)* | | Detailed Intra-Application Test result (Comparison) | |
| 3rd Parties | Tracker Requests | Domain/ Host | IP | Detected as Tracker | Third party hosts | IP | Address (based on A-Record [A] Or CNAME [C]) | Intra-Application $DT_5$ match | Intra-Application $DT_3$ Known tracker match |

Here, all the properties already discussed such as static/dynamic examination, off-/on-premises operation, forensic data types and data streams captured is maintained and the URL/tracker data and the matching certainty are recorded. A complete examination for a given publisher covers 3 separate tables and forms the semantics for the fingerprint formation.

Further, we are interested in inter-application matches for a given publisher as this could provide hints for cross-application tracking. The idea is to be able to speculate about cross application tracking by identifying shared URL and tracker channels. For evaluating inter-application matches by also applying the certainty categories we evaluate the detailed data returned from the tools (including A-Record and CNAME data).

### E. System landscape analysis for Science-Tracking Fingerprint examination

To get an understanding about the opportunities and limitations proposed by the infrastructure, in [6] a system landscape analysis is proposed. Here the connections between the components of interest and the data flows can be visualized and conclusions can be drawn. Figure 3 shows a simplified system landscape analysis for our examinations.

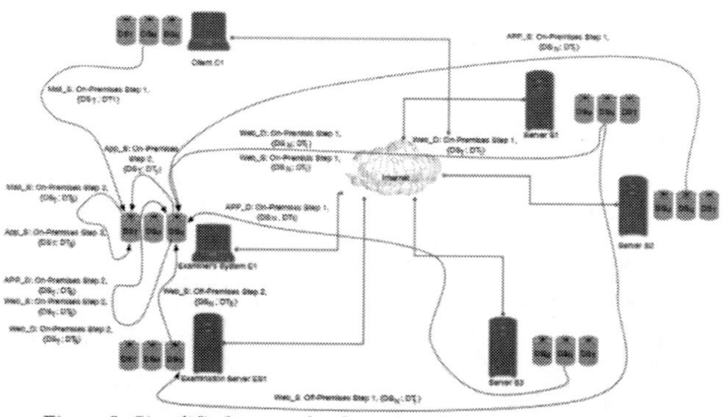


Figure 3: Simplified system landscape analysis for Science-Tracking Fingerprint (STF) examinations visualizing components connections and data flows during the forensic examination

All off-premises examination is performed by the Examination Server ES1. The examiner is located on the Examiner's System E1. Direct access to intermediate results, configurations and external data is only possible for tools running on E1. The data streams are represented as barrels and here the transformation process between data streams and data types during tool usage is visible. Data as input for the examination for the network data stream $DS_N$ is originating from the servers S1...3 representing the publisher's system. The email based examination is depicted by Client C1 retrieving the emails, which are then transferred using mass storage (USB thumb drive) to the Examiner's System E1. The system landscape is simplified, for an even more thorough examination, the data from the accessible network infrastructure elements such as routers, switches, etc. need to be considered.

## V. EXEMPLARY IMPLEMENTATION OF THE SCIENCE-TRACKING FINGERPRINT (STF)

We test our approach of the Science-Tracking Fingerprint (STF) and the intra- and inter-application matching on a laptop that is acting as the Examiner's System E1 (see Section III.E). It is a Lenovo E15 employing an Intel Core i7-1255U CPU, 16GB RAM and a 256GB SSD drive for mass storage. We use a Debian 11 Operating System [21] and the ungoogled chromium Version 95.0.4638.54 [23], both of which are configured to be reasonably passive on the network to avoid contamination of our dynamic recordings. To test the apps we setup Android x86 Version 7.1 inside the virtualization provided by Virtual Box Version 6.1 [20]. For static web investigations we use privacy score [12] public beta (unversioned) and webbkoll [12] in version ec39808 through their respective web interfaces. The website evidence collector is used in Version 1.0.0. For dynamic investigations we use wireshark [14] in Version 3.4.10. For static app examination we use exodus-standalone [16] in Version 1.3.1 and appchecker [17] in Version 2020.05 We use emlAnalyzer [22] (unversioned) and Version 0.5 of the self-implemented RA_email_forensics software. The latter is available as Open Source per email-request towards sec-by-design <at> iti.cs.uni-magdeburg.de.

### A. *Results of intra-/inter application comparison (URL/Tracker) on the example website of the IEEE*

The Table IX shows the result from our website visits of the IEEE (https://www.ieee.org) which are conducted on on June 6th 2023 with the exception of the privacyscore results, which date from June 16th, 2023. This is due to the off-premises scanning engine malfunctioned during the initial test and returned no results for 3rd party connections and known trackers.

We decide for a best-fit attempt when aggregating results for comparison of the static results of privacyscore, webbkoll and website evidence collector with the dynamic results of wireshark regarding the selection of A-Record or CNAME for the table. Greyed-out regions mark unavailable data, highlighting uncertainty through absence of data. Generally we apply the certainty result categories from Section IV.A. As can be seen in Table, we record the following occurrences of matches regarding URL information ($DT_5$):

- 23 plausible matches,
- 8 uncertain matches,

and regarding the tracker detection information ($DT_3$):

- 15 plausible matches,
- 6 uncertain matches,
- 10 mismatches (none).

Access to all tables (detailed and aggregated view) of all 4 publishers is available per email-request towards sec-by-design <at> iti.cs.uni-magdeburg.de.

### B. *Science-Tracking fingerprint of 4 selected publishers*

The complete aggregated view on our data regarding all 4 publishers is shown in Table IV.

TABLE IV. AGGREGATED SUMMARY OF ALL INTRA- AND INTER-APPLICATION RESULTS FOR URL (DT5) AND TRACKER DETECTION (DT3) DATA

| | aggregated $DT_5$ matches | | | aggregated $DT_3$ matches | | |
|---|---|---|---|---|---|---|
| | pl | unc | none | pl | unc | none |
| Intra-Web (ACM) | 19 | 5 | 0 | 5 | 9 | 10 |
| Intra-App (ACM) | 0 | 8 | 0 | 2 | 0 | 6 |
| Intra-Emai (ACM) | 3 | 1 | 0 | 1 | 0 | 3 |
| Inter-Application (ACM) | 0 | 1 | 35 | 1 | 0 | 35 |
| Intra-Web (Elsevier) | 5 | 12 | 0 | 2 | 4 | 11 |
| Intra-App (Elsevier) | 0 | 18 | 0 | 4 | 2 | 12 |
| Intra-Email (Elsevier) | 9 | 0 | 0 | 9 | 0 | 0 |
| Inter-Application (Elsevier) | 0 | 1 | 43 | 0 | 1 | 43 |
| Intra-Web (IEEE) | 23 | 8 | 0 | 15 | 6 | 10 |
| Intra-App (IEEE) | 0 | 15 | 0 | 1 | 3 | 11 |
| Intra-Email (IEEE) | 5 | 0 | 0 | 5 | 0 | 0 |
| Inter-Application (IEEE) | 2 | 3 | 46 | 1 | 3 | 47 |
| Intra-Web (SN-MME) | 11 | 11 | 0 | 2 | 6 | 14 |
| Intra-App (SN-MME) | 0 | 7 | 0 | 1 | 1 | 5 |
| Intra-Email (SN-MME) | 31 | 0 | 0 | 1 | 0 | 30 |
| Inter-Application (SN-MME) | 0 | 1 | 59 | 0 | 1 | 59 |

It represents all results of the intra-and inter-application area examination per publisher. Inter-application matches could hint towards cross-application tracking. The intra-application area results also form the basis of the Science-Tracking Fingerprint (STF) containing the BNF-style semantic cell description from Section IV.A and the syntactical vector from Section IV.B.

Table V shows the resulting Science-Tracking Fingerprint (STF) for the ACM publisher based on the data from Section III.B and tools from Section III.C.

TABLE V. SCIENCE-TRACKING FINGERPRINT (STF) OF THE ACM PUBLISHER USING THE SEMANTIC BNF-STYLE DESCRIPTION AND THE SYNTACTICAL VECTOR FORMED BY ELEMENT-VALUE PAIRS

| | A-Record 1st party | CNAME 1st Party | A-Record 3rd Party | CNAME 3rd Party |
|---|---|---|---|---|
| Web | 0 | 0 | $3_{PL,N,DT5;PL,N,DT3,L}$ | 0 |
| | 0 | 0 | $2_{PL,N,DT5;PL,N,DT3,L}$ | $2_{PL,N,DT5;PL,N,DT3,L}$ |
| | 0 | 0 | $6_{PL,N,DT5;UNC,N,DT3,L}$ | 0 |
| | 0 | 0 | $2_{PL,N,DT5;UNC,N,DT3,L}$ | $2_{PL,N,DT5;UNC,N,DT3,L}$ |
| | 0 | 0 | $1_{UNC,N,DT5;UNC,N,DT3,L}$ | $1_{UNC,N,DT5;UNC,N,DT3,L}$ |
| App | 0 | 0 | $1_{UNC,T,DT5;PL,T,DT3,L;\ UNC,N,\ DT5;\ PL,\ S,\ DT3,\ L}$ | $1_{UNC,T,DT5;PL,T,DT3,L;\ UNC,N,\ DT5;\ PL,\ S,\ DT3,\ L}$ |
| | 0 | 0 | $1_{UNC,T,DT5;PL,T,DT3,L;\ UNC,N,\ DT5;\ PL,\ S,\ DT3,\ L}$ | 0 |
| Email | 0 | 0 | $1_{PL,T,DT5;PL,T,DT3,M,\ 1PL,N,DT5;PL,N,DT3,M}$ | 0 |

Table VI shows the resulting Science-Tracking Fingerprint (STF) for the Elsevier Publisher based on the data from Section III.B and tools from Section III.C.

TABLE VI. SCIENCE-TRACKING FINGERPRINT (STF) OF THE ELSEVIER PUBLISHER USING THE SEMANTIC BNF-STYLE DESCRIPTION AND THE SYNTACTICAL VECTOR FORMED BY ELEMENT-VALUE PAIRS

| | A-Record 1st party | CNAME 1st Party | A-Record 3rd Party | CNAME 3rd Party |
|---|---|---|---|---|
| Web | 0 | 0 | $2_{PL,N,DT5;PL,N,DT3,L}$ | $2_{PL,N,DT5;PL,N,DT3,L}$ |
| | 0 | 0 | $2_{PL,N,DT5;UNC,N,DT3,L}$ | 0 |
| | 0 | 0 | $1_{PL,N,DT5;UNC,N,DT3,L}$ | $1_{PL,N,DT5;UNC,N,DT3,L}$ |
| | 0 | 0 | $1_{UNC,N,DT5;UNC,N,DT3,L}$ | 0 |
| App | $4_{UNC,T,DT5;PL,T,DT3,L;\ UNC,N,\ DT5;\ PL,\ S,\ DT3,\ L}$ | 0 | 0 | 0 |
| | $2_{UNC,T,DT5;UNC,N,DT3,L;\ UNC,N,\ DT5;\ UNC,\ S,\ DT3,\ L}$ | 0 | 0 | 0 |
| Email | $1_{PL,T,DT5;PL,T,DT3,M,\ 1PL,N,DT5;PL,N,DT3,M}$ | 0 | 0 | $1_{PL,T,DT5;PL,T,DT3,M,\ 1PL,N,DT5;PL,N,DT3,M}$ |
| | 0 | 0 | $8_{PL,T,DT5;PL,T,DT3,L,\ 8PM,N,DT5;PL,N,DT3,M}$ | $8_{PL,T,DT5;PL,T,DT3,M,\ 8PL,N,DT5;PL,N,DT3,M}$ |

Table VII shows the resulting Science-Tracking Fingerprint (STF) for the IEEE Publisher based on the data from Section III.B and tools from Section III.C.

TABLE VII. SCIENCE-TRACKING FINGERPRINT (STF) OF THE IEEE PUBLISHER USING THE SEMANTIC BNF-STYLE DESCRIPTION AND THE SYNTACTICAL VECTOR FORMED BY ELEMENT-VALUE PAIRS

| | A-Record 1st party | CNAME 1st Party | A-Record 3rd Party | CNAME 3rd Party |
|---|---|---|---|---|
| Web | 0 | 0 | $8_{PL,N,DTS\|PL,N,DTS,L}$ | 0 |
| | 0 | 0 | $5_{PL,N,DTS\|PL,N,DTS,L}$ | $5_{PL,N,DTS\|PL,N,DTS,L}$ |
| | 0 | 0 | $3_{PL,N,DTS\|UNC,N,DTS,L}$ | 0 |
| | 0 | 0 | $2_{PL,N,DTS\|UNC,N,DTS,L}$ | $2_{PL,N,DTS\|UNC,N,DTS,L}$ |
| | 0 | 0 | $2_{UNC,N,DTS\|PL,N,DTS,L}$ | 0 |
| | 0 | 0 | $2_{UNC,N,DTS\|UNC,N,DTS,L}$ | 0 |
| App | 0 | 0 | $1_{UNC,N,DTS\|PL,N,DTS,L;\ UNC,T,DTS,PL,S,DTS,L}$ | 0 |
| | 0 | 0 | $3_{UNC,N,DTS\|UNC,N,DTS,L;\ UNC,T,DTS,UNC,S,DTS,L}$ | 0 |
| Email | $5_{PL,T,DTS\|PL,T,DTS,M}$, $5_{PL,N,DTS\|PL,N,DTS,M}$ | 0 | 0 | $5_{PL,T,DTS\|PL,T,DTS,M}$, $5_{PL,N,DTS\|PL,N,DTS,M}$ |

Table VIII shows the resulting Science-Tracking Fingerprint (STF) for the Springernature-Macmillan Education Publisher based on the data from Section III.B and tools from Section III.C.

TABLE VIII. SCIENCE-TRACKING FINGERPRINT (STF) OF THE SPRINGERNATURE-MACMILLANEDUCATION PUBLISHER USING THE SEMANTIC BNF-STYLE DESCRIPTION AND THE SYNTACTICAL VECTOR FORMED BY ELEMENT-VALUE PAIRS

| | A-Record 1st party | CNAME 1st Party | A-Record 3rd Party | CNAME 3rd Party |
|---|---|---|---|---|
| Web | 0 | 0 | $1_{PL,N,DTS\|PL,N,DTS,L}$ | 0 |
| | 0 | 0 | $1_{PL,N,DTS\|PL,N,DTS,L}$ | $1_{PL,N,DTS\|PL,N,DTS,L}$ |
| | 0 | 0 | $3_{PL,N,DTS\|UNC,N,DTS,L}$ | 0 |
| | 0 | 0 | $3_{PL,N,DTS\|UNC,N,DTS,L}$ | $3_{PL,N,DTS\|UNC,N,DTS,L}$ |
| App | 0 | 0 | $1_{UNC,T,DTS\|PL,T,DTS,L;\ UNC,N,DTS,PL,N,DTS,L}$ | 0 |
| | 0 | 0 | $1_{UNC,T,DTS\|UNC,T,DTS,L;\ UNC,N,DTS,UNC,N,DTS,L}$ | 0 |
| Email | 0 | 0 | $1_{PL,T,DTS\|PL,T,DTS,ML}$, $1_{PL,N,DTS\|PL,N,DTS,ML}$ | $1_{PL,T,DTS\|PL,T,DTS,ML}$, $1_{PL,N,DTS\|PL,N,DTS,ML}$ |

As can be seen from Tables 5-7, the Science-Tracking Fingerprints are significantly distinct. The distinctiveness would be maintained if small changes appeared such as slightly changing the number of 3rd parties involved or changing characteristics thereof.

## VI. EVALUATION

Aggregated for the 4 publishers in total we identify 106 plausible, 85 uncertain and 0 mismatches for intra-application area URL matches per publisher out of 191 comparisons. For the tracker detection, we identify 48 plausible, 31 uncertain and 112 mismatches out of 191 comparisons. Additionally, covering all 4 publishers, we identify 2 plausible, 6 uncertain and 124 mismatches for intra-application area URL matches per publisher. For the tracker detection we identify 2 plausible, 6 uncertain and 125 mismatches.

The evaluation of the results leads to interesting findings regarding different name selections by the same domain owner. We propose to use whois [26] queries if some URL results seam similar, e.g.,www.google-analytics.com | firebase.google.com. This is partly backed by Google Inc. itself [27]. Such similarities result in uncertain intra- and inter-application matches Web/App for the publisher IEEE). Here we suggest to look for the entries of:

- Registrant,
- Admin,
- Tech.

If those entries match with regards to domain names (sometimes name server information differs), we would suggest this to be a manual match resulting to uncertain. Interestingly, such matches can also be found for URLs that at first look seem to be a sure mismatch (e.g., tiqcdn.com | tealium.com as intra- and inter-application match Web/App for the publisher IEEE). Again, we would opt for a manual match in that case. Also, the Adobe Ad cloud constituents from Marketo often have very dissimilar URLs (e.g., marketo.com | omtrdc.net | mktossl.com | mktoweb.com but all pointing towards Adobe Inc.). Those claims are partly backed by Adobe Inc. itself [28], [29].

Reliance on live DNS lookups in the case of wireshark is not recommended. In our experience in the case of multiple A-Records or multiple CNAMEs or a combination thereof often one hostname is chosen for display (with no easy detectable logic as to which one is chosen). Here we strongly suggest to look into the responses of the DNS server within the network data stream recording.

As already stated in Section II.B, automated tracker detection often relies on external data typically provided lists. Since the content is dynamic and thus differs between time $t_i$ and $t_{i+1}$, for the Science-Tracking Fingerprint to deliver comparable results, dates and contents of the respective lists need to be conserved. This calls for local installments for privacyscore and webbkoll, which is possible due to both tools being released as OpenSource. We leave this to future work due to time constraints.

The results from Section IV.B show, that each publisher out of the tested 4 can easily be individualized. This provides leads/hints towards an attribution by providing a similarity measure. However, it must be stated that the Science-Tracing Fingerprint alone is not deemed by the authors to be sufficient for attribution beyond reasonable doubt.

Also, in a quick exemplary evaluation using the IEEE publisher, 3 calls-for-paper emails were evaluated (intra-application only). They cover a time span from August, 9th, 2022 to August, 28th, 2023, and show similarities and differences compared to the email investigated in the main body of work from August, 9th, 2022 which announces the availability of a journal as content. Their STF is shown in Table X. Similarities include the usage of CNAMEs pointing towards usage of 3rd parties whilst the A-Record suggests 1st party (except for Table 10.b, where only 3rd parties are involved). Also, in Table 10.b, an image resource is used that is hosted by a server identified by the disconnect list [15], Arguably, this stems from the conference organization and not from the publisher.

Generally, from the viewpoint of the user, unnecessary tracking is also impacting resource use, so the proposed Science-Tracking Fingerprint (STF) can also be used to look at energy efficiency for sustainability purposes.

## VII. CONCLUSION AND FUTURE WORK

In this article we presented the Science-Tracking Fingerprint (STF) that provides a similarity measure to individualize and compare science publishers with qualitative and quantitative elements based on an existing model of the forensic process. The idea is to deliver hints/leads towards attribution of a specific science literature provider. Its semantics are based on a BNF-style representation of the Science-Tracking Fingerprint (STF).

Syntactically the elements are based on a vector representation of element-value pairs forming a matrix that contains a number of occurrences on the quantitative part also usable for general privacy measurements. URL information is based on DNS responses of the local DNS server and split into A-Record and CNAME information as part of the dynamic examination. This offers a considerably larger chance of finding matchs. A certainty result category as a metric in support of privacy measurements based on URL and tracker detection information forms the qualitative part. The Science-Tracking Fingerprint (STF) is tool-independent. We tested it during privacy measurements on the application areas of web, app and email of 4 publishers with existing on- and off-premises tools and implement the dedicated email tool of RA_email_forensics.

Part of the STF is the intra-application matching, where URL and tracker detection results are compared using the certainty categories. Our results using the Science-Tracking Fingerprint show promising pointers towards its discriminatory power. We also calculated inter-application area matches per provider, which could provide indicators for cross-application tracking. The proposed Science-Tracking Fingerprint (STF) can also be used to look at energy efficiency for sustainability purposes through analyzing the data packets used for science tracking by the publishers.

Future work includes the STF broad scale testing based on automation, which is supported by the BNF-style formalization. Further, a local installation of the section of the tools that is yet off-premises is necessary to remove the reliance on 3rd party administered updates of external data. This is because external data influences the tracker detection.

## ACKNOWLEDGEMENTS

The research from Robert Altschaffel is partly funded by the research project "CyberSec LSA_OVGU-AMSL, Security-by-Design-Orchestration_Booster" under the Grant Number ZS/2015/12/96222.

## REFERENCES

[1] Deutsche Forschungsgemeinschaft, "Data tracking in research: aggregation and use or sale of usage data by academic publishers" [Online] https://www.dfg.de/download/pdf/foerderung/programme/lis/datentracking_papier_en.pdf (2023.09.05).

[2] E. Bettinger, and M. Bursic, and A. Chandler, "Disrupting the Digital Status Quo: Why and How to Staff for Privacy in Academic Libraries" [Online] https://publish.illinois.edu/licensingprivacy/files/2023/06/Whitepaper-on-Privacy-Staffing-Licensing-Privacy.pdf (2023.09.05).

[3] R. Siems, "When your journal reads you – user tracking on science publisher platforms", Elephant in the Lab. https://doi.org/10.5281/zenodo.4683778, 2021.

[4] R. Altschaffel, and S. Kiltz, and T. Lucke, and J. Dittmann, "Introduction to Being a Privacy Detective: Investigating and Comparing Potential Privacy Violations in Mobile Apps Using Forensic Methods", in Proceedings of the Fourteenth International Conference on Emerging Security Information, Systems and Technologies (Securware), Valencia, Spain, 21-25/09/2020, ISBN 978-1-61208-821-1, pp 60-68, 2020.

[5] E. Casey, "Error, Uncertainty and Loss in Digital Evidence", In International Journal of Digital Evidence, Volume 1, Issue 2, pp. 1-45, 2002.

[6] S. Kiltz, "Data-Centric Examination Approach (DCEA) for a qualitative determination of error, loss and uncertainty in digital and digitised forensics", PhD Thesis, Faculty of Computer Science, Otto-von-Guericke-University Magdeburg, Germany, September, 2020.

[7] K. Inman and N. Rudin, "Principles and Practises of Criminalistics: The Profession of Forensic Science", CRC Press LLC Boca Raton Florida, USA, ISBN 0-8493-8127-4, 2001.

[8] W. Christl, "Corporate Surveillance in Everyday Life" [Online] https://crackedlabs.org/dl/CrackedLabs_Christl_CorporateSurveillance.pdf (2023.09.05).

[9] H. Mildebrath "Unpacking 'commercial surveillance': The state of tracking" [Online] https://www.europarl.europa.eu/RegData/etudes/BRIE/2022/739266/EPRS_BRI(2022)739266_EN.pdf (2023.09.05).

[10] C. Hanson, "User Tracking on Academic Publisher Platforms" [Online] https://www.codyh.com/writing/tracking.html (2023.09.05).

[11] D. Herrmann, "Welcome - PrivacyScore"[Online] https://privacyscore.org/ (2023.09.05).

[12] Dataskydd.net Sverige, "Analyze | Webbkoll - dataskydd.net" [Online] https://webbkoll.dataskydd.net/en (2023.09.05).

[13] European Data Protection Supervisor, "EDPS Inspection Software | European Data Protection Supervisor" [Online] https://edps.europa.eu/edps-inspection-software_en (2023.09.05).

[14] Wireshark Foundation, "Wireshark · Go Deep" [Online] https://www.wireshark.org/ (2023.09.05).

[15] Disconnect Inc., "GitHub - disconnectme/disconnect-tracking-protection: Canonical repository for the Disconnect services file" [Online] https://github.com/disconnectme/disconnect-tracking-protection (2023.09.05).

[16] Exodus Privacy, "GitHub - Exodus-Privacy/exodus-standalone: εxodus CLI client for local analysis" [Online] https://github.com/Exodus-Privacy/exodus-standalone (2023.09.05).

[17] J. Alemann, and N. Baier, and M. Streuber, and T. Nam, and L. Peters, "GitHub - Tienisto/AppChecker" [Online] https://github.com/Tienisto/AppChecker (2023.09.05).

[18] Exodus Privacy, "εxodus" [Online] https://reports.exodus-privacy.eu.org/en/trackers/ (2023.09.05).

[19] cwhung, "Android-x86 - Porting Android to x86" [Online] https://www.android-x86.org/ (2023.09.05).

[20] Oracle Inc., "Oracle VM VirtualBox" [Online] https://www.virtualbox.org/ (2023.09.05).

[21] Software in the Public Interest, Inc. , "Debian -- News -- Debian 11 "bullseye" released" [Online] https://www.debian.org/News/2021/20210814 (2023.09.05).

[22] F. Wahl, "GitHub - wahlflo/eml_analyzer: A cli script to analyze an E-Mail in the EML format for viewing the header, extracting attachments, etc." [Online] https://github.com/wahlflo/eml_analyzer (2023.09.05).

[23] ungoogled-chromium Authors, "GitHub - ungoogled-software/ungoogled-chromium: Google Chromium, sans integration with Google" [Online] https://github.com/ungoogled-software/ungoogled-chromium (2023.09.05).

[24] P. Mockapetris, "Domain names - concepts and facilites" [Online] https://datatracker.ietf.org/doc/pdf/rfc1034 (2023.09.05).

[25] Palo Alto Networks, Inc., "CNAME Cloaking: Disguising Third Parties Through the DNS" [Online] https://unit42.paloaltonetworks.com/cname-cloaking/ (2023.09.05).

[26] M. d'Itri, "whois(1) — whois — Debian bullseye — Debian Manpages" [Online]

https://manpages.debian.org/bullseye/whois/whois.1.en.html (2023.09.05).

[27] Google Inc., "What is Google Analytics for Firebase? - Firebase Help" [Online] https://support.google.com/firebase/answer/7388022?hl=EN (2023.09.05).

[28] Adobe Inc., "trackingServer | Adobe Analytics" [Online] https://experienceleague.adobe.com/docs/analytics/implementation/vars/config-vars/trackingserver.html?lang=en-US (2023.09.05).

[29] Adobe Inc., "Get started with tracking | Adobe Campaign" [Online] https://experienceleague.adobe.com/docs/campaign-classic/using/sending-messages/tracking-messages/about-message-tracking.html?lang=en (2023.09.05)

TABLE IX. AGGREGATED INTRA-APPLICATION COMPARISON FOR THE WEB APPLICATION ARE FOR THE PUBLISHER IEEE (HTTPS://WWW.IEEE.ORG, 2023.09.05)

| Application Web | | | | | | | | | |
|---|---|---|---|---|---|---|---|---|---|
| Static examination | | | | | | Dynamic examination | | | |
| Off-Premesis | | | | | On-Premesis | | | | |
| Privacyscore Web_S:Off Premesis $\{DS_N; DT_5, DT_3\}$ | | Webbkoll Web_S: Off Premesis $\{DS_N; DT_5, DT_3\}$ | | | Website Evidence Collector_S: On Premesis $\{DS_N; DT_5\}$ | Wireshark Web_D: On Premesis $\{DS_N; DT_5, DT_3\}$ | | Detailled Intra-Application Test result (Comparison) | |
| 3rd Parties | Tracker Requests | Domain/Host | IP | Detected as Tracker | 3rd party hosts | IP | Address (based on A-Record [A] or CNAME [C]) | Intra-Application $DT_5$ match | Intra-Application $DT_3$ known tracker match |
| insight.adsrvr.org | x | insight.adsrvr.org | 15.197.193.217 | x | insight.adsrvr.org | 52.223.40.198 | insight.adsrvr.org [A] | pl | pl |
| js.adsrvr.org | x | js.adsrvr.org | 18.165.129.129 | x | js.adsrvr.org | 18.64.82.184 | js.adsrvr.org [A] | pl | pl |
| | | | | | | 23.54.103.160 | www.ieeee.org [A] | unc | - |
| s3.amazonaws.com | | s3.amazonaws.com | 52.216.38.0 | | s3.amazonaws.com | 52.216.44.24 | s3.amazonaws.com [A] | pl | - |
| s3-us-west-2.amazonaws.com | | s3-us-west-2.amazonaws.com | 52.218.217.72 | | s3-us-west-2.amazonaws.com | 52.218.245.56 | s3-us-west-2.amazonaws.com [A] | pl | - |
| cdnjs.cloudflare.com | x | cdnjs.cloudflare.com | 2a06:98c1:3123:e000:: | | cdnjs.cloudflare.com | 104.17.25.14 | cdnjs.cloudflare.com [A] | pl | unc |
| 4490791.fls.doubleclick.net | x | 4490791.fls.doubleclick.net | 142.250.74.166 | x | 4490791.fls.doubleclick.net | 142.250.181.198 | 4490791.fls.doubleclick.net [A] | pl | pl |
| googleads.g.doubleclick.net | x | googleads.g.doubleclick.net | 2a00:1450:400f:80b::2002 | x | googleads.g.doubleclick.net | 142.251.209.130 | googleads.g.doubleclick.net [A] | pl | pl |
| stats.g.doubleclick.net | x | stats.g.doubleclick.net | 2a00:1450:4010:c0d::9c | x | stats.g.doubleclick.net | 142.250.147.155 | stats.g.doubleclick.net [A] | pl | pl |
| | | | | | | 142.250.181.194 | adservice.google.de [A] | unc | - |
| connect.facebook.net | x | connect.facebook.net | 2a03:2880:f013:d:face:b00c:0:3 | x | connect.facebook.net | 157.240.223.15 | connect.facebook.net [A] | pl | pl |
| www.facebook.com | x | www.facebook.com | 2a03:2880:f113:81:face:b00c:0:25de | x | www.facebook.com | 157.240.223.35 | www.facebook.com [A] | pl | pl |
| kit.fontawesome.com | | kit.fontawesome.com | 2606:4700::6812:1734 | | kit.fontawesome.com | 104.18.22.52 | kit.fontawesome.com [A] | pl | - |
| adservice.google.com | x | adservice.google.com | 2a00:1450:400f:801::2002 | x | adservice.google.com | 172.217.19.66 | adservice.google.com [A] | pl | pl |
| www.google.com | x | www.google.com | 2a00:1450:400f:802::2004 | x | www.google.com | 142.250.181.196 | www.google.com [A] | pl | pl |
| www.google.de | x | www.google.de | 2a00:1450:400f:801::2003 | x | www.google.de | 142.251.209.131 | www.google.de [A] | pl | pl |
| region1.google-analytics.com | | region1.google-analytics.com | 2001:4860:4802:32::36 | x | region1.google-analytics.com | 216.239.32.36 | region1.analytics.google.com [A] | pl | unc |
| www.google-analytics.com | x | www.google-analytics.com | 2a00:1450:400f:802::200e | x | www.google-analytics.com | | | unc | pl |
| www.googletagmanager.com | x | www.googletagmanager.com | 2a00:1450:400f:803::2008 | | www.googletagmanager.com | 142.250.181.200 | www.googletagmanager.com [A] | pl | unc |
| | | | | | securesso.ieee.org | 140.98.193.42 | securesso.ieee.org [A] | unc | - |
| code.jquery.com | | code.jquery.com | 2001:4de0:ac18::1:a:2b | | code.jquery.com | 69.16.175.42 | code.jquery.com [A] | pl | - |
| app-ab24.marketo.com | x | app-ab24.marketo.com | 104.16.96.80 | x | app-ab24.marketo.com | 104.16.96.80 | app-ab24.marketo.com [A] | pl | pl |
| munchkin.marketo.net | x | munchkin.marketo.net | 23.61.220.209 | x | munchkin.marketo.net | | | unc | pl |
| 756-gph-899.mktoresp.com | x | 756-gph-899.mktoresp.com | 192.28.144.124 | | 756-gph-899.mktoresp.com | | | unc | unc |
| up.pixel.ad | x | up.pixel.ad | 95.140.228.46 | | up.pixel.ad | 178.79.242.16 | up.pixel.ad [A] | pl | unc |
| di.rlcdn.com | x | di.rlcdn.com | 35.244.174.68 | x | di.rlcdn.com | 35.244.174.68 | di.rlcdn.com [A] | pl | pl |
| | | 6045067.global.siteimproveanalytics.io | 18.185.183.56 | | 6045067.global.siteimproveanalytics.io | 18.185.183.56 | 6045067.global.siteimproveanalytics.io [A] | unc | - |
| | | siteimproveanalytics.com | 2606:4700:e4::ac40:ad0c | | siteimproveanalytics.com | 172.64.173.12 | siteimproveanalytics.com [A] | unc | - |
| pixel.sitescout.com | x | pixel.sitescout.com | 98.98.134.241 | x | pixel.sitescout.com | 98.98.134.243 | pixel.sitescout.com [A] | pl | pl |
| tags.tiqcdn.com | | tags.tiqcdn.com | 2600:9000:2375:8a00:7:2bfb:7c00:93a1 | | tags.tiqcdn.com | 18.64.79.94 | tags.tiqcdn.com [A] | pl | - |
| www.youtube.com | | www.youtube.com | 2a00:1450:400f:80a::200e | x | www.youtube.com | 142.251.209.142 | www.youtube.com [A] | pl | unc |

TABLE X. SCIENCE-TRACKING FINGERPRINT (STF) FOR CALL FOR PAPERS EMAILS FROM THE IEEE PUBLISHER DATING FROM A) AUGUST, 9TH, 2022, B) SEPTEMBER,13TH, 2022, C) AUGUST, 28TH, 2023

**Fingerprint a) Mail from August, 9th, 2022**

| | A-Record First party | CNAME First Party | A-Record Third Party | CNAME Third Party |
|---|---|---|---|---|
| Email | $3_{PL,T,DT5;PL,T,DT3,M}$, $3_{PL,N,DT5;PL,N,DT3,M}$ | 0 | 0 | $3_{PL,T,DT5;PL,T,DT3,M}$, $3_{PL,N,DT5;PL,N,DT3,M}$ |

**Fingerprint b) Mail from September,13th, 2022**

| | A-Record First party | CNAME First Party | A-Record Third Party | CNAME Third Party |
|---|---|---|---|---|
| Email | 0 | 0 | $3_{PL,T,DT5;PL,T,DT3,M}$, $3_{PL,N,DT5;PL,N}$ | $3_{PL,T,DT5;PL,T,DT3,M}$, $3_{PL,N,DT5;PL,N,DT3,M}$ |

**Fingerprint c) Mail from August, 28th, 2023**

| | | | | |
|---|---|---|---|---|
| Email | $5_{PL,T,DT5;PL,T,DT3,M}$, $5_{PL,N,DT5;PL,N,DT3,M}$ | 0 | 0 | $5_{PL,T,DT5;PL,T,DT3,M}$, $5_{PL,N,DT5;PL,N,DT3,M}$ |
| | $1_{PL,T,DT5;PL,T,DT3,M}$, $1_{PL,N,DT5;PL,N,DT3,M}$ | 0 | 0 | $1_{PL,T,DT5;UNC,T,DT3,M}$, $1_{PL,N,DT5;UNC,N,DT3,M}$ |